THE KINGDOM OF OUR FATHER

Who is God the Father?

Thomas W. Petrisko

THE KINGDOM OF OUR FATHER

WHO IS GOD THE FATHER?

Interviews with Today's Visionaries about the First Person of the Trinity, their Mystical Experiences with Him, and their Prophecies for the New Millennium

THOMAS W. PETRISKO

St. Andrew's Productions

CONSECRATION
AND DEDICATION

This book is dedicated to my Godfather, William Petrisko. It is consecrated to the loving, paternal heart of God Our Father and Creator. May His Kingdom come to reign in the world and in the hearts of all His children.

Second Printing, *2001*
Third Printing, *2002*

ISBN: 1-891903-18-7

Published by:

St. Andrew's Productions
6111 Steubenville Pike
McKees Rocks, PA 15136

Phone:	(412) 787-9735
Fax:	(412) 787-5204
Internet:	www.SaintAndrew.com

Scriptural quotations are taken from The Holy Bible —RSV: Catholic Edition. Alternate translations from the Latin Vulgate Bible (Douay Rheims Version —DV) are indicated when used. Some of the Scriptural quotations from the New American Bible: St. Joseph Edition, The New American Bible— Fireside Family Edition 1984-1985, The Holy Bible—Douay Rheims Edition, The New American Bible— Red Letter Edition 1986.

PRINTED IN THE UNITED STATES OF AMERICA

ACKNOWLEDGMENTS

I am indebted to many for assisting and supporting me with this work, especially Father Guy and Armand Gerard, Georgette Faniel, Matthew Kelly, Barbara Centilli, Christina Gallagher, Father Gerard McGinnity, Father Richard Foley, Father William McCarthy, Father Robert Hermann, Father Richard Whetstone, Sister Agnes McCormick, Sister Margaret Mary Sequin, Tom Faye, Barbara Laboissonniere Ph.d (editing), Dr. Frank Novasack, Michael Fontecchio, Amanda DeFazio, Carole McElwain, Joe and Gerry Simboli, Mr. John Haffert, Carol Jean Speck, Joan Smith, Jim Petrilena, Clyde Gualandri, Mary Lou Sokol, Thelma Bugansky and the prayer group at the Pittsburgh Center for Peace.

As always, my loving appreciation to my family; my wife Emily, daughters Maria, Sarah, Natasha and Dominique, and sons, Joshua and Jesse.

ABOUT THE AUTHOR

D r. Thomas W. Petrisko was the President of the *Pittsburgh Center for Peace* from 1990 to 1998 and he served as the editor of the Center's nine special edition *Queen of Peace* newspapers. These papers, primarily featuring the apparitions and revelations of the Virgin Mary, were published in many millions throughout the world.

Dr. Petrisko is the author of seventeen books, including: **The Fatima Prophecies**, *At the Doorstep of the World;* **The Face of the Father**, *An Exclusive interview with Barbara Centilli Concerning Her Revelations and Visions of God the Father;* **Glory to the Father**, *A Look at the Mystical Life of Georgette Faniel;* **For the Soul of the Family**; *The Story of the Apparitions of the Virgin Mary to Estela Ruiz*, **The Sorrow, the Sacrifice and the Triumph;** *The Visions, Apparitions and Prophecies of Christina Gallagher*, **Call of the Ages**, **The Prophecy of Daniel**, **In God's Hands**, *The Miraculous Story of Little Audrey Santo*, **Mother of The Secret**, **False Prophets of Today**, **St. Joseph and the Triumph of the Saints**, **The Last Crusade**, **The Kingdom of Our Father**, **Inside Heaven and Hell** *and* **Inside Purgatory** *and* **Fatima's Third Secret Explained.**

The decree of the **Congregation for the Propagation of the Faith** (AAS 58, 1186 - approved by Pope Paul VI on 14 October 1966) requires that the *Nihil Obstat* and *Imprimatur* are no longer required for publications that deal with private revelations, apparitions, prophecies, miracles, etc., provided that nothing is said in contradiction of faith and morals.

The author hereby affirms his unconditional submission to whatever final judgment is delivered by the Church regarding some of the events currently under investigation in this book.

TABLE OF CONTENTS

17   *"Lo, I am about to create new heavens and a new earth; The things of the past shall not be remembered or come to mind.*

18   *Instead, there shall always be rejoicing and happiness in what I create; For I create Jerusalem to be a joy and its people to be a delight;*

19   *I will rejoice in Jerusalem and exult in my people. No longer shall the sound of weeping be heard there, or the sound of crying;*

20   *No longer shall there be in it an infant who lives but a few days, or an old man who does not round out his full lifetime; He dies a mere youth who reaches but a hundred years, and he who fails of a hundred shall be thought accursed.*

21   *They shall live in the houses they build, and eat the fruit of the vineyards they plant;*

22   *They shall not build houses for others to live in, or plant for others to eat. As the years of a tree, so the years of my people; and my chosen ones shall long enjoy the produce of their hands.*

23   *They shall not toil in vain, no beget children for sudden destruction; for a race blessed by the Lord are they and their offspring.*

24   *Before they call, I will answer; while they are yet speaking, I will hearken to them.*

25   *The wolf and the lamb shall graze alike, and the lion shall eat hay like the ox (but the serpent's food shall be dust). None shall hurt or destroy on all my holy mountain, says the Lord.*

— Isaiah 65:17-25

THY KINGDOM COME

Fr. Richard Foley, SJ

Nothing could be more timely than this new book by Dr. Petrisko. For it focuses directly on that Divine Person to whom 1999 is dedicated, yet towards whom we still pay relatively little devotion whether private or public. Hence, the author's urgent plea for the Church to promote a specific cultus of God the Father, a cultus to be marked annually by an octave of consecration culminating in a formal feast in His honor.

Dr. Petrisko's book is prophetic in as much as its central purpose is to focus our gaze on what the Father holds in store for us in time future (which in the event could well prove to be <u>near</u>-future.) Indeed, a prophetic note is what we would expect in any case from the subject-matter, given that every <u>Our Father</u> we say is oriented towards what lies ahead—notably the coming of the Father's kingdom. Nor would anyone deny that it's coming is exactly what our world sorely needs, steeped as it is in a neo-pagan culture of sin and death.

In speaking of things future, the author is careful to steer clear of millenarianism. That is, he does not claim that the Father's coming kingdom will take the form of a Messianic Utopia or a secular Shangri-la where righteousness and material abundance go hand in hand. Rather, the promised kingdom's keynote will be that special holiness, peace and love which originate from our loving Father and will lead us, His prodigal children, to our eternal home.

A valuable feature of Dr. Petrisko's book is that it musters an impressive chorus of chosen souls who in their various ways act as prophetic mouthpieces of the Father's intentions for this day and age.

Their message has one common denominator: we are on the threshold of a new era—the Era of the Father. Therefore we must honor, love and serve Him as never before. While at the same time we owe Him filial fear, we should never be afraid of our fatherly God. For He is tender mercy itself; besides, He cherishes each and all of us as the children of His creation, the treasures of His heart, His very own macushlas.

Readers will draw a wealth of doctrinal insights and devotional inspirations from these prophetic figures. Among them is Mother Eugenia Ravasio. She died in Italy some ten years ago. Hers were the first recorded messages from the Father to receive official Church approval. Among other things, she stresses the need for private and public devotion to the First Person with a special liturgical feast in His honor.

Another prophetic voice is that of Matthew Kelly, the remarkable and engaging young Australian. His message from God the Father is simple yet profound: mankind is soon to receive the great grace of a "mini-judgment" aimed at preparing the way for the coming era of peace and holiness.

Then there is Georgette Faniel. This French Canadian mystic and victim soul is a very special instrument of the First Person and zealous champion of devotion to Him both private and public. Another mystic and victim soul is the Irish woman, Christina Gallagher, some of whose spiritual messages come from the Heavenly Father; through her He pleads with mankind to return to Him before this time of special mercy runs out.

Luisa Piccarreta is another chose mouthpiece of God's desires and designs with regard to this present age. Her revelations bear strongly on the coming of the Kingdom as expressed in the Lord's Prayer.

In many ways the most significant of all these testimonies are those supplied by Barbara Rose Centilli—a mature and extraordinary American woman whose revelations also call for a feast day for the Father. Dr. Petrisko's book gives the text of many of the amazing dialogues she has held with God the Father. In them He comes across as being all merciful, forgiveness and exquisite tenderness towards His chosen daughter—as He is towards each single one of us. Indeed, He indicates that His love for our prodigal selves is simply overwhelming. In St. Paul's phrase, it surpasses all understanding.

What similarly comes across in the Centilli messages is a sense of imminence and urgency about the coming Age of the Father, and our corresponding duty and need to spread and formalize private and public devotion to Him without delay. A further insight we gain from her revelations is the close link between the Fatima prophecy of Mary's Triumph and the advent of the Father's kingdom on earth.

We owe a debt of thanks to Dr. Petrisko for presenting us with a book that so persuasively and powerfully states the case for the Father of Mankind. It has been said that nothing is so invincible as an idea whose hour has come. Already the dawn of this exciting new era is breaking over the horizon. Let us pray and work that it will radiate the Father's light and warmth far and wide.

INTRODUCTION

"Man is placed above all creatures, and not beneath them, and he cannot be satisfied or content except in something greater than himself. Greater than himself is nothing but Myself, the Eternal God."

— Dictated by St. Catherine of Sienna during a state of ecstasy while in dialogue with God the Father

A s a child, I remember that it was my mother who first told me about God the Father. Mom explained that our heavenly Father created me. He made all of us. He made the entire world and He was watching, always watching, to see if I was being good and remembering to say my prayers.

Prayers. I didn't know much about my heavenly Father except that He liked prayers, especially the one named after Him. Folding my hands together, with my fingers pointing perfectly towards heaven, I would begin "His" prayer on my knees every night by the side of my bed: *"Our Father, Who art in heaven, hallowed be Thy name, Thy Kingdom come, Thy will be done, on earth as it is in heaven...."*

I liked saying the *Our Father* prayer. And for some reason, I knew that when I did, this seemingly far-away Father of mine heard me every time. I was sure of this in my heart. I also felt good about saying this prayer. I felt good about it because mom said that when this prayer was said, it helped others who weren't as fortunate, people who were often hungry and sad.

As I grew in age and stature, I kept saying that prayer—for all the same reasons—and for a few new ones. I also became curious about why my Father in heaven was so far away. Why couldn't we see Him? Why didn't He reveal Himself to us? And why wasn't everyone as fortunate as we were? Why were there poor and sad people in the world? Didn't they know this prayer could assist them? Couldn't they ask their Father in heaven to help them like we did? I knew there were problems, but I wasn't sure why they existed.

A young mind now colliding with the drama of creation, I recognized that the world contained inequities, but through the grace of God, I somehow knew it wasn't God's fault that these problems existed. Such a determination, I sensed, would be wrong and would destroy my trust in God—my confidence in His providence. I concluded that I wasn't going to understand the problems of the world any better by surrendering my faith, especially the faith I had in my Father. As a young adult, I held tight to my convictions. I wasn't going to blame my Father in heaven for the injustice in the world. People were to blame, I reasoned, because of the choices they made. Trust, continue to trust in God, I told myself. Indeed, I continued to believe in Him— even though many people felt that there couldn't possibly be a Father in heaven who would allow so much suffering and injustice to exist in the world.

But I knew they were wrong. I also knew they didn't understand the Lord's Prayer.

The Our Father

"The Prayer"—that wonderful prayer Mom said was so special—contained the answer. "Give us our daily bread," "forgive us our trespasses," "deliver us from evil"— it was all there. The solution to the problems of the world was evident, and in my mind and heart, viable. It all came down to believing in that prayer. Brothers all are we, the song says. And in the words of the *Our Father*, I believed this brotherhood could be realized on earth, no matter how bad the world seemed to be. I believed this because I believed my Father in heaven would do anything and everything for His children — if only more people would pray to Him as I did.

Renowned author Fr. Louis Evely writes that "Christian prayer works miracles and lifts mountains, and when we have said 'Father' we have already said everything." Fr. Evely's deduction has a theological basis supported by two of Christ's teachings: "If you ask the Father anything in My Name, He will give it to you" and "Your Father knows what you need before you ask." Thus, with faith in the power of these words, Fr. Evely must have then concluded that once the word *"Father"* is spoken, the supernatural prayer of a Christian becomes absorbed into the degree of faith that launched it. Indeed, Christians pray in the name of Jesus, which means to pray in the Spirit of Jesus, who cries out within us *"Abba, Father!"* Christians also believe this because Christ's Father is our Father and in the Lord's Prayer, we are to cast ourselves aside as Christ did, and proclaim our trust in this Father who Scripture says we are someday meant to meet.

St. Thomas Aquinas

Trying to comprehend the mystery of God, His omnipotence, His infiniteness, exhausts and exhilarates a soul. No analogy can suffice. Philosophers, poets, scientists, and theologians rarely disclose satisfaction in their efforts to explain God. After completing his monumental *Summa Theologica,* even St. Thomas Aquinas, considered by many to have been the finest theological mind in Catholic history, admitted that he had not begun to truly understand God.

But in Aquinas' attempt to "sum up" all that is known about God and humanity's relations with Him, the great saint examined the profound meaning and implications of the seven petitions contained in the *Our Father.* With great care, Aquinas probed and analyzed their meaning and importance. He contemplated their potential and power. Moreover, he generated as many questions as he could about why God's people should pray this prayer. Finally, Aquinas arrived at a conclusion: what an extraordinary world this would be if the faithful actually believed that the words of the *Our Father* prayer could and would be fulfilled. Similar to my own simple conclusion, Aquinas felt that our Father in heaven wanted to answer the petitions of this prayer—if only His children, through their faith, would "let" Him. Aquinas also concluded that God wanted His children to understand that He was a Father they could depend on and trust in. And as a family depends on its earthly father, this God, our Father in heaven, said Aquinas, was always ready to help His children with any and all of their needs, just as the Old Testament reveals God had done with ancient Israel.

The Old Testament

Theologians tell us that the Personhood of God the Father is not completely revealed in the Old Testament. While these writings do establish God as a single deity—a belief the three major religions of the world still embrace today—they do not clearly show us how three persons make up this one and only God. They do, however, begin to unveil this truth and how God had a plan for His people. A plan He set in motion with Abraham. A plan which would eventually reveal the full reality of the Trinity.

Through His Old Testament covenants, God showed us how He desired to be loved and honored by His chosen people. Through His prophets, He told us that He would send His Son and His Spirit who would come to fulfill His will on earth as it was in heaven. Most of all, the Old Testament emphasizes that God desires to be recognized by His people as a father who provides and cares for His children—one who chastises them if necessary, in order to protect and guide them. All this, so His plan for them can come to fruition.

Christ Reveals the Trinity

With the coming of Christ, the truth of the Trinity was fully revealed. Almost immediately, Christ spoke of His Father in heaven. He also spoke of a second divine person, the Holy Spirit. And in explaining how He and the Father were one, Jesus revealed His own divinity. Jesus also revealed that as God's Son, His origin, as well the Holy Spirit's, comes from the Father. Thus, theologians tell us, God the Father is first and foremost and that He takes precedence. This is because in the Father everything that is God has its origin.

Scripture goes on to reveal how the Father, in sending His only Son to serve as a ransom for His sinful creatures, established an adoptive sonship for His Son's disciples. This made Christ's Father, our Father: "Call no one on earth your father — for One is your Father in Heaven" (Mt 23:9). Indeed, throughout Scripture, this teaching is supported. Even after His resurrection, Christ continued to remind His followers of this truth: "I am ascending to My Father, and your Father, to My God and your God."

Worshiping Our Father

Christ further revealed how He had come to reestablish God's

Kingdom on earth and that with His coming the reign of God was at hand. It was deliberately beginning small, the Lord said, like a mustard seed hidden in soil, but eventually would be so visible as to be undeniable. It was a kingdom that had to grow "within" each soul, He explained. And it was a kingdom in which true believers would come to worship the Father in spirit.

Most significantly, Christ taught that this ever-expanding Kingdom of God, though Trinitarian in its true nature, was best understood and acknowledged as being the "Kingdom of the Father," certain verses of Scripture support this truth, but we accept this teaching primarily because of the words contained in the Lord's Prayer, words which guide the faithful to petition their Heavenly Father for all their needs and concerns, including the coming on earth of His Kingdom. [Note: some theologians argue that the word *'Father'* in the Lord's prayer implies the Trinity.]

Over the centuries, the *Our Father* has been recited by millions and millions of people, perhaps billions and billions of times. Countless souls have prayed the Lord's prayer at one time or another in their lives, whether in times of trial and tragedy or appreciation and joy. It has been recited on many occasions and in diverse situations, as history records even evil movements, organizations, and individuals praying to the heavenly Father for divine assistance, and for His will to be done on earth as it is heaven.

His Will

Thus, such a reality reveals another truth that few of us ever find time to profoundly contemplate: along with our prayers to Him, our Father knows and has witnessed every thought, word, and deed since the beginning of the world. He has, therefore, because of His will and our pleas, been guiding the affairs of His children's lives to bring His Kingdom into the world, just as the Lord's Prayer invites Him to do. Indeed, the wisdom of Scripture teaches us that He takes all things bad and turns them into good. He has done this from the beginning, as all human events have been guided to fulfill the will of the Father, no matter how minuscule and unremarkable.

Léon Bloy writes in *Le Désespéré:* "Every man who performs a free act, projects his personality into infinity. If grudgingly he gives a penny to a poor man, that penny will pierce the hand of the poorman, will fall, will perforate the earth, will bore through the suns, will cross the filament and endanger the universe. Should he commit an impure act, he will perhaps darken the heart of thousands whom he does not know but who correspond mysteriously with him and need this man to be pure, just as a traveler dying of thirst needs the glass of water of which it is spoken in the gospel. An act of charity, a gesture of real pity will sing for him the divine praises from the days of Adam till the end of the world; it will cure the sick, console those in despair, calm the storms, ransom prisoners, convert the infidels, and protect the human race."

Bloy's words reveal, in short, how God so subtly, yet so perfectly, is guiding every action people undertake toward the coming of His Kingdom. This process has been underway from the beginning, but with Christ's introduction of the *Our Father*, it was divinely advanced.

The Catechism

The Church is in agreement with this timeless concept of the work of God. According to the Catechism of the Catholic Church, the coming of the Kingdom has been going on since the fall of man. We are all God's prodigal children who have abandoned our Father's house. And in our extreme misery, we all seek to return. Mercifully, despite our sinful nature, we are invited to return to His home, His Kingdom. For God through His only begotten Son, provided the path for our return through His forgiveness of our sins. We especially see this in the words Christ said to Peter: "I will give you the keys of the Kingdom of heaven, and whatever you bind on earth shall be bound in heaven, and whatever you loose on earth shall be loosed in heaven" (Mt. 16:19, cf Mt 18:18; 28: 16-20).

The Catholic Church not only recognizes that God is guiding history and the world to a climax, but declares that at the end of the world, the Kingdom of God will come in its fullness. For man, this will be the final realization of the unity of the human race, which God willed from creation. The visible universe, then, is itself destined, according to our faith, to be transformed so that the world itself, restored to its original state, will be at the service of the just in the risen Christ.

Praying for the Kingdom

But the question arises: why do we pray to see the Father's Kingdom "come on earth as it is in heaven" if this will not happen till the end of the world?

According to theologians, Scripture and Church Tradition reveal that while the "full" coming of the Kingdom will not happen before the end of the world, we pray that each day will see "more" of the coming of the Kingdom, that this plan of God's continues to unfold, and that all souls cooperate with God's will for the growth of His Kingdom on earth.

The Reign of the Temporal Kingdom

However, despite the fact that the full coming of the Kingdom will not come until the end of the world, it has also been prophesied that a limited, but distinguishable era in time, known as the "reign of the Kingdom on earth", will take place before the end of the world. This prophesied "temporal" Kingdom on earth has been clearly documented in the writings of the Fathers of the Church and sustained by many Doctors, Popes, Saints, and prophetic figures throughout Church history. Moreover, it has been handed down for centuries and is a prophecy, experts say, clearly established in the Old Testament. Unfortunately, the true meaning of this important teaching has been almost lost because of the many controversies surrounding the heresy of Millenarianism.

Millenarianism

The heresy of Millenarianism, which teaches that Christ will literally reign for 1,000 years on earth, has been repeatedly condemned in different versions over the centuries by the Church. This theory, and all millennium theories, have resulted from a misinterpretation of certain passages of Scripture and from the misinterpretation of the writings of some of the early Fathers of the Church. Likewise, this heresy, perhaps more than any other reason, is seen by some theologians to be perhaps the greatest reason that there is confusion in the discernment of the many prophecies which foretell the coming of a true, ordained era of peace in the world before the end of time.

But, as theologian Fr. Joseph Iannuzzi wrote, "The question of a millennium or temporal kingdom as promoted through the 'spiritual' writings of the Church Fathers, however — to be understood in a *spiritual sense* — remains open. In the words of Cardinal Joseph Ratzinger: *"Giacché la Santa Sede non si é ancora pronunicata in modo definitivo"* ["the Holy See has not yet made any definitive pronouncement in this regard"]."

On Earth as it is in Heaven

According to eschatological scholars, the coming of a temporal reign of God on earth is a completely separate prophecy and should not be confused with Millenarianism. This is because, they say, Scripture and Tradition provide strong evidence that from the beginning God willed that the earth would see a great period of peace in which the Church would reign over almost all people and nations. It is to be a period of great grace in which the Holy Spirit, as if ushering in a Second Pentecost, will guide the affairs of men in a special way that reveals God's great love and mercy for His people.

Since the 18th century, the apparitions and revelations of the Virgin Mary have continued to maintain the approach of this ordained era. Countless mystics, prophets, and visionaries have said that they have been given the understanding that the coming of "the Kingdom of the Father" on earth is near. It is not to be a literal reign of Christ on earth, they say, but rather it is to be a period in which Christ will reign through His mystical body, the Church.

At Fatima in 1917, the Virgin Mary foretold an era of peace for the world. This era, a commission of six theological experts appointed by the Bishop of Fatima concluded, implied a *"true reign of Christ, in the world."* This was because, the commission stated, *"there could be no other meaning of the word 'peace' on the lips of the Mother of Christ and no other meaning to her words "My Immaculate Heart will Triumph."* (We will discuss this matter more in Chapter Seven.)

The Holy Spirit Calls

In his Apostolic letter *Tertio Millennio Adveniente*, the Holy

Father writes that "the whole of Christian life is like a great pilgrimage to the house of the Father and that Christians are called to maintain their hope in the "definitive coming of the Kingdom." The Holy Father, expressing His great hope for what the Third Millennium will bring for the Church and the world, foresees in his apostolic letter a new springtime in the Church that would find it ready to receive "a special grace of the Lord for the Church and all humanity."

The Church, Pope John Paul II also said, was "on a journey to the Father" and would celebrate the year 2000 explicitly as a Great Jubilee. It is to be, the Holy Father said, "not a matter of indulging in a new Millenarianism: rather it is aimed at an increased sensitivity to all that the Spirit is saying to the Church and to the Churches (cf. Rev 2:7 ff) as well as to individuals through charisms meant for the whole community."

The Fulfillment of the Lord's Prayer

What is the Spirit saying to the Church? The Spirit announces the dawn of a new epoch, according to God's prophets of our age. And this new epoch, many believe, is none other than the long awaited, promised coming of the temporal Kingdom of God, the Kingdom of our Father on earth. Indeed, was it not Pope John XXIII who voiced his belief in a Second Pentecost when he announced the convening of the Second Vatican Council?

Most significantly, the Spirit has been revealing that this new era will be in many ways the fulfillment of the *Our Father* prayer. In fact, God's chosen ones say the very words of the petitions in the Lord's Prayer—*"Thy Kingdom come, thy will be done on earth as it is in heaven"*— alludes to such a future time of fulfillment and that these words were deliberately provided by Jesus to unite the voices of the faithful to plea to God "for peace on earth as it is in heaven." Surely over time, they say, God our Father intended to answer His people's cries, as He did when ancient Israel was held in bondage.

As Pope John Paul II stated in his general audience of December 16, 1998, "Thus, we set out on the journey, which, starting from the Father, leads creatures back to the Father, in accordance with the loving plan fully revealed in Christ." Indeed, this reality, and what it means to the future of the world, is said to be the essence of the new era.

A Kingdom Within

Finally, it is important to understand that the new era will be ushered in only by a fuller realization that the coming of the Father's Kingdom on earth will be spiritual. God's children must renounce this world through their own free will and desire God with all their heart.

Thus, spurred by a great infusion of grace, the coming Kingdom will be, as Christ said, a Kingdom within our souls. Our Father loves His people with an unconditional love and each is precious in His eyes, but for the Kingdom to come, countless souls have to turn to God, to spend time with Him, to get to know Him in the innermost recesses of their souls—their hearts. Then and only then, with this kind of relationship with souls, will God's presence be made more manifest throughout the world.

The Triumph Comes

While all this sounds almost impossible in light of our present world, the prophets of our times say God will bring much of this about Himself. Through a great epiphany, many will soon begin to turn toward God. They will come to perceive God in a more profound way, eventually becoming , if they so choose, subsumed into His love and transformed in a way that they will claim their inheritances as true children of God. This means that they will know, love, and honor God and permit Him to dwell in their souls. And they will lead countless more to want to follow.

According to visionaries, this process has already begun. The winnowing has commenced and the separation and differences between our age and the coming age will soon come into clear view. The consequences of the choices our errant culture has made will soon hasten the dissolution of the old age so that the dawn of the new era will become more evident.

Indeed, the clock cannot be turned back and the prayer of the ages will be answered. Clothed in the wisdom of God, the Triumph dawns—the Father's Kingdom comes—and true peace, the peace our forefathers desired, is said to be destined to cover the earth.

This book seeks to look closer at *who* our heavenly Father is, the unfolding of the great mystery surrounding the coming of His Kingdom on earth, and to support the belief that God's prodigal children are truly coming home — home to their heavenly Father.

CHAPTER ONE

I AM A FATHER TO ISRAEL

"We believe in one God, the Father Almighty, Creator of Heaven and Earth, of all that is seen and unseen."

With these words, Catholics, and certainly all Christians, affirm that their God not only exists, but has revealed within His Divinity and Trinitarian nature—through His only begotten Son, Jesus Christ—the mystery of His Divine paternity. And that in the fullness of this revelation, God Our Father reveals both who He is for us and in us.

The early centuries of the Church saw the formation of the Trinitarian dogma in the context of its defense against heresies that challenged the divinity of Christ and the existence of the Triune God. But the mystery of the Fatherhood of God was announced by Christ so many times and in so many ways that His Messianic mission in establishing this truth is incontestable. For Jesus, God was not merely the Father of Israel, or the Father of mankind, but "My Father."

Indeed, Christ spoke of "His Father" in such a literal sense that the Jews wished to kill Him (Jn 5:18). The Father, said Christ, is the origin of His being, of His messianic mission, of His teaching. And, so that we should follow His teaching with no misunderstanding, Christ said, "He who believes in Me believes not in Me, but in Him who sent Me" (Jn 12:44).

We proclaim this truth at the beginning of the Creed. The Eternal Father merits our first consideration because He is the "beginning without beginning" in the Trinitarian mystery. The Father is not made, nor created, nor generated by anyone. He is of Himself, the principle of the life which He has in Himself. This life, that is the divinity itself, is possessed in absolute communion with the Son and the Holy Spirit, who are consubstantial with Him.[1]

But how is Christ's revelation of the Father different from that of the Old Testament, in which God as Father is also revealed and contemplated?

The Fatherhood of God is Revealed

Biblical scholars say that the Old Testament did not reveal God's Fatherhood in the way that Christ explicitly announced this truth. Although it did prepare the way for Christ's revelation by revealing God's Fatherhood in His covenant with His people and through His Words to His prophets, no specific doctrine of the Father is found.

Scholars note that God's plan in the Old Testament is easily discernible as seen in the emergence of the Jew's monotheistic creed, something of a rarity in the pagan polytheistic era. They say the Old Testament can be understood to have been fashioned by God to, first and foremost, manifest the truth about one God, and that in His wisdom, God chose to withhold the fullness of the revelation of the Blessed Trinity.

Much like our gradual understanding of the mysteries surrounding the divine favors given to the Blessed Virgin Mary (especially her own Immaculate Conception), without directly stating such divine truths, the Old Testament reveals that the Messiah would have a divine nature and that God was an infallible Trinity of Persons.

But perhaps as much as any of His other divine attributes, the Fatherhood of God in the Old Testament is clear, irrefutable, and measurable. The God of the Jews can be understood in human terms by analogy with human fatherhood and this was designed to be clearly recognized by His people. Indeed, the allusions to God's Fatherhood are clear in the Old Testament and convey His moral authority over His people like a father with his family. Many verses reveal this truth:

> The Lord says: Israel is my first born son, and I say to you let my son go... (Ex 4:22-23).

Yet, Lord, you are our Father, we are clay and you are our potter; we are all the work of your hand. (Is 4:8; 63:16).

As a father pities his children the lord pities those who fear him so (Ps 103:13).

The Lord reproves him who he loves, as a father the son in who he delights (Prov 3:12).

O Lord, Father and Ruler of my life, do not abandon me to their counsel, and let me not fall because of them... O Lord, Father and God of my life, do not leave me at the mercy, of brazen looks (Sir 23: 1-4).

If the righteous man is God's son, he will help him, and will deliver him from the hands of his adversaries (Wis 2:18).

With weeping they had departed, and with consolations I will lead them back...for I am a father to Israel, and Ephraim is my first born (Jer 31:9).

A Father to Israel

As noted, the Old Testament, the hinge of monotheistic religion, consolidated the truth about one God, but not the truth of the triune God. This did not come until Christ. But, the fatherhood attributed to God in the Old Testament is above all a true fatherhood, and this is especially seen as it relates to the people of Israel as a whole.[2]

In the Old Testament, God showed Israel the way and gave them food, actions that can be interpreted as a father's love, a father who teaches his children to walk and who feeds them.[3] Likewise, the element of paternal reproof of Israel is cited: "Know then in your heart that the Lord, your God, disciplines his son "(Deut 8:5). Family disharmony, the consequence of sin, is also pointed out to the people of their God, their father: "I reared children and brought them up, but they have rebelled against me" (Is 1:2).

But God keeps asserting His paternal authority, reminding Israel that because of their filial relationship with and consecration to Him, they are not to follow the customs of others: "You are children of the Lord your God. You must not lacerate yourselves or shore your forelocks for the dead. For you are a people holy to your Lord your God, it is you the Lord has chosen out of all the people on earth to be his people, his treasured possession" (Deut 14:1-2). God also tells them they should honor Him as their Father: "A son honors his father, and servants their master. If then I am a father, where is the honor due me? And if I am a master, where is the respect that is my due? Says the Lord of hosts to you, O priests, who despise his name" (Mal 1:6).

A Father to Each of His Children

The Old Testament emphasizes Yahweh as a father of the community of Israel; it is a collective fatherhood as it relates to the needs of the people. But there are, scholars also explain, many references to God's fatherhood as it relates to individuals:

> Though my father and mother, forsake me, yet will the
> Lord receive me (Ps 27:10).

> As a father has compassion on his children, so the Lord
> has compassion on those who fear him. For he knows
> how we were made, he remembers that we are dust
> (Ps 103: 13-14).

Likewise, many individuals in the Old Testament speak of God as their father:

> Abimelek — "My Father is king."
> Abierzer — "My Father is ready to help."
> Abiyah or Joab — "Yahweh is My Father."
> Abiram — "My Father is great."
> Abinadab — "My Father is generous."

Indeed, as the Old Testament unfolds, an emphasis is found on individual paternal affections. The trials of Israel are seen in the trials of individuals, almost like paternal chastisements: "My child, do not dispense the Lord's discipline or be weary of his reproof for the Lord reproves the one he loves as a father the son in whom he delights" (Prov 3:11-12).

In the book of Sirach, God is petitioned by the name of Father on two occasions—once for protection and once for help in resisting temptation: "Who will set a guard over my mouth, and an effective seal upon my lips, so that I may not fall because of them, and my tongue may not destroy me? O Lord, Father and Master of My life, do not abandon me to their designs and do not let me fall because of them" (Sir 22:27-23:1), and "O Lord, Father and God of my life, do not give me haughty eyes and remove evil desire from me. Let neither gluttony nor lust overcome me, and do not give me over to shameless passion" (Sir 23:4-6).

In citing God's divine paternity of Israel in the Old Testament, both collectively and individually, a systematic and developed doctrine may be discerned. Some scholars argue, though, that this is not the case. They believe that God's Fatherhood is revealed in dispersed texts, but it is not a major theme of the Old Testament. Rather, it is linked to the major themes, such as covenant and salvation. However, the revelation of God's Fatherhood does reveal His mercy and His love for His people—an aspect of God's behavior that counterbalances the sovereign exercise of His omnipotence.[4]

A Foreshadowing of Christ

Most noted in the Old Testament is the foreshadowing of Christ's coming and His relationship with God: "You are my son, today I have begotten you" (Ps 2:7); "I will be his father and he shall be a son to me" (2 Sm 7:14). The latter passage is seen to be a device that a "king" will be truly the "son" of Yahweh. The idea is seen again in Psalm 110:3: "Yours is princely power in the day of your birth, in holy splendor, before the day star; like the dew, I have begotten you."

Fr. Jean Galot, SJ, an eminent Biblicist who teaches at the Pontifical Gregorian University in Rome, writes of the profound meaning of this in regards to God as Father:

The messianic king is so truly the son of the Most High

that he becomes in his image, "the most high" among the kings of the earth.   Fatherhood imprints a resemblance. "He shall cry to me, 'You are my Father, my God, and the Rock of my salvation!'" (Ps 89: 26-27).   This Psalm finds its inspiration in Nathan's prophecy which declared: "I will make you famous just like the great ones of the earth" (2 Sm 7:9). Yet it shows more clearly how the Messiah will be the image of God whom he calls his Father, since he possesses a facsimile of his supreme power.

The Father Takes Precedence

Overall, God's Fatherhood as revealed in the Old Testament is limited; it is a specific fatherhood to a specific people.[5] The other peoples and nations are not seen to benefit from His love and are even the objects of His hostility. But it does present the concept of a God who is closer to His people, to their human condition of suffering through trials.   And it begins to reveal the implications of knowing, loving, serving, and honoring the true God–a God that had to be understood as the one, true God before there could come any knowledge of the person of the Father.

Thus, to make God known, in which the Old Testament does, is to begin to make the Father known. And although knowledge of God and knowledge of the Father are not identical, to know who God is we need to enter into the mystery of a divine person who is totally paternal, the Father.[6] We also need to enter into the mystery of the Incarnate Son, for it is through Him we have access to the Father. Likewise, we must strive to fathom the mystery of the Holy Spirit. But it is the Father who should take precedence, theologians tell us.[7]   Because in Him, everything that is in God has its origin.

CHAPTER TWO

MY FATHER AND
YOUR FATHER

The Old Testament paved the way for the full revelation of the mystery of the Fatherhood of God. While confined to limits, it revealed a God close to human existence, aware and responsive to His people's trials and needs.

But it is with the New Testament that the divine personhood of God the Father, a distinct person apart from the Son and the Holy Spirit, is revealed. Christ reveals that this divine person is "Abba-Father" and that this term is to be understood in the strictest sense. Likewise, Jesus' divine Sonship is also revealed. "Didn't you know that I have to concern myself with my Father's affairs?" (Lk 2:49).

It must be noted that Fatherhood, as it relates to the Messiah, had found expression under the influence of the surrounding religions in which the king was considered to be "the son of God."[1] This mythology of the ancient Near East originated the belief that "deity" is the "father" of men or certain lines of men. These legends also taught that a divine ancestor is often found in the origin of tribes, families, and people. Therefore, the king, as representative of the people, gathered the privilege of his person.[2] He was regarded as the 'father' of his people because the term "father" denoted his authority, which was a special, unchallenged, divinely ordained authority. Sumerian-Accadian and Sumerian-Babylonian texts especially demonstrate that these traditions existed in the ancient cultures. The pharaohs of Egypt also claimed divine paternity.

The Father-God

But while such mythologies existed, the Old Testament writings held important differences. In the Old Testament verses, there is never, as in the mythologies, references to God as a physical ancestor, one who "begets." Rather, it is a divine fatherhood towards Israel, God's elect: "For you are a people holy to the Lord your God, to be a people for his own possession, out of all the peoples of the earth" (Deut 14:2). The word "Father" is found 14 times in the Old Testament but each time with significance. He is the Creator: "Is he not your Father, who created you, who made you and established you?" (Deut 32:6). He is majestic: "Who can measure his majestic power?...(Sir 18:5). He is love: "I have loved you with an everlasting love; therefore I have continued my faithfulness to you (Jer 31:3). He is merciful: "As a father pities his children, so the Lord pities those who fear him. For he knows our frame; he remembers we are dust." (Ps 103:13-14).

Most importantly, with this unique saving act of God, on which Israel's sonship is based, a foreshadowing of the mystery of the Messiah's divine Sonship and mission of salvation is also seen. This in turn strengthens the Jewish revelation of the Father-God, but it is also significantly different. It is richer, more profound and in many ways, altogether new.

Jesus Reveals His Father

The divine Fatherhood of God as revealed in the Old Testament was related to the nation, individuals, and concentrated in a paternal relationship to the coming of the messianic king. But Jesus reveals a father who is His Father, and that He is the only begotten Son. This relationship also allows the adoptive sonship of His disciples, as Christ's teachings about the Father permit the Father's paternity to be extended to all.

Scholars say that the most significant revelations in Christ's teaching is that this divine person is be addressed as "Father." This then means, that over and above Jewish teaching, God's Fatherhood is now no longer seen as a divine attribute of God but the specific characteristic of a divine person, a person to be called "Father." "Call no one on earth your father, for One is your Father-in Heaven" (Mt 23:9).

This revelation in turn also reveals how the Father is not the totality of God. The Son and the Holy Spirit are also revealed by Christ as well as the unity between The Three Persons. The story of the Annunciation begins to delineate the distinction between the divine persons. Fr. Galot explains the significance of this revelation:

> Whereas the Jews awaited a Messiah who would have been strictly a human person, the Savior sent into our world is at once God and man. Never had the prophets imagined a personage of this sort. It is the Son who, by coming to dwell among us, showed forth the surprising dimensions of His identity. Now, by this revelation he revolutionized thinking about God himself.
>
> In particular Jesus worked a veritable revolution in the way of conceiving the fatherhood of God. By presenting himself as the Son he claimed a relationship of God. By presenting himself as the Son he claimed a relationship to a Father in who he acknowledges his origin but with who he shared the divine riches totally since he had received them as God's Son. He conceived of his earthly life as an incessant relationship with the Father. Whereas other people are involved throughout their lives in their creaturely relationship with their Creator, Jesus always acted as a Son who maintained the most complete intimacy with his Father.
>
> Jesus has therefore shown the Father to be someone who has a Son before having human beings as His children. The Father does not monopolize within Himself the reality of God, since this reality exists quite as completely in the Son and the Spirit. Yet this Father possesses and expresses the fullness of divine fatherhood.

The Doctrine of the Father

What therefore is the distinction between the doctrine of God and the doctrine of the Father? Over time, many have concluded the God of the Old Testament, in lieu of Christ's revelation of the Father, to have been entirely the person of the Father. Some have even called this period the time reserved to the Father.

However, while the God of The Old Testament was surely called father, these revelations were actually pointing to a future revelation of the person of the Father, from Whom comes the Son and the Holy Spirit. In the Old Testament, God manifests Himself as endowed with various attributes which will later appear as belonging to three distinct persons.[3] These attributes reveal that He already possessed His Trinitarian constitution, which eventually, in the light of Christ, is shown. However, theologians say it would be an error to conceive of God in the Old Testament as being impersonal. For this would be a reduction in value of the Trinitarian mystery which must begin with the person of the Father. There is no God, then, who proceeds the Father. Fr. Galot explains this mystery:

> In Christian revelation, divine fatherhood relates to the
> very principle of divine eternity. It forms the person
> who is the origin of the other two. It is situated within
> the depths of God. As a result, it assumes its full
> consistency within the eternal Being and it possesses
> divine perfection. Divine fatherhood arises within the
> divine Being long before it reaches out to humanity.

The Father Takes Precedence

The significance of this, says Fr. Galot, is paramount to the entire mystery of God, His being three persons in one God, and how we can come to know Him clearly through Christ's revelations of Him:

> The Father takes precedence. He is the first person to
> be God. In him everything that is in God has its origin.
> This explains why, when the revelation of the Trinity
> was given us, the name of God, which designated the
> totality of God in the Old Testament in whom the
> distinction of the persons was not yet apparent, was used
> in the New Testament to designate more specifically
> the person of the Father. The Father is called God
> because in him is verified everything that had previously
> been revealed about God, and because he is the source

of the divinity of the Son and the Spirit. In the Father dwells the plenitude of divinity in its primordial ongoing. This plentitude is present in the Son and the Spirit, inasmuch as it is received from the Father.

In practice, this consideration, which might seem very abstract, means that everything we know about God, his eternity, his omnipotence, his infinity, his qualities and attributes, assumes the face of a Father when seen in the light of the New Testament. The Father's features come to life in a certain sense when we see the warmth of a fatherly glance that confers a new light and a new warmth to our vision. God's eternity is first of all the eternity of a Father who has always existed. His omnipotence is inherent in his paternal supremacy. His infinity is the immeasurable grandeur of a Father's heart. The other attributes have a similar hallmark, such as the simplicity through which everything in the Father is paternal in the most limpid and transparent way. God is first and foremost, a Father, and therefore all the characteristics of divinity first assume a paternal aspect. In order to know God, it is important to see his paternal face clearly.

Christ's Father is our Father

Of course, it is in Christ's words that we learn all about His Father, our Father, and about all of His paternal attributes. Christ taught about the Father in such a definitive way that there is no doubt about how we are to understand the Father and how He is to be approached. Indeed, Scripture shows us how Christ moved swiftly to reveal that since He and the Father are one, our approach to the Father should begin with Him. Jesus said this in many ways in the New Testament:

He who believes in me believes not in me, but in him who sent me (Jn 12-14).

I have not spoken on my own authority, the Father who sent me has himself commanded me what to say and what to speak (Jn 12:49).

Truly, truly I say to you, the Son can do nothing of his
own accord, but only what he sees the Father doing for
whatever he does, the Son does likewise (Jn 5:19).

For as the Father has life in himself, so he has
generated the Son also to have life in himself (Jn 5:26).

As the living Father sent me, I live because of
the Father... (Jn 6:57).

He who has seen me has seen the Father (Jn 14:9).

The Father "Almighty"

Christ's revelations that the Father and He are one confirm His
divine nature. But His obedience to the Father is just as significant, for
He was allowing us to understand the divine attributes of the Person of
the Father, unique to Him as Father.

For instance, Christ explains that the Father is almighty–a firm
truth not to be misunderstood. This, we inevitably recall in the Creed,
when we say: "I believe in One God, the Father almighty." Indeed,
of all the divine attributes, only God's omnipotence is cited in the
Creed.

The Catechism of the Catholic Church teaches that to confess
this power "has great bearing on our lives." We believe that His might
is universal, for God, who created everything also rules everything, and
can do everything [4] The Catechism also states that "God's power is
loving, for he is Father, and mysterious, for only faith can discern it when
it is made perfect in weakness." And that "God is the Father Almighty
whose fatherhood and power shed light on one another. God also
reveals his fatherly omnipotence by the way he takes care of our needs;
by the adoption he gives and by his infinite mercy."

In revealing the person of the Father, Christ not only revealed
His "almighty" power but that within that power the Father is also to
be understood as the Creator. He is the creator, we pray in the Creed,
"of heaven and earth, of all that is seen and unseen." Creation is the

beginning of the history of salvation which culminates in Christ, whose light then reveals the beginning: "God created heaven and earth and that this creation was envisaged in the glory of Christ."[5] The Catechism teaches that the Father Almighty, the Creator of the ordered and good world, then also cares for all His creatures.

The Profound Love of Our Father

But why then, the question arises, does evil exist? Did the Father create evil, too?

Here, in the drama of sin, do we come to understand God our Father even more profoundly. This is because Christ reveals how the Father, in His patient, enduring love, created a world with free creatures. These creatures have to journey toward their ultimate destinies through free choice. And although they go astray and sin, He permits it because He respects their freedom. Christ's reveals how the Father awaits the return of each of His children. Like the parable of the Prodigal Son, as soon as we turn His way, He rushes to meet us.

Scholars say that Jesus Christ's mission to reveal the Father's love, in the way that is seen throughout Scripture, is superior to the bond originally contracted by the Father with His creatures, simply as their Creator. Rather, it is a love of the Father grounded in the filial love of the Son's resurrection and, consequently, then granted to all souls. Indeed, Christ's words speak of "My Father and your Father." He uses the terms "your heavenly Father," "your Father" "their Father," and "our Father," all of which continue to confirm the truth of a wonderful mystery: that Christ's Father is also truly our Father.

CHAPTER THREE

OUR FATHER

Who is our Father in heaven, the Father that Christ revealed? Surely much can be said to answer this question. However, Christ's own words, and the words of those who heard Him speak of God the Father, are the best source, for they reveal the truth of who the Father is in the simplest and clearest manner.

Christ's Teachings on the Father

In his first letter, the apostle John gives us this revelation of the Father:

> What was from the beginning, what we have heard, what we have seen with our own eyes; what we have looked upon and touched with our hands; the Word, who is life—this is our subject. That life was made visible: we saw it and we testify and proclaim to you the everlasting life which was the Father and has been made visible to us. What we have seen and heard we now proclaim to you. (1 Jn 1:1-4).

No words more perfectly begin this mystery. For these men, the Apostles, experienced the specific moment in history in which God the Father revealed Himself. While John's Gospel refers to the incarnate Christ as the Word, it also states that the Word is with someone other than Himself: "The Word was with God" (1 Jn 1:1). While the Word made flesh is God, the phrase "the word was with God" reveals that from all eternity Christ was oriented to the Father.

Indeed, according to John, no one has truly seen the Father. But Christ, the only begotten Son, "is in the bosom of the Father" (Jn 1:18). This intimacy is intended to be shared, "for our fellowship is with the Father and with his son, Jesus Christ" (1 Jn 1:3).

John wrote of these things so we would understand that intimacy with the Father should be the goal, the great summit, of our lives—one which will give us an abundance of joy. For as John explains, "We are writing these things so that our joy may be complete" (1 Jn 1:4).

Moreover, with these words, the great evangelist is expressing the essence of Christ's teaching: communion with the Father is the highest goal to be sought through Christ, because Christ Himself taught this to His disciples. Indeed, His entire public life was focused on the Father.

Christ and the Father are One

From His earliest teachings, Christ testified that it was His oneness with the Father that permitted Him to speak as He did. Scripture tells us that the people were amazed at His teaching, at its authority and its wisdom (Mk 1:22) and that Christ Himself said His words would not pass away (Mk 3:31). But Christ quickly defined the source of His words and authority: "I have not spoken on my own, it is the Father Himself who sent me who has commanded me what to say and how to speak it... as the Father has spoken to me, so do I speak" (Jn 12:49-50); "I've called you friends because everything I've heard from the Father I've made known to you" (Jn 15:15). This, Christ said, included the miracles: "If I'm not doing my Father's works, don't believe me! But if I am and you still doubt Me, believe the works, so that you may realize that the Father is in me and I am in the Father" (Jn 10:37-38). Likewise, even His authority to work on the Sabbath is, Christ says, from the Father: "My Father is at work until now, and I am at work as well." (Jn 5:17)

Thus, Christ's earthly mission was the mission of the One who sent Him. And He made it a great part of His mission that this truth be realized by His listeners and followers. Throughout Scripture this teaching is emphasized: "My food is to do the will of the One who sent me and to bring his work to completion" (Jn 4:34).

To the Father Through the Son

The One Who sent Him and assigned His mission is revealed early in the New Testament: "Did you not know I must be about My Father's business?" (Lk 2:49). This Father is the one Christ calls "Abba" in prayer, a word based on Jewish tradition that theologians say is rich in its meaning. In using it, Christ shows us that His Father is to be understood as our Father. Indeed, even after His resurrection, He continues to remind His followers of this truth. At the tomb, He says to Mary Magdalene, "I ascend to My Father and your Father, My God and your God" (Jn 20:17).

Most of all, the Father of Christ is revealed in Scripture to be loving, merciful, and generous to His children: "If you who are evil know how to give good gifts to your children, how much more will your Father in heaven give good things to those who ask him!" (Mt 7:11) And those good things were available for the asking, Christ said, especially if asked through Him: "All things have been given to me by my Father" (Mt 11:27); "Father...everything of mine is yours and yours is mine" (Jn 17:1,10).

Thus, following Scripture's words, we must first turn to Jesus and pray that He grants us the grace of approaching the Father with our petitions: "No one knows the Son except the Father, nor does anyone know the Father except the Son, and anyone to whom the Son wishes to reveal him" (Mt 11:27). But first, to be favored by such a grace, Scripture says we must be humble of heart, like a child: "Father, Lord of heaven and earth, to you I offer praise; for what you have hidden from the learned and the lower you have revealed to the merest children. Father, it is true. You have graciously willed it so" (Mt 11:25-27).

Finally, Christ also taught that we should "pray in secret" under the watchful eyes of the Father (Mt 6:6), "address our petitions to the Father" (Mt 7:7:11, Lk 11:9-13), and to pray, addressing Him as "Our Father who art in heaven" (Mt 6:9).

The Father's Kingdom

Christ revealed that the Father already knows what our earthly needs are: "Your heavenly Father knows all that you need" (Mt 6:32). But, not surprisingly, the Father was especially concerned with the needs of our souls: "Seek first the Kingdom and his righteousness, and all these things will be given to you besides (Mt 6:33).

And so the question is, how does one seek the Father's Kingdom and what exactly is this Kingdom? How do we come to grasp the depths of this mystery?

According to Christ's words, it is a kingdom of humble souls who trust their Father in everything: "Your Father knows what you need before you ask Him" (Mt 6:8). They are souls that know that Christ, Himself, asked His Father to prepare them for the coming of the Kingdom: "Father, keep them in your name, that you have given me, so that they may be one just as we are" (Lk 10:22). And that, indeed, the Father is searching and desirous for such souls: "The hour is coming, and is here now, when true worshipers will worship the Father in spirit and truth, and indeed the Father seeks such people to worship Him" (Jn 4:23). Finally, they are souls who strive to be true children of their heavenly Father (Mt 5:45), and who will work to bring glory to the name of the Father, as Christ did in His life, suffering, and death: "Father, glorify your name. Then a voice came from heaven, "I have glorified it and will glorify it again" (Jn 12:28).

The Coming of the Kingdom

Since Christ's ascension, the mystical body of Christ has prayed for the coming of the Kingdom of the Father, "on earth as it is in heaven." However, over the centuries some of the meaning of this divine petition to the First person of the most Holy Trinity has become somewhat removed. Contemporary theologians note that Christians say the words of the Our Father without ever contemplating what they are asking for. Likewise, few think about God's Kingdom truly coming to exist in some greater form on earth.

But since the 19th century, the chosen ones of God, His prophets and visionaries, have said that there is greater meaning in this prayer than we may think and that we need to reexamine it more clearly to understand God's plans. At Fatima, Mary promised that God would bring a new era into the world. It is to be an era that honors God and gives Him the Glory He deserves. Mary says it is to be an era of peace. Most of all, experts who have studied Mary's words say it is to be an era that will more closely resemble the Father's "Kingdom on earth" than any time since the beginning—one that fulfills to a greater degree the words of the *Our Father* prayer—and one that finally brings to fulfillment an old prophecy, long held to be found in Judeo-Christian Scripture and Tradition.

CHAPTER FOUR

GOD SHALL REIGN
OVER THE NATIONS

A ccording to many theologians, Scripture clearly speaks of a coming period of universal peace on earth. Church history is also rich with related testimony. In fact, this prophecy can be traced back before the beginning of the Catholic Church. Therefore, it must be looked at in the proper tradition of examining such prophecy to grasp its importance for the Church and the world. In fact, our faith dictates as much, because contrary to current belief, our entire religion is based on prophecy and its subsequent, historical merit as related to the truth about our one, true God.

The Great Role of Prophecy in Christianity

Church historians tell us that the Judeo–Christian faith functionally begins in prophecy and history. The Fathers of the Church understood that Christianity and its root, Judaism, were radically different from other religions. Prior to Judaism, religions of the world were without historical perspective. But beginning with Abraham, promises of future events were prophesied and then fulfilled in history. From Sarai's conception to the coming of Moses, the liberator, God shared His foreknowledge of the future with His chosen people, and then proved His words were true through the unfolding of events. With the coming of the prophesied Messiah, the continuation of religion based on the hope found in fulfilled prophecy is seen again and becomes the foundation of the world's largest religion. Christianity, like Judaism, took on the form of a historic religion, as one prophesied event after another was fulfilled..

Moreover, the New Testament encourages that such a charism as prophecy is to be accepted, encouraged, and respected. Saint Paul in the first letter to the Corinthians says:

> Aim at charity, yet strive after the spiritual gifts, but especially that you may prophecy.

> He who prophesies speak to men for edification and encouragement and consolation.

> Now I should like you all to speak in tongues but still more to prophecy. For he who prophecies is greater than he who speaks in tongues.

In His first letter to the Thessalonians, St. Paul wrote:

> Do not extinguish the Spirit, do not despise prophecies. But test all things and hold fast to that which is good.

The Catholic Church's Magisterium concurs with this position and in Lumen Gentium, the Second Vatican Council recognized that the charism of prophecy extends down to our day. Likewise, the Church established that it's position is not restricted to Scriptural-based prophecy but also recognizes the value of private revelation. This is because God continues to communicate His Will to His people.

The Valuable Role of Private Revelation

Private prophecy holds an honored place in the history of the Catholic Church and often such events become authenticated within the Church in the form of devotions and sacramentals. Wrote Pope Benedict XIV, "Though an assent of Catholic faith be not due to such revelations, they, however, desire a human assent, according to the rules of prudence, by which they are probable, and piously credible, as the revelations of Blessed Hildegarde, St. Bridget, and St. Catherine of Sienna."

However, over the centuries and especially throughout the 20th century, prophecy and it's value to the Church has been questioned and gradually replaced by a false intellectualism driven by a contemporary incredulity in all matters of the supernatural. This has left the Church, and the average Catholic, with a weakened faith in the Church's teachings. We see this in many areas of the faith, but perhaps the polls that reflect the fact that many Catholics have lost belief in the True Presence of Christ in the Eucharist are the best and most recognized example.

This contemporary tidal wave of "disbelief in the supernatural," which includes the element of prophecy, has also found its way deep into the Church, where some scholars debunk the miraculous, supernatural events of Scripture, rationalizing why they are not to be accepted as the literal truth. Indeed, from the miracles of the multiplication of the loaves of bread and fish to Christ's resurrection, our faith in the historical accuracy of our religion is being dismantled piece by piece.

All of this is relevant for an important reason. Mary's message at Fatima of a new era, a reign "peace", must be seen as an assertion that the Lord of history is about to take control of history in such a visible way as to redirect the entire course of civilization, regardless of the present atmosphere of doubt. Furthermore, such a change may be seen as no less than miraculous, and will also then invite an entire reexamination of the importance of prophecy. This is because God has been announcing for centuries that this period was coming and that He willed it so, but few have wanted to take a look at what Scripture held and what the Fathers and Doctors of the Church, as well as many great saints, mystics, and popes, had written about this matter.

Prophecies of the Coming of the Kingdom in Scripture and Tradition

The prophecy of a coming, universal reign of God's peace on earth is one that has surfaced in the prophetic writings of almost every generation, But in order to arrive at a true understanding of the coming epoch and what it will hold, we must begin by looking beyond private revelation. This is because the Church has not recognized many of the prophecies of the saints, mystics, and visionaries that make up these revelations, and therefore, they have not been officially declared "worthy of the faith." This is not to say these revelations are to be discarded, ignored or mistrusted, for there may be great truth and even greater light on the new era in such writings. But the foundation for the proper understanding of such a prophecy as the coming of the "reign of the Kingdom" must first be established through

Scripture and Church Tradition. Likewise, the Catechism of the Catholic Church must be noted. Only after this can such an important prophecy be examined in the light of private revelation in order to see if there is harmony and perhaps any new disclosures that God may desire to reveal to His people.

The Millenarian heresies

It must be noted that this prophesied era is not to be confused with the prophecies that speak of the 1,000 year reign of Christ with His Saints on earth. These beliefs are known as "Millennium theories" and have also been called Millenarianism, Millenarism or Chilam. Through Origen, St. Augustine, and St. Jerome, such teachings were totally discredited by the 5th century and even as recently as the 20th century, Cardinal Ratzinger in his work *The Theology of History in St. Bonaventure* noted that the Church excluded these theories as heretical for they denied "Christ is the end of the ages." In 1994, the new Catechism again rejected even modified forms of these theories, calling them the falsification of the Kingdom to come under the name of Millenarianism, especially the "intrinsically precise' political form of secular messianism." Simply stated, true believers are not to look for a 1000-year reign of Christ Himself on earth and that such beliefs stem from a false understanding of the teachings of Scripture and Tradition.

A Reign of Peace on Earth

But what exactly is contained in Scripture and Tradition about the coming of an era that is foretold to be steeped in peace and strong faith?

According to scholars, the age of peace—the coming of the Father's Kingdom on earth—has been historically understood from Scripture and Tradition since the earliest times in the Church to be a future time that, after a unique series of events, witnesses a complete restoration of Christian culture in the West and then throughout the world.

Many theologians have upheld that an "unconditional age of peace" is foretold to come. It is unconditional, they say, because it *is* indicated in both Scripture and Tradition and because it will precede the end of time. Desmond Birch, in his book, *Trial, Tribulation and Triumph,* (Queenship Publishing, 1996) summarized what Church scholars have written concerning this prophecy in Scripture. "In the opinion of many sound Catholic Scripture scholars, there is a Scriptural basis for a significant "time of peace" that is an interlude......this is recognized by all the great eschatologists in the Church...."

The Writings of the Old Testament

To note all of these Scriptural passages would be prohibitive, but Scriptural scholars say that numerous verses of the Old Testament expect the coming of such an age. Some of these verses have also been viewed as foreshadowing references to the coming of Christ. In this context, they were, therefore, fulfilled in Him. However, scholars say these interpretations cannot be true because, although Christianity has changed the world, the world remains driven by secular, humanist philosophies and has not yet experienced what the verses of the Old Testament appear to be foretelling: an almost universal reign of God on earth:

> For God is the king of all the earth: sing ye wisely. God shall reign over the nations; God sitteth on his holy throne (Ps 47:8-9).

> And he shall rule from sea to sea, and from the river unto the ends of the earth... And all kings of the earth shall adore him: all nations shall serve him" (Ps 72:8,11).

> The wolf shall dwell with the lamb: and the leopard shall lie down with the kid: the calf, and the lion, and the sheep shall abide together, and a little child shall lead them. The calf and the bear shall feed: their young ones shall rest together: and the lion shall eat straw like the ox. And the sucking child shall play on the hold of the asp: and the waned child shall thrust his hand into the den of the basilisk. They shall not hurt, nor shall they kill in all my holy mountain, for the earth is filled with the knowledge of the Lord, as the covering waters of the sea (Is. 11 6-9).

> For he that made thee shall rule over thee, the Lord of hosts in his name: and thy Redeemer, the Holy One of Israel, shall be called the God of all the earth (Is 54:5).

And the Lord shall be king over the earth: in the day there
shall be one Lord, and his name shall be one (Zach 14:9).

The New Testament

There is evidence of the same in the New Testament. As in the
Old Testament, some say Christ's teachings hint to such a time. In
addition to the *Our Father* prayer (Matt 6: 9-13), Jesus speaks of the
Kingdom of God in several parables. Comparing it to a mustard seed and
unleavened bread (Lk 8:18-21), Christ explains that the Kingdom will
begin hidden and slowly rise, becoming so visible through its ever-
expanding growth, that there will be no doubt it is of God.

Also noted in Christ's teaching is the need for God's children to
understand that they were created with free will, and that the coming of the
Kingdom on earth before the end of time would only be realized through
an internal process of change, not by God forcing His will upon the world.
God's people would have to choose the teachings of Christ, then, to
become Christ-like. And in becoming Christ-like, they would, one by
one, establish the Kingdom of heaven on earth: "For Lo, the Kingdom of
God is within you" (Jn 4:24); "The Kingdom of God is not meat and drink
but justice, and peace, and joy the Holy Spirit" (Rom 14:17).

Most noted, experts say, are several passages in the Book of
Revelation. Fr. Herman Kramer, considered possibly the leading
authority of the 20th century on this subject, wrote a lengthy study on the
authentic and inspired prophecies of the Old and New Testament titled
Mankinds Final Destiny. Kramer, who read and wrote fluently in seven
languages and who wrote extensively on the Apocalypse, especially cited
Chapter 9 of the Apocalypse. He wrote "Verses 20 and 21 presage a *"time
of peace."* This "time of peace," according to Birch's interpretation of Fr.
Kramer's conclusion, is to be a time which follows our present time, and
is based upon the commentaries of all the great eschatological Scriptural
scholars in the history of the Church, especially the early Fathers.

The Catechism

Of course, it is especially in the writings of the early Fathers that
the Catechism of the Catholic Church formulated its interpretation of
what Christ meant when he spoke of the coming of the Kingdom on the

earth as it is in heaven. While not wishing to interpret any specific prophetic inferences to these words, which the Church has always refrained from doing with most eschatological mysteries, the Catechism provides insight and direction.

The Catechism states that the words *"thy Kingdom come,"* as recalled in Scripture, refers *"primarily"* to "the final coming of the reign of God through Christ's return," and that this will be "at the end of the world." Likewise, the Catechism addresses this question again in its interpretation of the meaning behind our Profession of Faith. Again, the Catechism states that the coming of the Kingdom will not come in the fullest sense of the words until the end of the world: "At the end of time, the Kingdom of God will come it its fullness. Then the just will reign with Christ forever."

The correct understanding of the meaning of the full coming of the Kingdom, therefore, is unequivocal. However, the Catechism, while not stating that a definitive period of profound bliss is promised to come and will be seen on earth, allows for the unfolding of such an historical development coming to fruition before the end of time. That is why it enjoins the word "primarily" when defining the meaning of the coming of the Kingdom, and then adds that it is the mission of the Church to work for the growth of such a kingdom *"now."*

Indeed, Christ Himself said the reign of God had begun with Him and indicated that the world would see more evidence of this truth as time passed (Lk 13). The Catechism of the Catholic Church, ever aware of Scripture and the writings of the Fathers and Doctors of the Church on this matter, clearly emphasizes that while the "full" coming of the Kingdom will not occur until the end of time, this reality must not discourage or impede progress in the growth of the reign of God in time: "Far from distracting the Church from her mission in the present world, this desire [the coming of the Kingdom] commits her to it all more strongly. Since Pentecost, the coming of the Reign is the work of the Spirit of the Lord who "complete(s) his work on earth and brings us the fullness of grace."

The Catechism also acknowledges that this is exactly what the Spirit seeks in our world in every generation: "The Kingdom of God is righteousness and peace and joy in the Holy Spirit. The end-time in which we live is the age of the outpouring of the Spirit. Ever since Pentecost, a decisive battle has been joined between "the flesh" and the Spirit:"

Only a pure soul can boldly say "Thy Kingdom Come."

One who has heard Paul say, 'Let not sin therefore reign in your mortal bodies and he who has purified himself in action, thought, and word will say to God: "Thy Kingdom Come!

Striving for the Kingdom

Finally, the Catechism of the Church states that we are to pray for the Kingdom on earth because God has made it known to us that this is part of the mystery of His will as He set forth in Christ:... "to gather up all things in Him, things in Heaven and things on earth. And therefore, we ask in prayer for this loving plan to be fully realized "on earth as it is already in heaven."

Thus, Scripture clearly holds prophetic inferences for the coming of a special time of peace on earth and the Church teaches that striving for the "Kingdom on earth" is more than appropriate, it is a duty. And if at such a time in history God grants the world, and especially the Church, the grace to experience a greater, universal reign of peace amongst nations and peoples as has been prophesied for centuries, then this is in no way a contradiction with what will occur at the end of time. In fact, all of this, according to the Catechism, is a matter of "discernment":

> By a discernment according to the Spirit, Christians have to distinguish between the growth of the reign of God and the progress of the culture and society in which they are involved. *This distinction is not a separation.* Man's vocation to eternal life does not suppress, but actually reinforces, his duty to put into action in this world the energies and means from the Creator to serve justice and peace. This petition is taken up and granted in the prayer of Jesus (The Our Father) which is present and effective in the Eucharist, it bears its fruit in the Beatitudes.

Once again, the *Our Father* prayer is exactly where, according to experts, we find the most insight in Scripture about this matter. Therefore, before we examine what Tradition and private revelation offer concerning the coming of an era foretold as the reign of the Father's Kingdom on earth, let us see what the Church has come to understand about this entire mystery as revealed in the Lord's prayer.

CHAPTER FIVE

THY KINGDOM COME

"Our Father, who art in heaven, hallowed be thy name. Thy Kingdom come. Thy will be done, on earth as it is in heaven."

For two thousand years, Christians have prayed the *Our Father* prayer, as revealed by Jesus, invoking the First Person of the most Holy Trinity and asking that His heavenly Kingdom of peace and love come on earth as it is in heaven. Given to us by Christ when one of His disciples said, *"Lord teach us to pray,"* the *Our Father* is the staple prayer of the Christian faith. Besides honoring the Father, the prayer is considered the perfect dialogue with God because of its emphasis on love, forgiveness, and protection from evil. It has served as common ground for Christians, and may perhaps be mystically seen in retrospect someday to be what God gave the Church to restore the unity necessary for a greater coming of the Kingdom *"on earth as it is in heaven."*

But what exactly, according to experts, is the reason we should want this? What exactly are we praying for when we pray the *Our Father?*

St. Thomas Aquinas

According to Church scholars, if we want to better understand the principles of the "Kingdom of God" so that heaven on earth can become more of a reality, we must better understand the "Our Father." In this, the Lord's prayer, we discover all that is necessary to seek and follow the plan of God for the world and for our own individual lives. And through it we are better able to understand the "Father" and "His

Kingdom" and why we pray for His Kingdom to come.

While many great men and women of the Church have written about the *Our Father* prayer, one especially is noted. St. Thomas Aquinas, the great theologian and Doctor of the Church, reportedly preached 10 sermons on the Lord's prayer in 1273, the last year of his life. Aquinas preached that among all the prayers, the *Our Father* was prominent because it excelled in five important areas: confidence, rectitude, order, devotion, and humility. Aquinas taught that in beginning to pray the *Our Father,* we must consider two things: (1) Why God is our Father and (2) what we owe Him because He is our Father. And according to Aquinas, we must call God Father because:

1. He created us.
2. He governs us.
3. He adopted us.

As a result, the great Doctor of the Church explains that we owe God a four-fold debt: honor, imitation, obedience and patience. Moreover, with this understanding of our heavenly Father, we are then better able to understand the words of the *Our Father*—especially, says Aquinas, what it means, to "pray for the coming of His Kingdom on earth as it is in heaven."

There are seven petitions in the Lord's prayer, of which, the first is "Thy Kingdom Come" and the second is "Thy will be done on earth as it is in heaven." The following is St. Thomas Aquinas's teaching on these two petitions:

St. Thomas' Aquinas Teaching On The Lord's Prayer

[First Petition] Since the kingdom of God always was, why must we ask for it to come? The answer may be understood in three ways:

1. **So that all things may become subject to Him.** Sometimes a king has only the right to a kingdom or throne, but as yet has not been proclaimed king because the inhabitants are not yet subjected to him. In this sense, his kingdom or throne will come when those men are subject to him.

Now, God by His very essence and nature is Lord of all. And Christ is Lord of all (not only as God, but as man by reason of His Godhead): "He gave Him power and glory and a kingdom". Consequently, all things ought to be subject to Him. However, they are not subject as yet, but will be at the end of the world: "He must reign until He hath put His enemies under His feet". Therefore, it is for this that we pray when we say, *Thy Kingdom come.*

In making this petition, we have a threefold purpose: a) the safeguarding of the just; b) the punishment of the wicked; and c) the destruction of death.

a. **The safeguarding of the just.** Man is subject to Christ in two ways either willingly or unwillingly. Since God's will is efficacious, it must be fulfilled outright; and since God wills all things to be subject to Christ, one of two things is necessary: either that men do the will of God by submitting to His Commandments (as the just do) or else that God wreak His will on men by punishing them (as He will do on sinners and on His enemies at the end of the world): "Until I make thy enemies thy footstool."[107] For these reasons, the saints are enjoined to ask that God's kingdom may come (i.e., that they may be wholly subject to Him).

b. **The punishment of the wicked.** To sinners, this is repellent, since their asking that God's kingdom may come is nothing less than their prayer that by God's will they may be condemned to punishment. "Woe to them that desire the day of the Lord."

c. **The destruction of death.** The result [of the coming of the kingdom] will be the destruction of death. Since Christ is life, in His kingdom there can be no death since it is contrary to life. Thus, it is said, "Last of all, the enemy, death, shall be destroyed." This will be fulfilled at the resurrection: "He will transform the body of our lowliness, that it may be made like to the body of His glory."

2. **Because kingdom signifies the glory of paradise.** We pray *Thy Kingdom come* because the kingdom of heaven signifies the

glory of paradise. This is easily understood. *Regnum* ("kingdom") is just another word for *regimen* ("government") and the best government is one in which nothing is done against the will of the governor. Now, since God wills men to be saved, God's will is the salvation of mankind which will be realized most especially in paradise where there will be nothing contrary to man's salvation: "They shall gather out of His kingdom all scandals." In this world, however, there are many things contrary to the salvation of mankind. When, therefore, we pray *Thy kingdom come*, we ask to be made partakers of the heavenly kingdom and of the glory of paradise.

Moreover, this kingdom is most desirable for three reasons.

a. **Its supreme righteousness**. It is desirable because of the supreme righteousness that obtains there: "Thy people shall be all righteous." Here below the wicked are mingled with the good, whereas there, are no wicked and no sinners.

b. **Its perfect liberty.** This kingdom is desirable because of its perfect liberty. Although all men desire liberty naturally, here there is none; but in heaven there is perfect liberty without any trace of bondage: "The creature itself will be delivered from the slavery of corruption."

In fact, not only will all be free, but all will be kings: "Thou hast made us to our God a kingdom." This is because all shall be of one will with God: whatever the saints will, God shall will, and whatever God wills, the saints shall will. Therefore, their will shall be done with God's will. In this way, all will reign, since the will of all will be done, and God shall be the crown of all: "In that day shall the Lord of hosts be for a crown of glory and for a diadem of beauty unto the residue of His people."

c. **Its wondrous wealth**. This kingdom is also desirable because of its wondrous wealth: "The eye hath not seen, O God, besides Thee, what things Thou hast prepared for them that wait on Thee." "Who satisfieth thy desire with good things."

Take note that whatever man seeks in this

world, he will find it more perfect and more excellent in God alone. If you seek delight, you will find supreme delight in God: "You shall see and your heart shall rejoice." And everlasting joy shall be upon their heads." Do you seek wealth? You will find in Him all things you desire in abundance: "When the soul strays from Thee she seeks things apart from Thee, but finds all things impure and unprofitable until she returns to Thee."

3. **Because sometimes sin reigns in this world**. We pray *Thy Kingdom come* because sometimes sin reigns in this world. This occurs when a man is so disposed that he follows at once the lure of sin and carries it into effect: "Let not sin reign in your mortal body" but let God reign in your heart ("who says to Zion, 'Thy God shall reign'"). This will be when you are ready to obey God and keep all His commandments. When therefore, we ask that His kingdom come, we pray that God (and not sin) may reign in us.

This fulfills the beatitude: "Blessed are the meek"

Thus, by this petition we shall obtain that beatitude of which it is said: "Blessed are the meek" by:

a. **Reliance on God**. According to the first explanation above [regarding our prayer that all may become subject to God], from the moment that a man desires God to be the Lord of all, he ceases to seek revenge for the injury done to himself and leaves that to God. For if you were to avenge yourself, you would no longer seek the advent of His kingdom.

b. **Detachment from earthly goods**. According to the second explanation above [regarding heaven as the reign of God in the glory of paradise], if you await the coming of His kingdom, i.e., the glory of paradise, you have no need to regret the loss of earthly goods.

c. **Meekness**. And according to the third explanation above [regarding the reign of sin in this world], if you pray that God may reign in you, Christ Who was most meek also will reign in you; and you will be meek in consequence: "Learn of me, for I am meek...."

The Second Petition of the Our Father

The second petition of the Lord's prayer, **Thy Will be done on earth as it is in Heaven** was also addressed by Aquinas. He says that to begin to want God's Will on earth we must desire the knowledge of God on earth. Once again, Aquinas explains this petition, and that it actually begins with our understanding of the gift of knowledge:

The gift of knowledge is the third gift bestowed on us by the Holy Spirit. For He bestows on the righteous not only the gift of fear and the gift of piety (which is a filial affection towards God, as already stated), but He also gives them wisdom. It is for this that David prayed: "Teach me goodness, discipline, and knowledge." By this knowledge the Holy Spirit teaches us to lead a good life.

Now of all the signs of man's knowledge and wisdom, none is proof of greater wisdom than that a man does not cling to his own opinions: "Lean not upon thine own prudence." For those who cling to their own judgement so as to mistrust others and trust in themselves alone, invariably prove themselves fools and are judged as such. "Seest thou a man wise in his won conceit? There is more hope for a fool than for him." But if a man distrusts his own judgement, that is a proof of his humility (which is why it is said, "where humility is, there also is wisdom") whereas the proud are too self confident.

Accordingly, we learn from the Holy Spirit (by His gift of knowledge) to do not our own but God's will, and by virtue of this gift we pray to God that His Will may be done on earth as it is in heaven. It is in this that the gift of knowledge is proved, so that when we say to God, *Thy Will be done*, it is as when a sick man consults a physician. He takes the medicine not precisely because he wills it himself, but because it is the will of the physician. If he only took what he willed himself, he would be a fool.

Hence, we should ask nothing of God but that His will be done in our regard (in other words, that His will be fulfilled in us). For man's heart is right when it agrees with the divine will. Christ did this: "I came down from heaven to do, not my own will, but the will of Him that sent me." For as God, Christ has the same will as the Father; but as man, He has a distinct will from the Father and in respect of this will, He says that He does not His own but His Father's will. For that reason, He taught us to ask and pray, *Thy will be done.*

But how can this be explained in the face of the words of the Psalm: "He hath done whatsoever He hath willed"? If He has done whatever He pleased in heaven and on earth, what does He mean when He makes us say, *Thy will be done on earth as it is in heaven*?

This is explained by observing that God wills three things in our regard, which we pray to be fulfilled.

1. **Eternal life**. God wills that we may have eternal life, because whoever makes a certain thing for a certain purpose wills that purpose for it. God made man, but not without a purpose, for as the Psalm says, "Hast Thou made all the children of men of vain?" Therefore, He made man for a certain purpose; but not for the sake of material pleasures, since dumb animals have them, but that He may have eternal life. For it is the Lord's will that man have eternal life.

When a thing attains the end for which it was made it is said to be saved, whereas when it fails to reach that end, it is said to be lost. Now God made man for eternal life; and consequently, when man obtains eternal life, He is saved, which is God's will: "This is the will of my Father Who sent me, that whosoever beholdeth the Son and believeth in Him, have eternal life." This will is already fulfilled in angels and saints, who are in heaven, who see, know, and enjoy God.

But we desire that as God's will is fulfilled in the blessed who are in heaven, even so may it be fulfilled in us who are on earth. This, then, is the sense of our prayer, *Thy will be done*: namely, that it be done in us who are on earth, even as it is fulfilled in the saints who are in heaven.

2. **Obedience to the commandments**. God wills that we keep His commandments, because when we desire a particular thing, we do not only will what we desire, but we also will whatever enables us to obtain it. Thus, a physician, in order to restore a man to health, also wills his diet, his medicine, and so on. Now God wills us to obtain eternal life: "If thou wouldst enter life, keep the commandments."

Therefore, He wills us to keep the commandments: "Your reasonable service...so that ye find out what is the *good* and the *well-pleasing* and the *perfect* will of God."

a. **God's will is good**: "Who teaches thee to profit."

b. **God's will is well-pleasing**, and though displeasing to others, yet delighted to those who love His will:

"Light is risen for the righteous and joy for the upright in heart."

c. **God's will is perfect**: "Be ye perfect as also your heavenly Father is perfect."

So when we say, *Thy will de done*, we pray that we may keep God's commandments; and this will of God is fulfilled in the righteous, but is not yet fulfilled in sinners. Now the righteous are signified by *heaven* and sinners by *earth*. Hence, we pray that God's will be done on *earth*, i.e., in sinners, even as it is done in *heaven*, i.e., in the righteous.

We must observe here that we have something to learn from the very manner of expression. For He does not say *Do* or *Let us do* but *Thy will be done*. This is because two things are required in order to obtain eternal life: the grace of God and man's will. And although God made man without man's help, He does not sanctify him without his cooperation. As Augustine says, "He Who created thee without thyself, will not justify thee without thyself," because He wishes man to cooperate: "Turn ye unto me and I will turn unto you." "By the grace of God I am what I am, and His grace in me hath not been void." Presume not therefore on yourself, but trust in the grace of God; nor be neglectful, but do your utmost.

Hence Christ does not say, *Let us do* (lest He seem to imply that God's grace counts for nothing); nor does He days, *Do* (lest He seem to state that man's will and effort are of no account). Rather He says, *Be it done*—by God's grace, with solicitude and effort on our part.

3. **Restoration of the original dignity of man**. God wills that man be restored to the state and dignity in which the first man was created, which was so great that his spirit and soul experienced no rebellion on the part of his flesh and sensuality. For as long as the soul was subject to God, the flesh was so subject to the spirit that it felt no corruption, whether of death or of sickness or of other passions.

But from the moment that the spirit and soul that stood between God and the flesh rebelled against God by sin, there and then the body rebelled against the soul. It began to be aware of death and infirmity, as well as of the ceaseless rebellion of sensuality against the spirit: "I behold another law in my members, warring against the law of my mind." "The flesh lusteth against the spirit and the spirit against the flesh."

Thus, there is continual war between flesh and spirit, and man is ever being worsened by sin. Hence, it is God's will that man be restored to his pristine state, namely that the flesh be wholly delivered from all that rebels against the spirit: "This is the will of God, your sanctification."

But this will of God cannot be fulfilled in this life, whereas it will be fulfilled at the resurrection of the sins, when bodies will arise in glory and incorruption, and in a state of great perfection: "It is sown in dishonor; it shall rise in glory." In the righteous, however, God's will is fulfilled with regard to the spirit by their righteousness, knowledge, and life. And therefore, when we say, *Thy will be done,* we pray that this may be fulfilled also in the flesh. In this way, we take heaven to signify the spirit and earth to indicate the flesh. So the sense is, *Thy will be done* on earth (i.e., in our flesh) *as it is done in heaven* (i.e., in our spirit) by righteousness.

This fulfills the beatitude: "Blessed are they who mourn" By this petition, we reach the blessedness of those who mourn, of which it is said: "Blessed are they who mourn, for they shall be comforted." This applies to each of the three explanations given above:

a. **Because eternal life is delayed**. In accordance with the first explanation (above), we mourn because we desire eternal life, but it is delayed:

"Woe is me that my sojourn is prolonged." In fact, in the saints this longing is so great that because of it, they desire death which in itself is repellent: "We have the courage even to prefer to be exiled from the body and to be at home with the Lord."

b. Because keeping the commandments is painful. In accordance with the second explanation (above), we mourn because we desire to keep the commandment, yet, however sweet the commandments are to the soul, they are bitter to the flesh, which is continually buffeted: in the flesh, "going they went and wept" but in the soul, "coming they shall come with joy."

c. **Because flesh and spirit conflict**. In accordance with the third explanation (above), we mourn because of the continual conflict between our flesh and our spirit

[which frustrates our desire to be restored to the dignity
of the first man], yet it is impossible for the soul not to
be wounded at least by venial sins due to the flesh. This
is why, until the soul is healed, it mourns: "Every night"
(i.e., in the darkness of sin) "I will wash my bed" (i.e.,
my conscience).

And they who weep thus reach their heavenly
country, to *which may God bring us all.*

Church Tradition

St. Thomas Aquinas's writings firmly solidify our understanding
of the Father and His Kingdom and why we should pray for it to come.

But it is in Church Tradition where we especially find a wealth
of information concerning the prophecy of a golden era of the Church,
an era to be known for its "peace" —an era of the reign of the Father's
Kingdom, on earth as it is in heaven. This is because many saints, popes,
and great historical figures of the Church have written about the coming
of "the Kingdom."

It is to be a time, they have stated, when a truly universal peace
will reign, one in which many governments are once again Christian,
vocations abound, and a series of great popes and rulers reign. Most of
all, Tradition holds that the reign of the Father's Kingdom on earth is to
be an age of Eucharistic reign, as mankind comes to more deeply
understand the depths and potential of this profound mystery of God
dwelling amongst His people in His Sacramental form. Thus, it will be
the fulfillment, many Church greats have said, of the prophecy of "one
flock and one shepherd."

CHAPTER SIX

ON EARTH
AS IT IS IN HEAVEN

Because Church Tradition holds so many documented references to the coming of the Father's "Kingdom on earth," it is important that some of these writings be reviewed and referenced. This is done to better establish how God has clearly revealed this is to be His Will for His people on earth before the end of the world, and to show how contemporary revelations of such an age are not new, but have long been foretold by generations of prophets.

According to the very oldest of such prophecies, a very unique set of events will come about to augment the arrival of a renewal of creation. This subject, known to theologians as the coming of the temporal Kingdom, is seen as an undisputed deposit of the faith and is comprised of the teachings and the writings of the Apostolic Fathers and Magisterial documents.

The Apostolic Fathers

The writings of the Apostolic Fathers, which the Catechism of the Church acknowledges as the teachings of Christ to the Apostles, reveals that this teaching, the coming triumph and renewal of Christianity, was accorded much speculation and is directly traceable to the Apostles.

According to Fr. Joseph Iannuzzi's's, OSJ, in his book, *The Triumph of God's Kingdom in the Millennium and End Times*, Papias of Hierapolis (floruit c.a. 130 A.D.) a Catholic Church Bishop, Father and Martyr, received direct teaching from the Apostle John concerning the reign of the temporal Kingdom. But because of a misunderstanding on the part of the noted 4th century historian, Esubius, Papias's writings became submerged in the heresy of Millenarianism. However, writes Fr. Iannuzzi, "Papias conveyed ... nothing but the truth according to the Apostolic Tradition." Papias writes that there will be on earth the establishment of "Christ's Kingdom where the just will reign." This reign, notes Iannuzzi, is not a literal reign that Papias speaks of for "Papias makes no mention whatsoever of Christ coming down to reign in the flesh, but rather speaks of a 'Kingdom.'"

St. Jerome

Papias's writings were upheld by St. Jerome, who Esubius preceded by 80 years. Papias, notes Iannuzzi, must also be properly credited with correctly taking a spiritual view of many of the symbolic passages of St. John's Revelation. He understood these not to have meant to be in the literal sense, but were referring to Christ's Church. This means that arguments dismissing the possibility of a literal millennium in the early Church Father's writings should not be used, as Iannuzzi writes, "to dismiss the possibility of a 'holy age' to come or a 'true millennium' (as opposed to false Millenarianism)."

St. Justin

St. Justin (100-165 A.D.), another Church Father and martyr who was beheaded, also wrote of an era of peace. In his apology of the Christian faith, *The Dialogue with Tripho*, Justin explained that it was un-Christian not to accept that the prophet Isaiah was speaking of the coming of the temporal Kingdom on earth. "If you ever encountered any so-called Christians who do not admit this doctrine (of the millennium), but dare to blaspheme the God of Abraham... do not consider them real Christians."   Furthermore, noting that the 1,000 year reign was "symbolic", Justin wrote, " A man among us named John, one of Christ's apostles, revived and foretold that the followers of Christ would dwell in Jerusalem for 1,000 years, and that afterwards the inevitable and, in short, everlasting resurrection and judgement would take place.   Writes Iannuzzi, "Because Justin was born just one generation from the Apostles, his testimony, like that of Papias (the disciple of St. John,) bears weight to its orthodoxy and unmodified influence."

St. Irenaeus

St. Irenaeus of Lyons (140-202 A.D.) is also credited with writing of the coming of the temporal Kingdom on earth. He is known as the "Father of Catholic Dogmatics" and was educated in his youth by St. Polycarp (69-156 A.D.), who also directly heard St. John the Apostle. Irenaeus wrote the classic *Adversus Haereses*, which addressed Gnostic heresy. In the second part of this writing, Irenaeus addressed the temporal Kingdom: "Days will come when vines will shoot ten thousand branches...and all around... will be at peace and in harmony with one another, completely at man's beck and call."

The Nicene Fathers

The Nicene Fathers also wrote about the coming of the temporal Kingdom. According to Iannuzzi, Tertullian, (155-240 A.D.), a Church Father, refers to a "millennial interspace" in which, notes Iannuzzi, "the Lord fills the earth with His glory." St. Hippolytus of Rome (d.235 A.D.), another Church Father, notes the coming of such an age of peace as does St. Methodius of Olympus (300 A.D.) and the theologian, Lactantius (250-317 A.D.).

Fr. Iannuzzi, in summarizing the Apostolic Tradition found in these writings and many more, noted that the Second Vatican Council advised that it was wise counsel to remain faithful to the Apostolic Tradition when no definitive pronouncement has been made by the Church, "as we see with the possibility of a Temporal Kingdom beginning to take shape and form a reality":

> Through her ordinary Magisterium, The Church consistently taught, as she continues to do, that it is not contrary to Catholic teaching to believe or profess "a hope in some mighty triumph of Christ here on earth before the final consummation of all things. Such an occurrence is not excluded, is not impossible, it is not all certain that there will not be a prolonged period of triumphant Christianity before the end" (*The Teaching of the Catholic Church: A*

Summary of Catholic Doctrine, Burns, Oates, & Washbourne, 1952 p. 1140). Since the Church has assumed, on the one hand, an inexorable stance in condemning the doctrines of Chiliasm or Millenarianism, while legitimizing the possibility of an intermediary reign of Christ on the other, she wisely sets forth the crucial distinctions of the good and bad doctrines concerning the millennium. In addition to the Magisterium, another equally important source in the formulation of doctrine is the Apostolic Tradition, which provides us with the confirmation of the existence of a temporal kingdom based upon the principle of unanimous reliability that the Apostolic Fathers enjoyed ...

The Tradition on a temporal kingdom, which the Fathers carefully conveyed, while scarcely passing as a simple explanation of a formal statement of biblical revelation, nonetheless, possesses strong ties with the revelation of the Apostles. Peter, Paul, John, Matthew, and many of the Old Testament writers attest to the permanence of a theology on the millennium, unlike the theology of *Millenarianism.* These doctrines, ... were not invented but developed by the Fathers, thereby attesting to their life-history, a "living tradition" that maintains a continuity and homogeneity with the doctrines of the Apostles.

Fr. Iannuzzi, concludes:

This temporal Kingdom appears, from the writings of the aforementioned Church Fathers, to be an 'age', commonly known as a thousand years (signifying a period of time), in which God's elect or saints will reign in perfect accord with God's Will. All creation will, furthermore, exult rejoicingly such that all humans, animals, plants, trees, fruits, etc. will not only abound in virtue of the divine fecundity of almighty God's blessing, but also abide in perfect harmony. This divine fecundity is not to be taken in the carnal sense as, for example, of the sheer propagation in quantity, but in a divine and spiritual sense, according to the good pleasure of the Lord who "fills the earth with his glory.

The Church Doctors

By the 4th century, many such writings advanced the coming of an ordained time of peace on earth and that the authors of these writings were aware of what had already been written and handed down on this matter. The writings of the Church Doctors especially revealed a thread that speaks of this temporal kingdom on earth as envisioned in the writings of the Fathers. St. Augustine of Hippo (354-430 A.D.) clearly wrote of such an era. While firmly denouncing the notions of Millenarianism, he traced out the distinction between the doctrines of the Fathers and the heresies and saw a spiritual resurrection of Christianity to occur during an epoch before the end of the world.

St. Cyril of Jerusalem, who was declared a Doctor of the Church by Pope Leo XIII in 1882, spoke of the time of a coming Kingdom and how such a future age had already been recognized in the "tradition" of the early Church. This era would appear, he writes, when "the end of the world is drawing near." St. John Chrysostom, who is also a Father and Doctor of the Church, also spoke of such a "Kingdom" and of the reign of a golden era of the Church. St. Cataldus spoke of a similar time as did St. Methodius, whose writings appear to be curiously similar to what Mary has been saying in her modern day apparitions. "A day will come when the enemies of Christ will boast of having conquered the whole world." But, he added, they "would be defeated and peace will be given to the world." It will be, Methodius added, "a long duration of peace, a splendid fertility of the earth." Likewise, St. Anthony of the desert spoke of a time when "the Church and the world are one," as did St. Regimus (5th century) who proclaimed the coming of a great "Kingdom."

St. Ephraem, an early 5th century Syrian Deacon, is both a Father and Doctor of the Church. His writings earned him the title "Harp of the Holy Spirit." In writing about the latter times, St. Ephraem stated that God would bring a period of peace, an era in which the "Kingdom" shall be established: "Then the Lord from His glorious heaven shall set up His peace. And the Kingdom of the Romans shall rise in place of the latter people, to establish its dominion on earth, even to its ends, and there shall be no one who will resist it."

St. Ceasar of Arles (6th century) writes that there would be "a reformation of the whole earth" and that "all nations shall recognize the Holy See of Rome and shall pray homage to the Pope." He also wrote, "many nations that are living in error and impiety shall be converted and an admirable peace shall reign among men during many years, because the wrath of God shall be appeased..."

These writings of the early doctors and others historic figures of the Church are open to criticism, but St. Jerome and St. Augustine noted that such opinions had been "handed down by all the ecclesiastical writers." Moreover, theologians agree that references to the establishment of an era of peace, or a holy Roman empire or Kingdom, are all the same—the foretelling of a spiritual reign that is to come into the world before the end of time and is not to be confused with a host of millenarian heresies.

The Medieval Period

The Medieval period finds a continuation of the prophecies of a coming kingdom of peace on earth. St. Hildegard saw a great purification that was to be followed by a "peace" for the "world." "During this period of peace," writes the great saint, "people will be forbidden to carry weapons... and many Jews, heathens and heretics will join the Church." St. Edward (11th century) and St. Thomas Beckett (12th century) also wrote of such a time as did St. Malachy (12th century). Another respected prophet of the age, Abbot Joanchin Merlin of the 13th century, proposed that "after many long sufferings endured by Christians, after too great an effusion of innocent blood, the Lord shall give peace and happiness to desolated nations." St. Thomas Aquinas, perhaps the most respected of the Doctors, also refers to the concept of a "terrestrial kingdom." St. Thomas notes it is only after the temporal "kingdom of light" that there will take place what he called "the cessation of the movements of the heavenly bodies." St. Mechtitilde of Helfta, a highly celebrated mystic of the 13th century, whose revelations scholars suspect formed the basis of Dante's Divine Comedy, sees an age of evangelization and a new order of preachers who would cover the world during the era of peace.

Likewise, a group of celebrated prophets of this age treat the coming of the Kingdom. Werdin d' Otrante, of the 13th century, believed that after years of war "peace will reign over the earth." John of

Vatiguerro (13th century) prophesied that "after many tribulations, the whole world shall venerate the Church for her sanctity, virtue and perfection." Monk Hilarion (15th century) suggested that "The Holy Man will bring peace." And a prophet named Dolciano (14th century) stated that "Under a holy pope there will be a universal conversion."

In the 15th century, St. Frances of Paula mentioned of the era of peace, saying that a new order known as the Knights of the Cross would be instrumental in a evangelization process. Around the same time, a very famous prophet emerged whose prophecies are still circulated. Brother John of the Cleft Rock (1340) boldly foresaw a future time of peace and property that will reign in the world.: "There will no longer be Protestants and Schismatics, the Lamb will reign and the bliss of the human race will begin. Happy will be those who escape the perils of that terrible time, for they can taste of its fruits through the reign of the Holy Ghost and the sanctification of mankind." St. Nicholas of Flue (15th century) saw a great suffering for the Church to be followed by a great victory. "The Church" will be exalted in the sight of all doubters," he wrote. In the 16th century, a prophet named, Tele-sphorus of Cozensa described the same golden era: "After terrible wars... They (a leader and a Pope) will convert the world and bring universal peace." St. Robert Bellarmine also believed in a temporal "terrestrial" kingdom of God that would come before the end of the world.

But perhaps one of the most concise versions of the prophesied coming of the Kingdom during the Medieval period came from St. Vincent Ferrer who wrote that "there would be a new reformation in the world." "This would occur," said Ferrer, "in the days of peace that are to come after the desolation, revolutions and wars, before the end of the world."

The Late Middle Ages

The late Middle Ages until the beginning of the Modern Marian Era, recognized by theologians to have started at Rue Du Bac, Paris, in 1830 with the apparitions of the Virgin Mary to St. Catherine Laboure, abounds with numerous prophecies on the "coming of the Kingdom on earth," the long awaited era of peace. Here are some of the most compelling:

—Blessed Mary of Agreda (17th century): "It was revealed to me that through the intercession of the Mother of God, all heresies will disappear. The victory over heresies has been reserved by Christ for His Blessed

Mother. In the latter days, the Lord will, in a special manner, spread the renown of His mother. Mary began salvation and by her intercession it will be completed. Before the second coming of Christ, Mary, more than ever, must shine in mercy, might and grace in order to bring unbelievers into the Catholic faith. The power of Mary in the latter days will be very conspicuous. Mary will extend the reign over the heathens and the Mohammedans, and it will be a time of great joy when Mary is enthroned Mistress and Queen of Hearts."

— St. Louis de Montfort (18th century): "The power of Mary over the devils will be particularly outstanding in the last period of time. She will extend the Kingdom of Christ over the idolaters and Moslems, and there will be a glorious era when Mary is ruler and Queen of Hearts."

— Bernard Rembordt (18th century): "A Roman emperor will give peace to the world. A good and happy era will follow. God will be praised on earth..."

— Elizabeth Cani-Mora (18th century): "After the frightful punishment, I saw a great light coming upon the earth which was a sign of reconciliation of God with men. All men shall become Catholics.

— Venerable Holzhauser (18th century): "When everything has been ruined by war, when Catholics are hard-pressed by traitorous co-religionists and heretics, when the Church and her servants are denied their rights, when the monarchies have been overthrown and their rulers murdered, then the hand of Almighty God will work a marvelous change, something seemingly impossible according to human reason... Persecution will cease and justice shall reign. All nations will adore God, their Lord, according to Catholic teaching. There will be many wise and just men. People will love justice, and peace will reign over the whole earth, for Divine Power will bind Satan for many years until the coming of the Son of Perdition...

— Fr. Nectou (18th century) "the triumph of the Church will rise."

— Sister Marianne (18th century): "The triumph of religion will be so great that no one has ever seen the equal. All injustice will made good. Civil laws will be made in coming with the laws of God and the Church."

— Sr. Jeanne le Royer (18th century): "I saw in God and Our Mother, that the Holy Church will spread in many countries and will move her fully in abundance to compensate for the outrages she will have suffered from the impiety and the persecution of her enemies."

— Ven. Ann Catherine Emmerich (18th century): "After a period of great tribulation, Almighty God will, in His mercy, put an end to this confusion and a new age will begin."

— Marie Steiner: (18th century) "The Lord showed me how beautiful the world will be after this awful punishment."

— Sr. Marianne Gaultier (18th century): "The Triumph of religion will be so great that no one has ever seen the equal."

— Brother Louis Rocco (19th century): "The cross will replace the half-moon of Islamisn."

— Blessed Anna Marie Taigi (19th century): "Christianity, ... will spread throughout the world.... a Holy Pontiff, chosen by God to withstand the storm.... shall be praised over the whole earth. Whole nations will come back to the Church and the face of the earth will be renewed. Russia, England, and China will come into the Church."

— Pope Pius IX (19th century): "All erring souls will return to the path of truths and justice, after the darkness of the minds has been dispelled, and there will be one flock and one shepherd."

— Marie Julie Jahenny (19th century) (From Jesus to her):
"The Church is destined to put up with the most awful
affronts.   It will vanish away like the bodily life of
Christians; but it will rise again in the midst of trials, and
its triumph will be secured. Tell my children not to
harbor any doubts about her for coming triumph..."

— Palma Maria (19th century): "The Triumph of the
Church will make people quickly forget all evils."

Perhaps the words of Sr. Bertina Bouquillon (19th century) best
summarizes the prophecies of the coming of the Kingdom during this period.
Her words resound confidently that an era of peace will reign. Known as the
Nursing Nun of Belay, she received the stigmata and was known for her gift
of prophecy and visions. Concerning the temporal Kingdom, she wrote,
"What I see is so wonderful that I am unable to express it."

The Age of Mary

In light of this teaching being held so strongly in Scripture and
Tradition, we can more easily understand and accept what the Virgin
Mary has been saying in her apparitions for the last two centuries— that
an era of peace, a visible coming of the "Kingdom on earth"—is part of
God's plan for man before the end of the world. Indeed, talk of peace
has been the cornerstone of Mary's mission since Rue Du Bac in 1830.
One hundred years later, this central theme of our Lady's was solidified
and approved by the Church when it ruled in 1930 that the apparitions
at Fatima were *"worthy of the faith."*
But the apparitions of Mary over the last two centuries brought
something additional to our understanding of the "coming of the
Kingdom" on earth. Unlike the many previous prophecies, Mary's
words not only confirm the coming of such a future time but that this
new era is imminent. Clothed in a series of events that are to bring great
upheaval in the world, Mary's revelations announce that the new
springtime of the Church is about to dawn, and that the world as we
know it is about to pass away before our very eyes.

CHAPTER SEVEN

AN ERA OF PEACE

For centuries, prophecies have foretold a "coming of the Kingdom on earth." But it is with the apparitions and revelations of the Virgin Mary over the last one hundred and seventy years, that we learn *how* and *when* this era is to be ushered into the world. In fact, the words of the God's chosen ones make it clear: the fullness of time is at hand and a new period of understanding the truth, mysteries, and splendors of God is about to dawn.

The Era of Mary

The modern era of Mary not only continued and confirmed the many prophecies of a coming glorious era of God, but revealed even more the reasons why God wills to bring such an age into the world for His people. While a foreshadowing of Mary's words can be found in Scripture and Tradition, the wonder and awe of how such a visible transformation of the world is to take place is at the core of the revelations and is the primary difference between what had been revealed before and what has been revealed by Mary to her chosen ones over the last two centuries. Moreover, Mary's revelations give God's children a plan of action to help and assist in the transformation of the times, as well as an understanding of the difficulties this transition will bring for many. Thus, the Virgin's revelations reveal the extraordinary significance and uniqueness of the times at hand, for what is to occur is no less than what the faithful of every other generation for centuries has prayed for and worked towards in some form or another.

Rue du Bac

At Rue Du Bac, Mary made no bold or profound announcements of the approach of such historical times, but if one reads between the lines, the stage can be seen to have been being set. Mary's words spoke of evil coming to cover the world and of the antidote given at Rue Du Bac for the problem, the Miraculous Medal, which revealed Mary standing on "the whole world" and, as she said to St. Catherine," each person in particular." Likewise, the graces seen pouring from Mary's hands during her final apparition at Rue du Bac can be understood to represent how God would "transform the world" from evil and darkness to the love and light Mary would be bringing from heaven. This image revealed that the whole world would, indeed, come under Mary's feet, and that the evil, as represented in the crushed head of the serpent on the medal, would be defeated.

La Salette

At La Salette in 1846, the Virgin Mary's prophetic words to Melanie Calvat and Maximum Girard went well beyond anything ever before given by her and confirmed the world was to soon be transformed by God and that a reign of His peace would come. The looming, exponential growth of evil in the world, as revealed at Rue Du Bac, was repeated. But Mary also declared unequivocally at La Salette, that **"peace will be made"** and **"man will be reconciled with God."**

Fatima

At Lourdes (1858), Pontmain (1871), Pellovoisen (1876), and Knock (1879), the implicit underlying message of the revelations continued to reveal the approaching crossroad in human history. A new era was coming and Mary, while not explaining such a revelation in detail during these apparitions, was laying the groundwork for what was to be clearly announced at Fatima in 1917: God wished to grant the world an era of peace, a peace to be experienced by men and nations like never before.

At Fatima, Mary revealed that a universal peace would come into the world. She said World War I would end and that regardless of future "errors" to be spread by Russia (atheism, wars, persecution...etc), peace would still follow. Most significantly, Mary asserted this peace would be an "Era of Peace" for the whole world, with the word "era" clearly defined by theologians as being an extended period of time, an epoch. This prophecy, of all her prophecies at Fatima, is the most profound and mysterious. This is because Mariologists and laity alike have asked repeatedly what the true implications of such words are. What exactly did Mary mean when she said an era of Peace would take place?

An Era of Peace

Many books on Fatima note this prophecy without serious contemplation of its meaning, while some writers have engendered opinions that range the gamut. Some say the Era of Peace began with the 1984 collegial consecration of the world to the Immaculate Heart of Mary by the Pope (and those bishops who chose to participate in the liturgical act) and that we are now living in the Era of Peace, although there has been little change in the world. Other commentators have written of almost story book scenarios that reduce the world during the Era of Peace to a state best described as pre-modern, agricultural and anti-economic—a world of very holy people who pray constantly and live by a barter-system. However, the Virgin Mary's words at Fatima and since then, when closely examined, reveal a different scenario; one that is practical, realistic, and most importantly, compatible with Tradition on an era of peace, "a reigning of the Kingdom on earth."

For the most part, the Virgin has revealed that a series of painful, purifying events, primarily brought on by the consequences of the choices of man, but permitted by God in His plan of merciful justice for the world, will finally and completely propel people away from the root of their present day woes—lack of faith, hope and charity—and towards one another. Through a unique epiphany of grace, the Virgin Mary has revealed that mankind will come to disdain anger, envy, and pride and realize what it has brought upon itself through such sin. It will then turn en masse away from such behavior in order to seek the love, joy, and peace of God, who will be most ready to give it in a special way—just as the father in the parable of the Prodigal Son, who upon seeing his son returning from a distance, races to welcome and embrace him.

Mary describes the Era of Peace as beginning slowly, just as the era of Satan gradually revealed its face. But over time, because of God's will for man and the world and because of an extraordinary amount of grace, this new era will blossom into what can only be described as that which many saints, popes, and prophets have said has been destined for centuries: a golden age of the Church, an age of peace that no previous generation could have imagined the world would experience before the end of time, a true reign of the "Kingdom on earth." But how can we truly believe that such a transformation of the world is near?

The Definitive Message of Fatima

Once again, this is where the importance of Fatima and its message is seen. For the Church not only approved Fatima in 1930 but also studied and released a definitive opinion on the message of the apparitions. At Fatima, the bishop appointed a commission of six experts to interpret the message given by Mary there and, most significantly, what the Virgin meant in her revelation that God would grant the world an "Era of Peace." After thoroughly studying this issue, the commission stated that the Era of Peace promised by the Virgin Mary at Fatima implied a *"true reign of Christ"* on earth. This was because, they said, *"there could be no other meaning of the word 'peace' on the lips of the Mother of Christ, and no other meaning to her words. 'My Immaculate Heart will Triumph.'"* This was also the opinion of Eugene Cardinal Tisserant, Dean of the Cardinals of the Catholic Church. The Cardinal said, "the Virgin Mary will obtain the necessary graces of conversion and re-awaken an authentic sense of unity in Christ and in the Church for a 'true world peace.'"

In light of such authoritative statements by respected Church officials, a confident approach to a better understanding of what God is trying to tell His people may be undertaken. Indeed, as Pope John Paul II has stated, the Church needs to recognize the importance of Fatima's message and even "has a duty to be mindful of it." It is a message the Holy Father said on May 13, 1982, that is "deeply rooted in the Gospel and the whole Tradition of the Church feels that the message imposes a commitment upon her."

This commitment lies in our responsibility to understand what Mary was telling the world and the Church at Fatima, for her prophetic message there, as the commission confirmed, was not ordinary and insignificant. She had come to Fatima with good news, the news of the Gospel as Pope John Paul II noted, and, therefore, her words need to be welcomed in no less a manner than the way Scripture says the angel was received by the shepherds the night Christ was born, in the spirit of good tidings and with great joy. Indeed, how else should we respond to the Queen of Heaven's pronouncement of a coming Era of Peace?

The Temporal Kingdom and the Era of Peace are One

Some theologians have noted these revelations and, not surprisingly, have concluded in accordance with their knowledge of Scripture and Tradition, that it is clear that Mary's prophecies at Fatima of an era of peace are one and the same as those handed down for centuries —a temporal reign of God's Kingdom on earth is to come. Only now, according to Fr. Iannuzzi, the fulfillment of such a prophecy appears to be more recognizable and is perhaps what Pope John Paul II and other Church leaders have been alluding to in their writings:

> In order to arrive at a certitude of faith in matters regarding eschatology, in particular a temporal kingdom, we must base our ideas upon the guidance of the Church's universal Magisterium. The Second Vatican Council, in its document *Lumen Gentium* mentions the two-fold magisterial office exercised by the Pope and the Bishops. There is present in the Church her charism of *extraordinary* Magisterium as well as the guidance of her *ordinary*, to which all the faithful are obliged to lend loyal respect (*Lumen Gentium*, n.25; CCC 2034, 2039. Apropos of her ordinary Magisterium, the false chilastic concept of *millenarianism* is clearly distinguished from the concept of a temporary kingdom, *also known as an era of peace, as prophesied by the Blessed Virgin Mary at Fatima...*
>
> The millennium or temporal Kingdom of God, as evidenced in the writings of the Sacred Scriptures, Church Fathers and Doctors, ecclesiastical writers and in issued statements from her ordinary Magisterium, bear one common thread that runs all throughout history, the veritable reality of a period of peace that precedes the great and universal day of judgment of all the dead. The doctrinal fidelity to the traditional teachings of the Church contained in these writings attest to the veracity of its existence. As our Holy Father has so often quoted, this millennium will

be marked by "a new springtime in Christianity," be "intensely Eucharistic," at its dawn "make Christ the heart of the world," and have as its "goal and fulfillment... the life of each Christian and the whole Church in the Triune God" (Passim Apostolic Letter, *Tertio Millennio Adveniente*).

Contemporary Revelations Concur with Fatima

Since Fatima, dozens of lesser known visionaries, mystics, stigmatists, and prophets have reported receiving messages that concur with the Fatima commission's interpretations of Mary's promise of an "era of peace," although most of these visionaries and apparitions have not been approved by the Church.

It would not be possible to address all of the revelations that speak of the new era. Needless to say, many sound alike and reiterate the same essential understanding of what was revealed at Fatima. However, a look at several such revelations as received by the Italian locutionist, Fr. Stefano Gobbi, is reflective of the great body of these messages.

On August 15, 1991, the Virgin Mary gave the following message (which received the Imprimatur of Cardinal Escherria Ruiz of Ecuador) concerning the "new era" to Father Gobbi:

> **Today, beloved sons, contemplate me in the splendor of my glorified body, assumed into the glory of paradise. Live in joy and confidence the last times of this, your Second Advent, by looking to me as to the sign of sure hope and of consolation.**
>
> **The new era, which awaits you, corresponds to a particular encounter of love, of light and of life between paradise, where I am in perfect blessedness with the angels and the saints, and earth, where you my children live in the midst of many dangers and innumerable tribulations. This is the heavenly Jerusalem, which comes down from heaven upon earth, to transform it completely and to thus shape the new heavens and the new earth.**

The new era, toward which you are journeying, is bringing all creation to the perfect glorification of the Most Holy Trinity. The Father receives his greatest glory from every creature which reflects His light, His love and His divine splendor. His son restores his reign of grace and of holiness, setting free every creature from the slavery of evil and of sin. The Holy Spirit pours out in fullness his holy gifts, leads to the understanding of the whole truth, and renews the face of the earth.

The new era, which I announce to you, coincides with the complete fulfillment of the divine will, so that at last there is coming about that which Jesus taught you to ask for from the Heavenly Father: 'Your will be done on earth as it is in heaven.' This is the time when the divine will of the Father, of the Son and of the Holy Spirit is being accomplished by the creatures. From the perfect fulfillment of the divine will, the whole world is becoming renewed, because God finds there, as it were, his new garden of Eden, where He can dwell in loving companionship with his creatures.

The new era, which is just now beginning, brings you to a full communion of life with those who have preceded you and who, here in paradise, enjoy perfect happiness. You see the splendor of the heavenly hierarchy; you communicate with the saints of paradise; you relieve the purifying sufferings of the souls who are still in purgatory. You experience, in a strong and visible way, the consoling truth of the communion of saints.

The new era, which I am preparing for you, coincides with the defeat of Satan and of his universal reign. All his power is destroyed. He is bound, with all the wicked spirits, and shut up

**in hell from which he will not be able to get out
to do harm in the world. Herein, Christ reigns
in the splendor of his glorified body, and the
Immaculate Heart of your heavenly Mother
triumphs in the light of her body, assumed into
the glory of paradise.**

Mary's words in describing the new era to Father Stefano Gobbi
reiterate many often repeated terms that have been used to describe the
coming of the temporal Kingdom: the Second Advent, the Heavenly
Jerusalem, the Triumph of the Immaculate Heart, the new Garden of Eden.

But it is, in her words concerning the Eternal Father and the glory
that He is to receive in the new era, that we once again understand that no
terminology perhaps better describes the new era than the fact that it is to
be the Era of the Father—the coming of the Father's Kingdom.

Indeed, perhaps three messages received by Father Gobbi from the
Virgin Mary on July 3, 1987, December 31, 1991, and May 8, 1997
especially illustrate this point:

**These are the times of the great return. Yes, after
the time of the great suffering, there will be the
time of the great rebirth and all will blossom again.
Humanity will again be a new garden of life and
beauty and the Church a family enlightened by
truth, nourished by grace, consoled by the
presence of the Holy Spirit. Jesus will restore his
glorious reign. He will dwell with you and you will
know the new times, the new era. You will at last
see a new earth and new heavens.**

**These are the times of the great mercy. The
Father thrills with ardor and wills to pour out
upon this poor humanity the torrents of his
infinite love. The Father wants to mold with His
hands a new creation where His divine imprint
will be more visible, welcomed and received and
His fatherhood exalted and glorified by all. The
breath of this new creation will be the breathing**

of the love of the Father who will be glorified by all, while there will spread everywhere in an increasingly fuller way, like water which springs from a living and inexhaustible fount, the fullness of His divine love.

And Jesus will reign: Jesus for whom all has been created, Jesus who became incarnate, who became your brother, who lived with you, who suffered and died on the Cross to redeem humanity and bring it to a new creation and so that his reign might gradually be disseminated in hearts, in souls, in individuals, in families and in all society. (July 3, 1987)

Prostrate yourselves with me in an act of fervent thanksgiving for all the favors that have been given to you, by the love and the providence of your Heavenly Father. It is the Father who arranges for you every minute of you life, as an expression of his love and of his divine mercy. You are living within time, in order to bring to realization a great loving plan of His. Even when you draw away from Him, He never abandons you, but prepares for, awaits and brings to completion your every return. His divine mercy is a heavenly dew which comes down to make fertile the great dryness of this world and to make the desert in which you live blossom with holiness and with life.

You are now entering into the times when the miracle of divine mercy will become manifest to all. See how humanity lies prostrate and wounded, lacerated and defeated, threatened and stricken, diseased and dying. Of itself it can no longer rise again, unless a great mercy lifts it up.

The moment is at hand when the heavenly

Father will take it up in His arms, will relieve it of evil, will heal it and bring it with Him into His delightful garden. (DECEMBER 31, 1991)

I have caused to spring up here, for twenty-five years now, my Marian Movement of Priests so that the message of Fatima, often contested and rejected by many, might in your days come to its complete fulfillment.

Its fulfillment is necessary for you, my children, threatened and stricken, so that you may attain salvation.   Its fulfillment is necessary for the Church, so wounded and crucified, so that from its painful and bloody trial, it might emerge all beautiful, with-out spot or wrinkle, in imitation of its heavenly Mother.   Its fulfillment is necessary for all humanity, so that it may return to the arms of its Father and come to know the new times of its full communion of love and of life with its Lord and God.

As of now, this plan of mine is being fulfilled with the triumph of my Immaculate Heart in the world. (May 8, 1997)

Mary's words to Father Gobbi firmly establish that while the new era will be a Second Pentecost, a time of the reign of Christ, a time of the reign of the Two Hearts, it will perhaps be most of all a reflection of the love of the Eternal Father. His Kingdom of love will have finally arrived and all mankind will honor His Fatherhood.

Therefore, in order to more intimately examine this coming era of God our Father, a look at the words of some of those who have been chosen by the Father, who have received revelations directly from Him, is perhaps one of the best ways to the profoundly grasp the great mystery at hand. For in their words, in their knowledge of the Father and His Kingdom, we can come to share in a special way, a true understanding of what awaits the world and all of God's children.

CHAPTER EIGHT

MOTHER EUGENIA ROVASIO

I n 1932, an extraordinary but almost totally unknown event occurred in Italy that may someday be considered of unprecedented importance in the history of the Church and the world. A nun named Mother Elisabetta Eugenia Ravasio reported that the Eternal Father appeared to her in apparitions on July 1, 1932, and again on August 12, 1932. Thirteen years later, the Church fully approved the visions as worthy of the faith.

Mother Eugenia Elisabetta Ravasio was born on September 4, 1907, in San Gervasio d' Adda (now Capriato, San Gervasio), a small village in the providence of Bergamo, Italy. She came from a peasant background and received only an elementary education. After working several years in a factory, Eugenia entered the Congregation of Our Lady of the Apostles. She was twenty years old. By the age of twenty-five, the young nun was elected Mother General of the Congregation. Mother Eugenia then served in this position from 1935 until 1947.

While her spiritual work is the subject of this story, her worldly contributions were also significant. In twelve years of missionary work Mother Eugenia opened seventy relief centers in some of the most distant and removed locations in Asia, Africa, and Europe. She is credited with being the first to discover a cure for a form of leprosy, extracting it from the seed of a tropical plant. This process was later advanced at the Pasteur Institute of Paris. She further planned and developed a project for a "Lepers City" at Azopte (Ivory Coast). This center serviced an area of over 200,000 square miles and is still today a leading center for the care of leprosy sufferers. In recognition of this achievement, France conferred upon Mother Eugenia its highest national honor for social work. She further acted as a catalyst for the work of Raoul Follereau, who, in imitation of his mentor, Mother Eugenia, continued an apostolate dedicated to the service of lepers. He is regarded as the "apostle of the lepers."

Mother Eugenia Ravasio eventually left her order and reportedly became the subject of a great persecution. For years she remained a recluse and reportedly lived a hidden and pain-filled life of irony and tragedy. She died in Rome on August 10, 1990. But her life was extraordinary in many ways, and this was noted by her bishop, Alexander Caillot in great detail.

Bishop Caillot's report

In his final report on the Church's review of the apparitions received by Mother Eugenia, Bishop Caillot, noted that Mother Eugenia was humble and that her own life reflected the beautiful doctrine of the revelations given to her. Indeed, he noted that from the beginning of her religious life, Mother Eugenia had attracted her superiors attention because of her "piety, obedience and humility." She had endured trials because of her exemplary conduct and over the years of the investigation into the apparitions, she showed great patience and the utmost docility in submitting without complaint to a battery of medical tests, numerous theological and medical questions, and to the fact that there were often contradictions and trials which would emerge and reemerge. However, throughout it all her simplicity was praised even by the investigators.

Most noted, according to the bishop, was the fact that Mother Eugenia demonstrated the practice of virtue to a heroic degree. According to the theologians on the committee, an especially striking feature was her obedience during Father Auguste Valenin's inquiry in June, 1934, and her humility on another difficult day, December 20th, 1934.

In his statement of approval, the bishop launched high praise on her in a sweeping fashion confronting all her strong points as greater evidence of the correctness of his decision to approve the visions. From his words, we come to know who she was a little better:

I can attest that, while she was Superior General, I found

her very devoted to her duty, dedicating herself to her task–which must have seemed all the more difficult to her as she was not prepared for it–with great love for souls, her Congregation, and the Church. Those close to her are struck, as I myself am, by her strength of spirit in facing difficulties.

I am impressed not only by her virtues but also by the qualities she displays in exercising her authority. Also striking is the fact that a relatively uneducated nun should come to fill her Congregation's highest office. In this there is already something extraordinary and from this point of view, the inquiry conducted by my Vicar General, Mgr. Guerry, on the day of her election, is very significant. The answers given by the Chapter members and by the superiors and delegates of the various missions showed that they were choosing Mother Eugenia as their Superior General–in spite of her youth and the canonical obstacles which would normally have caused the idea of her nomination to be rejected–because of her qualities of judgement, balanced temperament, energy, and firmness. Reality would seem to have far surpassed the hopes that her electors placed in her.

What I especially noticed in her was her lucid, lively, and penetrating intelligence. I said that her education had been inadequate, but this was for external reasons over which she had no control: her mother's long illness had compelled her, at a very early age, to look after the house and to be absent from school very often. Then, before she entered the convent, there were the hard years she worked in industry as a weaver. Not withstanding these basic gaps, the consequences of which are evidenced in her style and spelling, Mother Eugenia gives many lectures in her community. It is worth nothing that she herself compiles her Congregation's circulars and the contracts with municipal authorities or administrative councils regarding the hospital institutes of Our Lady of the

Apostles. She has also compiled a long directory.

She sees every situation clearly and correctly, as if it were a matter of conscience. Her instructions are straightforward, precise, and very practical. She knows each of her 1400 daughters personally, and also their attitudes and their virtues; hence she is able to select those who are most qualified to perform various tasks. She also has an accurate personal knowledge of her Congregations's needs and resources. She knows the situation in every house and has visited all her missions.

We wish to emphasize also her spirit of far-sightedness. She has taken all the necessary measures for every hospital or school to have qualified nuns and whatever they need to live and develop. I find it particularly interesting to note that Mother Eugenia seems to possess a spirit of decisiveness, a sense of reality and a creative will. In six years she has founded 67 institutes and has been able to introduce very useful improvements in her Congregation.

If I single out her qualities of intelligence, judgment, and will, and her powers of administration, it is because they seem to me to rule out definitively all the hypotheses about hallucinations, illusions, spiritism, hysteria or delirium. These were examined during the inquiry but proved incapable of giving a satisfactory explanation of the facts.

Mother Eugenia's life is a constant demonstration of her mental and general equilibrium, which, to the observer, seems to be the dominant feature of her personality. Other hypotheses, about suggestibility and manageability, led the investigators to wonder whether they might be dealing with a very impressionable temperament, like a multi-faced mirror which reflects all influences and suggestions. These hypothesis were also rejected for reasons of everyday reality. Although Mother Eugenia is gifted with a sensitive nature and an emotional disposition, she has shown that she has never favored anyone, and far from letting herself be influenced by human considerations, she has always been able to determine her own projects and activities and to gain the acceptance of others thorough her personal insight.

The Apparitions

But it is the apparitions and divine revelations given to Mother Eugenia in 1932 that made her life truly extraordinary and most memorable, for no such similar event is recorded in Catholic mystical history.

On July 1, 1932, Mother Eugenia reported that she had begun to hear and see angels which she described as "*the entire Heavenly Court.*" According to the book, *God Is Father*, there was beautiful singing, incomprehensible harmony, and then finally the appearance of the Eternal Father Himself. She said God the Father then sat next to her and revealed a profound message of His desires for mankind to her. The Eternal Father told her He was now coming among men in order to love them and to help make them know His love and that, most of all, He desired a feast in His honor. It is also noteworthy that this message was given to Mother Eugenia in Latin, a language totally unknown by her.

In 1935, Bishop Alexander Caillot of Grenoble, France, convened a Commission of Inquiry to investigate the reported events. The commission took ten years to complete its work before recommending to the Bishop that he declare his opinion in favor of the apparitions. He did this in 1945. [Note: This decision has never been reversed, but because of events within Mother Eugenia's Order, according to Fr. Rene Laurentin's 1997 investigation, it is difficult to ascertain the facts surrounding the entire issue.]

The inquiry also discovered, in examining the Father's requests for a feast day, that many of the faithful did not have a good understanding of God the Father. Subsequently, an extensive survey of the faithful revealed that the faithful, across all class lines and even among priests and religious, did not know God the Father. The survey revealed that "*few pray to Him*" and "*nobody thinks of Him.*" The survey also discovered that many Christians keep distant from the Father, preferring to turn to Jesus because of His Humanity. It even found that many ask Jesus to protect them from the Father's rage. Thus, the commission and

Bishop Caillot concluded the request for a feast day by the Eternal Father to Mother Eugenia would effectively reestablish order in many Christian's piety as well as address Christ's words in His prayer concerning the coming of the Father's Kingdom. Historically, it was the first and only Roman Catholic Church-approved apparition and message of God the Father.

The Feast of the Father of all Mankind

The bishop's words in his final report left no doubt about the thoughtfulness and care that went into the decision to approve the apparitions. He stated that he had followed the dictates of his soul and conscience, with a keen eye on his responsibility to the Church, in arriving at his decision. He also stated that the events were supernatural and that the facts supported this explanation beyond any other conclusion.

Bishop Caillot held that the revelations were supernaturally *"rich"* and seemed to him to be noble, lofty, and a call to true devotion to God Our Father. He found no error in them and concluded they were of sound doctrine.

While Bishop Caillot wrote that the Church would have to consider as a separate matter the requests the Eternal Father made of Mother Eugenia, he did not hesitate to comment on whether or not in his opinion the requests were meritorious and needed, especially the Father's ardent desire for a feast day. Moreover, the Bishops noted that he believed the request for a feast day to be timely and legitimate.

The feast would make God the Father known and honored and was in keeping with Catholic practice as a whole, said the Bishop. He especially noted how Catholic prayer ascends to the Father, through the Son, in the Spirit as shown by the prayers of the Mass and the liturgical oblation to the Father during the Holy Sacrifice. For the most part, Bishop Caillot noted that it was "strange" that there is no feast day in honor of the Father. He noted how the Most Holy Trinity, The Holy Spirit and the Son are honored through feasts that celebrate their mission or external manifestations. Thus, the bishop wrote that a special feast would have the effect of allowing the faithful to raise their eyes toward heaven to the one the apostle St. James called, *"the Father of light, from whom every gift comes...."* The feast, said the bishop, would accustom souls to consider God's goodness and his fatherly providence.

The Revelations

Overall, the bishop's words reflected His awe of the revelations. Even investigating theologians, who had continually challenged Mother Eugenia, arguing that apparitions of the Father were impossible and that they had never occurred before in history, were eventually convinced of the miraculous aspects of the case. Finally, the Bishop concluded that the Father had indeed manifested Himself to Mother Eugenia, presenting her with a beautiful doctrine–true devotion to the Father.

The complete revelations to Mother Eugenia can be characterized as no less than unfathomable. Throughout His message to her, the Eternal Father outlined His plan, a plan that entreats all men and all nations to turn to Him. Most significantly, The Father said He desired mankind to turn to Him not in trepidation, but in total abandonment and love. The Eternal Father also touched on various subjects ranging from the story of His love for men as revealed to Moses and Israel in the Old Testament, to acknowledging the spiritual differences among His present-day children.

Indeed, the revelations were prophetic and evangelical. And the Eternal Father asserted from the beginning to the saintly nun that the Mystical Body of Jesus Christ, the Catholic Church, truly held within it the supernatural gifts and graces which He wanted to give to all mankind. Most significantly, in telling her this, the Eternal Father conveyed to Mother Eugenia Ravasio that the time of times has come. It was time, He told her, for the fulfillment of His Son's prayer, the *"Our Father."* And that this fulfillment, which would allow Him to be better known, loved and honored, would be best accomplished by a *special feast* in the Church dedicated in His name:

I desire to be known, loved, and honored with a special devotion, I do not ask for anything extraordinary. I desire only this: that one day, or at least a Sunday, be dedicated to honoring Me in a special way under the title Father of all Mankind. For this feast, I would like a special

Mass and Office. It is not difficult to find the texts in the Holy Scriptures. If you prefer to offer Me this special devotion on a Sunday, I choose the first Sunday of August. If you prefer a weekday, I would like it to be always the seventh of that same month.

But, the Father told the nun, this request for reasons known only by the Father, needed to be fulfilled before the end of the 20th century—or else the grace would be lost:

This century is privileged above all others. Do not let this privilege pass, for fear that it might be withdrawn! Souls need a certain divine touch, and time presses; do not be afraid of anything, I am your Father, I will help you in your efforts and your work. ...

Time presses. I wish men to know as soon as possible that I love them and that I feel greatness happiness in being with them and talking with them, like a father with his children. ...

I turn to you, My beloved son, My Vicar, before all others, to place this work in your hands. It should rank first among all your tasks and, because of the fear inspired in men by the devil, it will be accomplished only at this time.

Besides the paramount request for a feast day, the Father enlightened Mother Eugenia about many issues, first and foremost was why He was now coming to her, to all mankind with His message:

This is the real purpose of My coming:

1. I am coming to banish the excessive fear that My creatures have of Me, and to show them that My joy lies in being known and loved by My children—that is, by all mankind, present and future.

2. I am coming to bring hope to men and nations. How many have long since lost it! This hope will make them live in peace and security, working for their salvation.

3. I am coming to make Myself known just as I am, so that men's trust may increase together with their love for Me, their Father. I have but one concern: to watch over all men and love them as My children.

The painter delights in contemplating the picture he has painted. In the same way, it is My pleasure and delight to come among men, the masterpiece of My creation!

After clearly stating His purpose for coming, our Father told Mother Eugenia how His coming now was not for Himself but for His children:

May everyone recognize My infinite goodness towards all men and especially towards sinners, the sick, the dying and all those who suffer. Let them know I want only one this: to love them all, to give them my grace, to forgive them when they repent, and most of all to judge them not with My justice but with My mercy, so that all may be saved and numbered among My elect.

The Eternal Father also specifically addressed the Pope:

I turn to you, My beloved son, My Vicar, before all others, to place this work in your hands. It should rank first among all your tasks and, because of the fear inspired in men by the devil, it will be accomplished only at this time.

Oh, how I would like you to know the range of this enterprise, its greatness, its breadth, its depth, its height. I would like you

to understand the immense wishes that I have for mankind, now and in the future!

If only you knew how much I desire to be known, loved, and honored by men with a special devotion! I have had this desire for all eternity and since the creation of the first man. I have expressed this desire to men at various times, especially in the Old Testament. But man has never understood it. Now this desire makes Me forget all the past, if only it can become a reality now, in My creatures all over the world.

I am stooping down to the poorest of My creatures to talk to her, and through her to all men, even though she cannot realize the grandeur of the work I wish to accomplish among them.

I cannot talk of theology with her, I would be sure to fail, for she would not understand Me. I am doing this in order to realize My plan through simplicity and innocence. But now it is your turn to examine this work and bring it to a speedy fulfillment.

To be known, loved, and honored with a special devotion, I do not ask for anything extraordinary, I desire only this:

1. I desire that one day, or at least a Sunday, be dedicated to honoring Me in a special way under the title of Father of All Mankind.

For this feast, I would like a special Mass and Office. It is not difficult to find the texts in the Holy Scriptures.

If you prefer to offer Me this special devotion on a Sunday, I choose the first Sunday of August. If you prefer a weekday, I would like it to be always on the seventh day of that same month.

2. I desire that all the clergy should undertake to promote this devotion and, most of all, make Me known to men as I am and as I will always be for them—that is to say the most tender and the most lovable of all fathers.

3. I desire them to bring Me into all families, hospitals, laboratories, workshops, barracks, conferences halls of the ministers of nations - in short, wherever My creatures are, even if there were only one of them!

I desire that the tangible sign of My invisible presence be a picture to show that I am really present. Thus, all men will carry out all their actions under their Father's gaze and I Myself will have before Me the creature that I have not only created but adopted. In this way, My children will be, as it were, under their tender Father's gaze. Even now I am everywhere, certainly, but I would like to be represented in a tangible way!

4. I desire that during the year the clergy and the faithful should perform some acts of piety in My honor, without detriment to their usual occupations.

Let My priests go fearlessly everywhere, among all nations, bring the flame of My fatherly love to men. Then souls will be enlightened and conquered, not only among unbelievers, but in all those sects which are not of the true Church.

Yes, I want these men also, who are My children, to see this flame shining before them, to know the truth, to embrace it, and to put all the Christian virtues into practice.

5. I would like to be honored in a very special way in seminaries, in novitiates, in schools, and homes for the elderly. May everyone, from the youngest to the oldest, be

able to know and love Me as their Father, Creator and Savior.

6. Let priests set about seeking in the Holy Scriptures what I said in former times and what has remained unknown up to now concerning the worship I wish to receive from men. May they work to make My desires and My will known to all men, specifying what I wish to say to people in general and to priests, monks, and nuns in particular. Those souls are the ones I choose, more than others in the world, to pay Me great homage.

Of course, it will take time to realize completely these desires that I have for mankind and which I have revealed to you! But one day, through the prayers and sacrifices of generous souls who will give themselves for this work of My love, yes, one day I will be satisfied I will bless you, My beloved son, and I will reward you a hundred fold for all that you will do for My glory.

On August 12, 1932, during the second apparition of the Eternal Father to Mother Eugenia, the Father again made a special note of this burning desire: a feast day to bring Him honor and to fulfill what Scripture noted was to come:

I am the ocean of charity, My children, and this is another proof of the paternal love I feel for all of you, without exception, regardless of your age, your status or your country. Nor do I exclude different societies, sects, believers, unbelievers the indifferent. I enfold in this love all the rational creatures who make up humanity.

Here is the proof of this: I am the ocean of charity. I showed you the spring which pours from My Breast to quench your thirst, and now, in order to let you see My goodness towards everyone, I am going to show you the ocean of my universal charity, that you may dive into it blindly. Why? So that, diving into the ocean, souls rendered bitter by faults and sins may lose that bitterness in this bath of love. They will emerge from this ocean better, happy at having learned how to be good and charitable. If, because of ignorance or weakness, you yourselves happen to fall again into this state of bitterness, I shall still be an ocean of charity, ready to receive this bitter drop, transform it into charity and goodness and make you holy as I, your Father, am.

My children, do you want to live your life on earth peacefully and joyfully? Come and cast yourselves into this immense ocean and remain in it forever. As you work and live your normal life, this life will be sanctified through charity.

As for My children who do not follow the truth, I wish all the more to enfold them in My fatherly predilection, so that they may open their eyes to the light which now shines more clearly then ever.

This is the time of graces, foreseen and awaited since the beginning of time! I am here personally to talk to you. I come as the most tender and loving of fathers. I stoop down, forgetful of Myself, to raise you up to Me and ensure your salvation. All of you who are now living and you, too, who are in the void, but who will live century after century until the end of the world, remember that you are not alone: a Father thinks of you and offers you a share of the unfathomable privileges of His love. Approach the spring which will gush forever from My fatherly Breast. Taste the sweetness of this health-giving water, and when you have felt all its delicious power in your souls satisfying all your needs, come and cast yourselves into the ocean of My charity, so as to live only in Me, to die to yourselves and to live eternally in Me.

(Mother Eugenia's note: "Our Father told me in an intimate dialogue: 'The spring is the symbol of My knowledge; the ocean is that of My charity and of your trust. When you wish to drink from this spring, study Me in order to know Me and, when you know Me, dive into the ocean of My charity, trusting Me with a confidence so deep as to transform yourselves; this I shall be unable to resist. I shall then forgive your errors and lavish the greatest favor upon you.'")

I am among you. Happy are those who believe this truth and who take advantage of this time about which the Scriptures have spoken thus: "There will come a time when God must be honored and loved by men as He desires."

The Scriptures then go on to ask: "Why?" and answer: "Because He alone is worthy of honor, love and praise forever!"

Moses received from Me as the first of the ten commandments, this command to be communicated to men: "Love and worship God!"

Those who are already Christians may say: "We have loved you since we were born or since our conversion, as we often say in the Lord's Prayer: 'Our Father, Who are in heaven!'" Yes, My children, it is true, you to love Me and honor Me when you say the first part of the "Our Father," but continue with the other requests and you will see:

"Hallowed by They name!" Is My name being blessed?

Continue:

"Thy kingdom come!" Has My kingdom come?"

You honor very fervently the Kingship of

My Son, Jesus, it is true, and in Him you are honoring Me! But will you deny your Father this great glory of proclaiming Him "King," or at least, of letting Me reign until all men can know and love Me?

I desire you to celebrate this feast of the Kingship of My Son in reparation for the insults He received before Pilate and from the soldiers who scourged His holy and innocent humanity. I ask you not to suspend this feast, but, on the contrary, to celebrate it enthusiastically and fervently; but in order that everyone may really know this King, they must know His kingdom as well. Now, to achieve this dual knowledge perfectly, it is also necessary to know the Father of this King, the Maker of this kingdom.

Truly, My children, the Church–this society I entrusted My Son to found–will complete its work by honoring Him Who is its Author: your Father and Creator.

Some of you, My children, may reply: "The Church has grown continuously. Christians are more and more numerous: this is sufficient proof that our Church is complete!" Know, My children, that your Father has always kept watch over the Church since its birth and that, along with My Son and the Holy Spirit, I wanted it to be infallible through My vicar, the Holy Father. However, is it not true that if Christians knew Me as I am, the tender and merciful, good and liberal Father, they would practice this holy religion more fervently and sincerely?

My children, is it not perhaps true that, if you knew you had a Father Who thinks of you and loves you infinitely, you would in your turn make an effort to be more faithful to your Christian duties, as well as to your duties as citizens, to be just and to render justice to God and to men?

Is it not true that, if you knew this Father Who loves you all without distinction and Who, without distinction, calls you all by the sweet name of children, you would love Me as affectionate children, and that this love, under My impulse, would become an active love, extending itself to the rest of humanity who still do not know this Christian society and who know even less Him Who created them and is their Father?

If somebody went and talked to these souls, abandoned to their superstitions, or to so many others who call Me God because they know I exist but not hat I am close to them; if somebody said to them that their Maker is their Father as well, and He thinks of them and is concerned with them, that He surrounds them with intimate affection in their sorrows and dejection—this would obtain the conversion of the most stubborn ones, and these conversions would be more numerous and firm, that is, more preserving.

Some of you, examining this work of love I am carrying out among men, will find cause for criticism and will say: "But don't the missionaries, after arriving in those distant countries, talk to the non-believers about God, His goodness, and His mercy? What more could they say about God, since they speak of Him all the time?"

The missionaries have spoken and still speak of God as far as they know Him, but I assure you, you do not know Me as I am, because I am coming to proclaim Myself the Father of all and the most tender of fathers, in order to transform your love, which has become distorted by fear.

I come to make Myself similar to My creatures, to correct the idea you have of a terrifying just God, as I see men spending their whole lives without confiding in their only Father, Whose only wish is to make their earthly life easier and then give them a divine life, in heaven.

This is a proof that souls do not know Me any more than you do, not having overcome the idea you have about Me. But now I am giving you this light. Remain in the light and bring it to everybody, and it will be a powerful means both to obtain conversions and to shut, if possible, the gates of hell, for I now repeat My promise, which will last forever:

ALL THOSE WHO CALL ME BY THE NAME OF FATHER, EVEN IF ONLY ONE, WILL NOT PERISH, BUT WILL BE SURE OF THEIR ETERNAL LIFE AMONG THE CHOSEN ONES.

And to you who will work for My glory and commit yourselves to making Me known, honored, and loved, I give you assurance that your reward will be great, because I will count everything, even the smallest effort you make, and I will reward you a hundredfold in eternity.

As I have told you, it is necessary to bring to fulfillment in the holy Church the devotion which honors in a very special way this society's Author, the One Who came to found it, and the One Who is its soul, God in three Persons: Father, Son and Holy Spirit.

Until the three Persons are honored by a special devotion in the Church and the whole of mankind, there will be something lacking in this society. I have already made some souls aware of this lack, but most of them, too timid, have not responded to My call. Others have had the courage to speak about it to the appropriate people, but, in the face of their failure, they have not persisted.

Now My hour has come. I Myself am coming to make men, My children, know what, until today, they have not understood completely. I Myself am coming to bring the flame of the law of love so that, by this means, the enormous layer of ice that surrounds mankind can be melted and destroyed.

Oh, beloved humanity, oh, men who are My children, set yourselves free from the bonds in which the devil has chained you until now, inspiring in you fear of a Father Who is pure love! Come, come closer to Me, you have every right to approach your Father; open up your hearts, pray to My Son that He may help you to know even better My goodness towards you.

You who are prisoners of superstition and the laws of the devil, leave this tyrannical slavery and come to the truth. Recognize the One Who made you and is your Father. Do not try to claim your rights, paying worship and homage to those who have led you to spend your life uselessly until now, but come to Me, I am waiting for you all because you are all My children.

And you who are in the true light, tell them how sweet it is to live in the truth! Say also to those Christians, to those dear creatures, My children, how sweet it is to think that there is a Father Who sees everything, knows everything, provides for everything. Who is infinitely good, Who forgives easily, and Who punishes only reluctantly and slowly. Tell them to come to Me: I will help them, I will lighten their burden and sweeten their hard life. I will inebriate them with My fatherly love, to make them happy in time and eternity.

And you, My children, who have lost the faith and live in the darkness, raise your eyes. You will see shining rays coming to illuminate you. I am the sun that shines, warms and re-warms. Look, and recognize that I am your Creator, your Father, your one and only God. It is because I love you that I come to make you love Me, so that you may all be saved.

I am speaking to all men, the world over, making this appeal of My fatherly love ring out, this infinite love that I want you to know is a permanent reality.

Love, love, love always, but also show others how to love the Father, so that from today on I will be able to show you all the Father Who loves you so passionately.

And you, My beloved sons, priests and monks, I exhort you to make known this fatherly love that I have for men, for you in particular. You must work so that my will may be accomplished in all men and in you. It is that I should be known, honored, and loved. Do not leave My love inactive for a long time, because I am thirsty in My desire to be loved!

This century is privileged above all others. Do not let this privilege pass, for fear that it might be withdrawn! Souls need a certain divine touch, and time presses; do not be afraid of anything, I am your Father; I will help you in your efforts and your work. I will sustain you always and make you enjoy, already here below, peace and joy of soul, making your ministry and your zealous works bear fruit. This is an inestimable gift, since the soul which is peaceful and joyful already has a foretaste of heaven while awaiting its eternal reward.

I communicated to My Vicar, the

Supreme Pontiff, My Representative on earth, a very special predilection for the missionary apostolate in distant countries and, most of all, a great zeal to spread throughout the world the devotion to the Sacred Heart of My Son, Jesus. Now I am entrusting him with the work that this same Jesus came on earth to accomplish: to glorify Me by making Me known as I am, just as I am telling all men, My creatures and children.

If men could penetrate the Heart of Jesus in all Its desires and Its glory, they would realize the Its most ardent desire is to glorify the Father, the One Who sent Him, and , most of all, not to let His glory be diminished as it has been until now. He desires the complete glory that men can and must give Me, as their Father and Maker, and still more as the Author of their Redemption!

I am asking of man what he is able to give Me: his confidence, his love, and his gratitude. It is not because I need My creature and his adoration that I desire to be known, honored, and loved; the only reason why I am stooping down to him is to save him and give him a share in My glory. Further, in My goodness and My love I realize that the beings I have drawn from nothing and adopted as My true children are falling in great numbers into eternal unhappiness with the devils. They are thus failing to fulfill the purpose of their creation and are losing their time and their eternity!

If there is something that I desire, above all now, it is simply to see more fervor on the part of the just, a smooth path for the conversion of sinners, sincere and persevering conversion, and the return of the prodigal sons to their Father's house. I am referring in particular to the Jews and to all others who are

My creatures and children, such as the schismatics, the heretics, the free-masons, the poor infidels, the sacrilegious, and the various secret sects. I want this whole world to know that there is a God and a Creator. This God, Who will address their ignorance twice over, is unknown to them; they do not know that I am their Father.

Believe Me, you who are listening to me as you read these words; if all men who are far from the Catholic Church heard people talking about this Father Who loves them, Who is their Creator and their God, about this Father Who desires to give them eternal life, then many of these men, even the most obstinate ones, would come to this Father of whom you have spoken to them.

If you cannot go to them and talk to them directly, look for other means: thousands of direct and indirect ways. Put them into effect with the true spirit of disciples and with great fervor. I promise you that your efforts will soon be crowned with success by a special grace. Make yourselves apostles of My Fatherly goodness, and because of the zeal I will give you all, you will be strong and powerful in your work among souls.

I will always be close to you and in you: if there are two of you talking, I will be with you; if there are more, I will be among you; thus you will say what I inspire you to say and I will put your listeners in the right frame of mind to hear you. In this way, men will be conquered by love and saved for all eternity.

With regard to the means of honoring Me as I desire, all I ask of you is great confidence. Do not think I want austerities or mortifications; I do not want you to walk barefoot or to lay your faces in the dust, or to cover yourselves with ashes. No, no! My dearest wish is that you behave as My children, simply and trusting in Me!

With you I will become everything for everyone, the most tender and loving Father. I will be on intimate terms with you, giving Myself to you all, making Myself small so as to make you great for eternity.

Most of the unbelievers, the impious, and various communities remain in their iniquity and unbelief because they think that I am asking the impossible of them, that they have to submit to My commands like slaves of a tyrannical lord, whose power and pride keep him distant from his subjects, to oblige them to show Him respect and devotion. No, no, My children! I know how to make Myself small, far smaller than you can imagine.

However, what I do require is the faithful observance of the commandments I gave the Church, so that you will be rational creatures and will not be like animals because of your lack of discipline and your evil inclinations, so that you will preserve the treasure which is the soul I gave you, clothed in fullness of its divine beauty!

Then, according to My desire, do what I have already instructed you to do: honor Me with a special devotion. May this make you know My will to give you many benefits and to let you share in large measure in My power and My glory, simply in order to make you happy and save you, and to show My sole desire; to love you and be loved in return by you.

If you love Me as faithful children you will also have loving and obedient respect for My Church and My representatives. Not a respect such as you show now, which keeps you distant from Me because you are afraid of Me. This false respect that you have now is an injustice to justice. It is a wound you cause to the most sensitive part of My Heart; you are forgetting, scorning, My Fatherly love for you.

What most grieved Me about My people, Israel, and what most afflicts Me still about present-day humanity, is this ill-conceived respect you have of Me. Man's enemy has, in fact, used it to lead you to fall into idolatry and schisms. He is still using it and will continue to use it against you to keep you distant from the truth, from My Church, and from Me. Oh, do not allow yourselves to be led any longer by the enemy; believe in the truth that is being revealed to you and walk in the light of this truth.

You, My children, who are outside the Catholic Church, should realize that you are not excluded from My fatherly love. I am making this tender appeal to you because you too are My children. If you have lived up to now in the devil's snares acknowledge that he has cheated you. Come to Me, your Father, and I will receive you with joy and love!

And you, who only know the religion in which you have grown up, and that religion is not the true one, open your eyes. Here is your Father, He Who created you and Who wants to have you. I come to you to bring you the truth and salvation. I can see that you do not know Me and do not realize that all I want is for you to know Me as your Father, Creator, and Savior. It is because of this ignorance that you cannot love Me. Understand, therefore, that I am not as far from you as you think.

How could I leave you alone after having created you and adopted you through My love?

I follow you everywhere, I protect you always, so that everything may become a confirmation of My great liberality towards you, in spite of your forgetfulness about My infinite goodness. This forgetfulness makes you say: "Nature provides us with everything; it makes us live and die." This is the time of grace and light. Recognize, then, that I am the only true God!

In order to give you real happiness in this life and in the next, I want you to do what I am suggesting to you in this light. The time is propitious; do not lose this love which is being offered to your hearts so tangibly. I ask everyone to take part in the Holy Mass according to the liturgy; this pleases Me greatly! Later on I will suggest some short prayers to you, but I do not want to overburden you! The most important thing will be to honor Me with the simplicity of true children of your God, Father, Creator, and Savior of the human race.

Here is another proof of My fatherly love of men. My children, I will not speak to you about the whole greatness of My infinite love, because you have only to open the holy books, to look at the crucifix, the tabernacle and the Blessed Sacrament, to realize the extent to which I have loved you!

Nevertheless, in order to show you that you need to satisfy My will for you to make Me better known and loved, I wish, before ending these words, which only set out the basis of My work of love among men, to point out to you some of the innumerable proofs of My love for you!

As long as man does not live in the truth, he cannot taste real freedom. You, My children, think you have joy and peace, you who are outside the true law, for obedience to which I created you. But deep in your hearts you feel that you have neither true peace nor true joy and that you do not enjoy the true freedom of the One Who created you and is your God and Father!

But you, who abide in the true law, or rather, who have promised to follow the law that I gave you to ensure your salvation, have let vice lead you into evil. You have strayed from the law by behaving badly. Do you think you are happy? No. You feel that your hearts are not at ease. Do you suppose that looking for pleasure and other human joys, your hearts will finally be satisfied? No. Let Me tell you, you will never fell truly free not truly happy until you recognize Me as your Father and submit to My yoke, to be true children of God, your Father.

Why? Because I created you for a single purpose, to know Me, love Me, and serve Me, as a simple and trusting child serves its father!

Once, in the Old Testament, men behaved like animals; they did not preserve any sign of their dignity as children of God, their Father. So to make them realize that I wanted to raise them to the great dignity of God's children, I sometimes had to show Myself as dreadfully severe. Later, when I saw some of them were endowed with sufficient reason to understand, eventually, that it was necessary to distance themselves from the animals, I then began to lavish benefits on them, to give them victory over those who were still unable to recognize and preserve their own dignity.

And as they were increasing in number, I sent my Son to them. He was adorned with all the divine perfections because He was the Son of a perfect God. It was He Who showed them the ways to perfection. Through Him I adopted

you in My infinite love, as real children. Since
then I have never called you simply "creatures,"
but "children."

I clothed you in the true spirit of the new
law which not only distinguishes you from
animals, like the men of the old law, but raises
you above those men of the Old Testament. I
raised you all to the dignity of children of God.
Yes, you are My children and you must tell Me
that I am your Father. But trust in Me as
children do, because without this trust you will
never be truly free.

Everything I am saying to you is intended
to make you realize that I come to carry out this
work of love, to give you powerful help to cast
off the tyrannical slavery which imprisons your
souls, and to let you enjoy real freedom, whence
real happiness comes. Compared with this
freedom, all earthly joys are as nothing. Raise
yourselves to the dignity of children of God and
learn how to respect your own greatness. I will
then be your Father more than ever, the most
lovable and merciful of fathers.

I have come to bring peace with this
work of love. I will let a ray of peace fall upon
anyone who honors Me and trusts in Me, so that
he will be relieved in all his troubles, all his
worries, sufferings and afflictions, especially if
he calls Me and loves Me as his Father. If
families honor Me and love Me as their Father,
I will give them My peace together with My
providence. If workers, businessmen, and
artisans invoke and honor Me, I will give them
My peace and My strength, I will show Myself to
be the good and merciful Father. If each
Christian community invokes and honors Me, I
will give it My peace; I will show Myself to be a
most loving Father, and through My power I

will ensure the eternal salvation of souls.

If all mankind invokes and honors Me, I will bring down upon it the spirit of peace like a benevolent dew.

If all nations, as such, invoke and honor Me, there will be no more discord, nor wars, because I am the God of peace and where I am, there no war can be.

Do you wish to gain victory over your enemy? Call upon Me and you will triumph over him.

Finally, you know that I can do everything because of My power. Well, I am offering this power to all of you, to use now and for eternity. I will always show Myself to be your Father, provided that you show yourselves to be My children.

What do I desire to achieve with this work of love, if not to find hearts able to understand Me?

I am the holiness of which I possess the perfect and full expression; I offer you this holiness, of which I am the Author, through My Holy Spirit, and I instill it in your souls through My Son's merit. It is through My Son and the Holy Spirit that I am coming to you and into you, and it is in you that I seek My repose.

To some souls, the words "I am coming into you" will seem a mystery, but it is not a mystery! Because, having instructed My Son to institute the Holy Eucharist, I intended to come to you every time you receive the Sacred Host!

Of course, nothing prevented Me from coming to you even before the Eucharist, as nothing is impossible to Me! But receiving this Sacrament is an action that is easy to understand and it shows how I come to you!

When I am in you, I can more easily give

you what I possess, provided that you ask Me for it. Through this Sacrament you are intimately united with Me. It is in this intimacy that the outpouring of My love makes My holiness spread into your souls.

I fill you with My love, then you have only to ask Me for the virtues and perfection you need and you can be sure that in those moments when God is reposing in His creatures, nothing will be refused you.

Since you know My Favorite place of rest, are you not going to offer it to Me? I am your Father and your God; will you dare refuse Me this? Oh, do not let Me suffer because of your cruelty towards a Father Who is asking you for this one favor for Himself.

Before ending this message, I want to express a wish to numerous souls who are consecrated to My service. You, priests and religious, are those souls. You are dedicated to My service, whether in the contemplative life or in charitable and apostolic works. For My part, this is a privilege granted through My goodness; for your part, it is faithfulness to your vocation, together with your good will.

This is My desire: you who find it easier to understand what I expect of mankind, pray to Me. So that I will be able to accomplish My work of love in all souls. You know all the difficulties that have to be overcome to win a soul! Well, this is the effective mans of helping you to bring a great number of them to Me: this means is that of making Me known, love and honored by men.

I want you to be the first ones to start doing this. What joy for Me to enter first the houses of priests and religious! What joy to find Myself, as Father, amid the children of My love!

With you I will converse as with intimate friends! I will be for you the most discreet of confidants! I will be everything to you, I will satisfy all your needs! Most of all, I will be the Father Who receives your requests, Who lavishes His Love, His benefits, and His universal tenderness upon you.

Do not refuse Me this joy which I desire to enjoy with you! I will give it back to you a hundredfold and, since you will honor Me, I will honor you too, by preparing great glory for you in My Kingdom!

I am the light of lights: where it penetrates there will be life, bread, and happiness. This light will illumine the pilgrim, the skeptic, the ignorant. It will illumine you all, O men who live in this world of darkness and vice. If you did not have My light, you would fall into the abyss of eternal death!

Finally, this light will lighten the ways which lead to the true Catholic Church for its poor children still victims of superstition. I will show Myself as a Father to those who suffer most on earth, the poor lepers.

I will show Myself to be the Father of all those who are abandoned, the outcasts of every society. I will show Myself as a Father to all families, to orphans, widows, prisoners, workers and the young. I will show Myself as the Father of kings, the Father of their nations, You will all feel My goodness and my protection; you will all see My power!

My fatherly and divine blessing on everyone. Amen!

Especially to My Son and Representative. Amen!

Especially to My son, the Bishop. Amen!

Especially to My son, your spiritual Father.

Amen!
Especially to My daughters, your mothers.
Amen!
To all the congregations of My love. Amen!

To order the full message of the Eternal Father to Mother Eugenia Ravasio you may write to:

Casa Pater
PO Box 1260
Emmitsburg, MD 21727

CHAPTER NINE

THERESA WERNER

In the spring of 1988, a string of supernatural signs and events began to be reported at Saint John Neumann Church in Lubbock, Texas. Three parishioners claimed locutions from the Blessed Virgin Mary and one of them, Theresa Werner, revealed that she was receiving messages from God the Father.

Theresa Werner's story is contained within the events at Lubbock which, although relatively brief, were marked by a series of reported supernatural phenomena that not only included the locutions, but also apparitions, miraculous odors and scents, interior visions, healings, conversions, and celestial phenomena. These events peaked on the afternoon of August 15, 1988 when, in expectation of the fulfillment of a prophecy from one of the locutionists, 20,000 people gathered at St. John Neumann on the Feast of Mary's Assumption to hopefully witness a miracle. A Mass was held that day and sometime before the Mass, and then after the reading of the Gospel, a series of solar miracles and heavenly visions were reportedly witnessed by great numbers in the crowd. Thousands upon thousands began to cheer as witnesses would later claim to have seen the sun pulsating and swirling and giving off bursts of lights, visions of Jesus, Mary, and Saints passing before their eyes in the sky, and a mystical "doorway to heaven," which repeatedly appeared on polaroid photographs. Some claimed their Rosaries turned from silver to gold and, later in the evening, that the moon changed colors. There were also reports of physical healings throughout the crowd.

News of the miracles spread far and wide and the Church eventually appointed a committee to study all of the related events at

Saint John Neumann Church. But although the story of Lubbock continues to this day, the account of Theresa Werner and her experiences with God the Father is confined to a series of prophecies she reportedly received from May 16, 1988 through August 8, 1988.

The third child of Peter and Earlene Steiert, Theresa Marie Werner was born on January 11, 1955, in Plainview, Texas. She grew up on a 200-acre cotton and corn farm in Hart, Texas, along with her older brother Jim and younger brother Pat. Her fondest memories include horseback and tractor riding and indulging in her favorite hobby, painting. The family practiced its faith too, as most evenings included the family Rosary, always prayed on the knees.

Theresa married Mark Werner at St. Elizabeth's Church in Lubbock, Texas, in 1983. The couple then lived in Alaska for a year before returning to Lubbock. In early 1985, as the couple expected their only child, Mark and Theresa decided on St. John Neumann as their permanent parish. A prayerful and friendly atmosphere led them there and on September 6, 1985, their son Joseph Earl Peter Werner was baptized at the church. The couple remained at St. John Neumann until 1988, when at that time they were briefly forced, because of scheduling restraints, to attend another parish.

But because St. John Neumann was open 24 hours a day, and had been designated the Marian shrine for the diocese during the 1988 Marian year, Theresa returned one evening to pray and light some candles. And this then was when it all began.

That night, Theresa Werner sat in front of a statue of the Virgin Mary in a small alcove within the chapel. Crying, and in deep prayer, Theresa says she suddenly experienced the strong scent of fresh-cut flowers, although only plastic flowers were in the chapel. Theresa said she then was stuck by a strong feeling that the Blessed Virgin Mary was there with her, in the chapel. The feeling got so strong within her that she even instinctively thought that Mary was going to appear to her.

Not feeling worthy of such an experience, she prayed that nothing would happen and hurriedly left the chapel for her car. On the way home, she told her husband who had been waiting for her what had happened. With that, the matter was over, neither being aware that others at St. John Neumann had reported similar experiences and that one parishioner was reportedly receiving messages from the Virgin Mary.

The next day, Palm Sunday, Theresa, along with her baby, returned to St. John Neumann where Monsignor Joseph James revealed during Mass the reported miracles that were occurring there. Stunned, Theresa couldn't believe what this meant as far as what had happened to her the night before, and while the emotion of the day wreaked havoc on her, she primarily felt frightened by it all.

Reconciled that God was working in her life, Theresa and her husband joined the Monday night Rosary meeting at St. John Neumann. From this time on, she says her experiences with the Blessed Mother, especially a "feeling" of her presence, grew. Likewise, her desire to pray the Rosary grew and more and more her house would come to be unexplainedly filled with the smell of roses.

Then one night at the Rosary, Theresa says she felt an inner, urgent feeling that led her to write down a message that was from the Virgin Mary. These experiences continued until on Mary 2, 1988, Theresa received a message that was given in a strange, archaic language, similar to "old" English. The message contained words such as "thee" and "thou" and had a style similar to verses found in some older versions of the Bible.

The Eternal Father speaks to Theresa

But it was on May 16, 1988, that Theresa Werner says that God the Father spoke to her. That night, before she received the first message, she says she saw in an interior vision, clouds and angels that seemed to be falling around her. Then, she says, she saw God Himself, God the Father. Theresa's own words perhaps disclose her experiences the best:

> On Monday, May 16, 1988, I believe that God came to speak to His people through me. I was very frightened. As He was speaking that first time, my handwriting was so bad it looked like a "polygraph test". I was very afraid and had no control of my hands. Before He delivered His message, I saw whirling clouds and angels that seemed to be falling around me. I saw Him mount His magnificent throne, and there were two mighty lions on either side of Him. The lions were great winged-beasts

with their heads going round and round; praises to God
were coming forth from their mouths with belches of
fire. God, Himself, was brighter than the mightiest sun,
and I couldn't look upon Him. If I attempted to look,
my eyes would water, even with my eyes closed, so
bright was His glory. I knew that if I were to look upon
God, I would surely die. Only through His Will could
I gaze upon His glorious countenance.

As God sat on His mighty throne surrounded by
clouds, He would lean over and speak, telling me what
He wanted me to relate to His people. His voice was
a strong, masculine one, full of authority, yet filled with
loving gentleness. Like thunder did it roar, but it was
clear and very regal sounding. I could see His face, but
not as I normally see—He would put visions into my
mind of the things He wanted me to see. He had a long
white beard, white hair, and His eyes were like fire—they
had a cast of red in them. His face seemed to glow with
a glorious radiance; it was full of wisdom and great age
but "youthful." Sometimes He seemed like He was
robed in pure gold. His arm was full of power and
strength.

The only way to describe what I saw is to
explain it this way: If I were to look at someone, then
close my eyes, I could still visualize how they look. The
visions I received were locutions—interior visions, but
these were like nothing I've ever seen before.

Sometimes God would scold me gently but
firmly and remind me of the task I was doing for Him,
because I was so busy looking at the creatures that were
surrounding His throne. He loves animals so much that
He surrounds Himself with them. I saw things like
huge, tusked-elephants which were decorated with
ornate jewelry. Also, I was distracted by the handsome
beauty of Saint Michael who is so big and muscular.
Often I had to force myself to pay attention to the words
being spoken.

Still, I am human, and at one point, I felt as

though I had reached my breaking point, I just didn't know if I could handle these visions and messages anymore, I began to wonder if I was making all of this up or that maybe a demon had gained possession of me. I needed confirmation that the messages and visions I was receiving were from God. One overcast day, God finally granted my prayer for peace in my soul. He told me to go out of my apartment door and take a picture of the clouds in the sky. I started to think that it was my own imagination telling me to do this, when I heard Him tell me to go outside before He was gone. I had two shots left in my camera, and I took a picture of the eastern sky. When it was developed, the picture showed Jesus Christ on the cross. On the next day, which was the 19th of the month, I was told to go out again and take another picture. Again, I took a picture towards the east, and this time the picture showed our Blessed Mother standing on a pillar of clouds with her Son, Jesus, right beside her. In this photo, all the mysteries of the Rosary could be seen. The five Joyful, the five Sorrowful, and the five Glorious were all visible.

The Messages

From this time on, the messages Theresa Werner would receive always left her emotionally drained. So intense, she said, it was "almost like giving birth to a child." Each week an internal tension would build within her as the day (Monday) the message was to be given got closer. The palpable tension also came from the content of the messages, as some of the messages dealt directly with the coming the Eternal Father's justice upon the world. Theresa was given to understand this justice symbolically in one vision, which involved an angel with a sword, who would soon come upon the earth, striking all four corners with God's justice. Theresa explained this vision:

> I felt the Lord was trying to show me that chastisements would soon fall on the earth with the striking of his mighty sword... God loves His people...all the human

race. He wants all the people to convert, to repent, and
to come back to him. He is a loving and merciful God,
but I feel His emotions are mixed. I believe that He is
grieved...angry...He doesn't want to inflict punishment,
but like an earthly father would punish his child for
being disobedient, so would our Heavenly Father. In
the messages I received from Him, He spoke of the
chastisements to come for our disobedience. When
these punishments will come and exactly what they will
be, I do not know, only the Father knows. I do believe
that these disasters could be adverted if we would only
turn   back   towards   Him   by   following   the
Commandments He gave to Moses on Mount Sinai
(Exodus 20: 1-17) and by praying for deliverance.

While many of the messages continued to note this coming
time of justice, Theresa's visions and messages not only involved God's
justice but many other elements of the faith. She was especially given
insight into the great events that were prophesied and then witnessed by
many on August 15, 1988 at St. John Neumann's Church in Lubbock.
This would also be the day she would learn that her work for the Father
was coming to an end:

As the time for Our Lady's Feast approached, I was
given various personal prophecies by both the Blessed
Mother and by the Father about what would happen
that day. I kept getting the number "20,000" which
was interpreted as meaning that this many people would
be there that day, and that we should make preparations
to receive and minister to them. I saw through visions
that there would be miracles of the sun, I saw the falling
rain that would wash away the curious and give relief to
the faithful.

On the Feast of the Assumption, I believe that
the Lord was here on Earth. I felt as though a bit of
Heaven had come to us. Everyone was at peace that
day...the way it should be. While I was witnessing the
"miracle of the sun," I heard my name being called. I

looked down and there in front of me two women were standing. One was wearing a light blue garment, while the other was in white. I looked upon the one in the blue garment, and her eyes were very big and blue. She had brown hair cut in a short style, and she was very fair. She said to me, "Theresa, I have come to tell you that your mission for the Father is complete. You may rest now."

I continued to stare at her, and she lifted one of her eyebrows as if to say, "You'd better listen to me, now." I thought to myself, "What if this is an angel...I'd better respect this person's wishes." Then I hugged her, (I remembered later that there hadn't been very much to hug) stepped back, and looked away for just an instant. I turned back toward her and her companion, and both had seemingly vanished! After this, I immediately started praying, because I felt as if I needed some sort of confirmation of this message.

Besides seeing the sun arrayed in many colors dance and spin, I also saw what appeared to be an eagle flying, coming down. Mounted on its back, I thought I saw the Blessed Mother. Later, I saw her profile in the sky. She turned her head towards the vast crowd and had in her hands a Rosary. She put her hands together as if to say, "Pray."

The next day, I was supposed to attend a meeting with the rest of the messengers, but I didn't go. I had assumed that since I was told that my mission was over that I was no longer a messenger. However, I found out later that the Blessed Mother had appeared to the other two messengers, Mike and Mary, and had scolded them because of my absence. During that meeting, Our Lady confirmed that a woman had been sent on the Feast to tell me that my service as God's instrument was over. I was amazed because I had told no one about my experience. However, this was the confirmation for which I had been praying.

Theresa Werner says she will always remember the day the

messages from God the Father to her ended. For her it was a day of very strong yet mixed emotions. On one hand, she says she felt relieved that day, unburdened by the vast responsibility of it all. Yet that evening, she said she broke down and cried as if the Lord had told her "goodbye."

But although the messages from God the Father were over, her mission was not. The messages still needed to go out to the world and the seriousness of the content of the revelations indicated that God had chosen her as a prophet who was given a message of great importance, and whose timing and significance may not yet have been realized.

Indeed, the revelations are poignant and profound with a divine quality that strikes of authenticity. While perhaps puzzling as to why the Father chose to speak to her in such an antiquated form of English, the style of the messages does in no way detract from the content.

In fact, because of the content, the old Testament biblical style phrasing of the revelations seems to convey an even more urgent reality and importance. The Father of the past remains the same Father of the present and the future. And in Theresa's revelations, His Divine authority as the author of all history is undeniable. An old age must pass, the revelations state, and a new era will definitely dawn. But a chasm must first be crossed and in this transition, those who are outside of God's will remain the most affected, disillusioned and lost. Therefore, a period of preparation has been given through Mary's intercession, and those who have rejected her help will apparently suffer the consequences of their choice.

Moreover, the Father tells Theresa, as He has to His other chosen ones, that He has not been honored as Scripture clearly reveals He should and desires. Therefore, it is time now for a new generation to give Him this honor and praise. His reign, he says, is at Hand, and the truth and light of this is about to be revealed. For His name's sake, a purification will come so that His Divine Will will reign. Most significantly, God Our Father told Theresa, **"The world, I, the Lord God, will make a new. The old shall pass away. Again the peoples will call Me their God and I shall have them as My people. It is in this that praise and glory shall be given unto Me again...and worship, once more."**

Many of the revelations given to Theresa Werner reflect the wisdom and truth found in Scripture. The following are some of the more thought-provoking messages given to her from May 10, through

August 8, 1988:

Repent and reflect upon all that has been set before you in words and actions. "Spurn not the Lord you God." Test Him no longer. Merciful and just is the Lord your God. All life He satisfieth with His mighty hands and will sustain thee. (May 16, 1998)

The Lord your God is calling to His faithful: Forsake Me not. Come, (the) time is at hand! There shall be not comfort by mere man, but from the Blood of the Lamb, Jesus Christ. (May 16, 1998)

See, alas, the storm cometh! Gather My people together. Wait no longer, for many will the wails be...and afflictions. Come to the refuge. Come to the abode with the Blood of the Lamb, Jesus; for there you shall be spared and blessings bestowed and peace (restored) to you. (May 16, 1988).

Fear, for it is in fear that you are wise. In wisdom, there shall be blessings (untold). It is My Eyes of Life that (tremble) the mountains. It is of My wisdom that the eagle is taught to build his nest. If is of My hands that thou shalt be filled with all good things. (May 23, 1988)

My glance is continually upon this Church...it's people. It is I (that) knoweth the directions of the winds. It is I that shall deliver thee thy miracle...on which you shall await. As of this day and hour, this will be My holy people, My holy church. For it is here I find the prayers of homage. (May 23, 1988)

My blessings I bestow upon ye - for which the appointed angels of heaven shall guard and guide thee from this day forth. So it shall be by My Son's most holy Blood. So it shall be by My Divine Will. Mine eyes shall be ever watchful upon ye. (May 23, 1988)

(Woe) unto those (whose) hearts laugh and make light their days of (gaiety), for their days soon will turn to darkness and sorrow, full of lamentations. They laugh and tease of (there) being no God. Oh, but come forth the days of wrath unto ye! (May 30, 1988)

For lo, seest the winds do stir and violently they shall toss to and from by the commands of My mighty hands. I say unto ye, old and young alike: No one knows the day nor hour. For it is in My Divine Will that thou shalt taste the bitterness of My chastisements. (May 30, 1988)

The days are at hand. Be not asleep as those (of) long ago. Be alert and wait upon thy Lord God. Keep the lamps lit for darkness approaches. Though the (cries) may by many, I hear not. My wrath shall strike! (May 30, 1988)

Yea, though, I say unto ye again: Look unto the east for there (thou) shalt beat thy hearts and gnaw thy teeth, for there thy many hearts shalt be laid bare. So it is. So it shall be. (May 30, 1988)

I, the Lord your God, say unto ye: As that of long ago, I seek and find not the choirs of thanksgiving and homage unto Me. I call, but thou hast had answered not. (June 6, 1988)

O, land of milk and honey, as of sucklings of
days past, when your mother's breast was full of
the sweetness of life, and (the) limbs of your
fathers of long ago (bent) and paid homage unto
Me, the Lord your God...(During the sorrowful
mysteries, Jesus in the Garden in Prayer) (June 6,
1988)

Though you may suffer the affliction from those
who slander ye and persecute ye, praise your
Heavenly Father. For it is in this that your
strengths will be multiplied and your graces
added. (June 6, 1988)

Console thy Mother. Console her, (because of)
those who bring blasphemies and torments
against her most Sorrowful Heart. The hour
draws near. It is at hand. So it is! So it shall be!
(June 6, 1988)

The brook (laughs) with praise unto Me. The
birds of the air take flight into the heavens to
touch My heavenly face. (June 13, 1988)

So I say unto ye: I, the Lord your God, (am)
great, and so say unto ye to do homage unto Me.
Sing to Me as long ago. Think upon Me with
your minds - as complex in creation that they
can be, yet all subconscious and consciousness
alike (know) the Divine Truth. (June 13, 1988)

Prepare thyselves as that of a bride to make
ready for her wedding day. As that of a warrior
who places his breastplate in a great detail to
keep his life from perishing. So it is with this
that is to be. (June 13, 1988)

Yea, I say unto ye: Though many shall perish,

those who are worthy of My new world shall therefore flourish in it. And bring forth a new life which shall rekindle that which has been lost. (June 13, 1988)

The chastisements are just. Rejoice in My "Fire of Love." For it is in being that those who remain faithful unto Me shall have everlasting life. (June 13, 1988)

Doest ye know that Mine enemies slandered Me? Tormented Me? Sorrowed My most Sacred Heart? So do I (see) thy afflictions but, I say unto ye: "Rejoice, Rejoice, for thy inheritance is at hand, 'The Glory of Heaven'." (June 13, 1988)

Behold! The earth (cries) in its pains of labor! Yea, I say unto ye again, the days are at hand. The days have been numbered. Yea, though many say the Lord God slumbers, it be not so. For I say unto ye: No man knows the hour nor day! (June 20, 1988)

Look about you. Does not your mind grasp what is happening? Your lands will be given over to those who are not of your own blood - (kin). Your food shall be sparingly reaped...as your prayers (have) been (sparing) unto Me, the Lord your God. (June 20, 1988)

Oh, if it were only like that of long ago when sackcloth and ashes were worn in (place) of (merriment) and wine! Repent! I say unto ye. Repent, for My wrath shall be great. (June 20, 1988)

Yea, the signs are at hand and that which (is) of

a thief in the night shall steal away from thee without thine (awareness). (June 20, 1988)

I shall make (you) Mine again! No longer shall ye run after your lovers! How foolish are you! How time races from your hands without knowledge of its passings. I shall strip you and make you naked before your foes. I shall shame you, for thou hast sinned against the Lord your God! (June 20, 1998)

The days (have passed) of your jewels and (delicacies). No more shall you adorn yourselves with fragrances and shadow your eyes! I shall make you return unto Me. I shall (shackle) thy (ankles) and make you a slave of your own weaknesses. You shall weep, but none shall comfort you. Holding (out) your arms which were so richly adorned, (they) shall be bare. And none shall come to your aid. (Contempt) shall be at your reach from all others who spy you. (June 20, 1988)

Oh, My beloved, My children from where you come from My own designs. What are you? (Who) are you without the Lord your God? Pray and beg that mercy shall be with you! For never hath thou tasted the bitterness (which) I, the Lord your God, will make ready for your drinking. (June 20, 1988)

Doest thou not see thy afflictions before you? The earth itself trembles at My mighty glances. The floodgates of heaven have been closed unto those who beg for rains to fall. Thine afflictions are yet but many. I say unto ye, daughter of Moses and all your forefathers: "Convert your lives while there is still time!" Yea, I say unto

ye: Thy days of merriment and dancing are at
an end. Your children shall be famished for their
parents' afflictions against Me, the Lord God.
(June 27, 1988)

I say unto ye: Woe upon the earth and all its
inhabitants; for theirs is grief and no comfort
shall be at their reaches. Yea, (thou) shalt be
rightly so to say the Lord your God has closed
His ears to your prayers. I am a God of jealousy,
for I am the only God. There shall be no other
gods before me. Yet you pay homage to all your
earthly possessions. (June 27, 1988)

Your profanities are often and yet there are no
regrets in the use of your slanders. Yours are the
defilement of the body and mind. Your
offspring acknowledge ME (themselves), not
the Lord God. Your men burn with lust for one
another which sickens My very Heart! Your
women spurn their rightful places and have
turned to one another for their cravings of the
flesh. Defilement! Defilement! Woe to you, for
thou art sinful and death before My Eyes of
Justice. (June 27, 1988)

Afflictions I shall give unto ye. Afflictions of
drought (and) flood. The earth shall tremble
and shake your towers you have adorned.
Famine shall befall ye; disease for which there
shall be no cure! Woe unto ye. Woe, for thou
are (truly) a cursing! (June 27, 1988)

I say unto ye: This be holy ground. Those who
come forth unto it (from) far and near shall be
blessed with the fruits they find here. It is here
My beloved have sung to Me. It is here they seek
My face and find it. Thou shalt have Fruits of

Life here, for the Lamb of God is here. His blood was shed unmercifully for all men. (June 27, 1988)

There shall not be the burning chastisement here, for it is here the grounds are holy. My beloved children, gather before Me and ask for pardon. For it is in asking that thou shalt receive it! Yea, though many shall perish, there will be a new world, a new life, a new generation which shall honor Me and not put the Lord God far from their minds. (June 27, 1988)

Yea, man's days may seem but long to them, but it is only a whisper in the wind. They who have done great things shall be forgotten. It is your soul that is your life. It is the Blood of Jesus, Who is the eternal hope and life. (June 27, 1988)

I say unto ye, My beloved: What purpose does it serve man to be learned and yet know not from whom his wisdom cometh? I say unto ye, My beloved: Adorn thineselves in (exquisiteness), yet (the) moth cometh to destroy and rotteth away. I say unto ye, My beloved: Riches may be stored up and locked away, but the thief comes in the night and takes from you all your savings and (possessions). (June 27, 1988)

The Lord your God saith unto ye: I, the Creator of all life great and small, looked upon ye in your lowliness. I spied you in your nakedness. There in your blood, I, the Lord your God, found you. I raised you from your lowliness and lifted you up. The Lord your God hath taken you into His divine care and nurtured your every need. (July 11, 1988)

You were fed of the finest wheat, flour and oils. Milk and honey were your foods. The poor He has given every good thing, the rich (he has) sent away. I adorned you in silk and satin. And there I placed upon you bracelets of gold and necklaces to adorn your neck. A ring in your nose I gave to you. And a (diadem) for your head. (July 11, 1988)

Behold, thou hast looked upon your very self with love and (begun) to seek your comforts and love elsewhere...not remembering from whence thou hast come. Your oils, wheat and flour you have given to your lovers that thou hast lusted after...making (thrones) of your silk and (satin) for others, not reflecting on (whence) they come. Thou hast become the (harlot). Your lusts burn forth with no control and with no regrets of your sins. (July 11, 1988)

And unto ye My (shepherds): Thou hast fed off My chosen. Thou hast misled them and scattered them about to foreign lands...leaving them to hunger and be abandoned to their foes. I say unto ye: Behold, the Lord God shall go forth and gather His lost sheep. He shall feed the hungry and bind up the crippled and nurse the sick back to health. But the fattened lambs and goats, I, the Lord your God, shall drive away. (July 11, 1988)

I shall send forth the pestilences of My jealous wrath. It shall burn till it shall be appeased. There shall be drought. There shall be famine. There shall be war. (July 11, 1988)

For it was said long ago and still stands firm to

this day...those who are first shall be last and the last shall be first. But, I, the Lord your God, in your lowliness I shall lift ye up again. I shall put between My people a covenant which shall be sweet to My (nostrils). I shall (anoint) ye and make ye Mine again. And I will be your God and ye My people. (July 11, 1988)

In your goodness given, your shame shall be upon ye and thou shalt behold the mercy of the Lord your God. Sing unto the Lord your God all you peoples of every race and tongue! Praise Him for He is good and His mercy endureth unto all generations! (July 11, 1988)

Bring forth your blind; your deaf, mute and crippled; your sick and lame; your downtrodden. Rejoice, for miracles will be at hand unto ye who gather forth in the glory of Jesus Christ and to the Heavenly Father. (July 11, 1988)

For lo, the Lord God is angered by the nations; and the Lord God will have His day of chastisements. The Lord God will have His day of vengeance; for His mighty sword shall be with blood. (July 18, 1988)

My brethren, My beloved–like that of a lamp...you leave it out that the light may be seen by many. You would not put it under a basket. So, I say unto ye, My beloved: In its time the Truth and the Light shall be revealed. I say unto ye: The ax surely is laid to the root of the tree. Whoever bears not fruit will be cut down and cast into the fire. (July 18, 1988)

Thou seekest (a sign). It has been given, ye of little faith. Yea, thou mayest have eyes, but do not see. Ears, but hearest not. I say unto ye...I, the Lord your God, shall make the lame run like the spirited stag, the mute to sing, the blind to give witness...so it is, so it shall be. (July 18, 1988)

The Lord your God saith unto ye: In the beginning the Spirit of God dwelled about in a great vastness. The Lord God gave forth creation...making the lands and great oceans, the dome in which to hold the planets and stars (which) the Lord God placed with His holy hands. I, the Lord God, created all life great and small...every creature that crawls and every fowl that flies in the sky. My mighty glance smolders the mountains and My breath is that of fire. (July 25, 1988)

I give unto ye another sign. Yea, I say, it is in faith and hope that you be here. Signs you (seekest) and (thou) shalt receive them. One I give unto ye...(a weeping Madonna). She mourns with joy to see her faithful gathered and she mourns for those who continue to follow the road—which is wide and smooth—to destruction. (July 25, 1988)

For, yea, I (am) near unto ye. I (am) at thy door now! Glory to the Lord Jesus, for in His reign there is no ending. (July 25, 1988)

The Lord God saith unto ye: Hast ye not all the one Father? If it is this, where is the honor unto Me...the (reverence) from ye? (August 1, 1988)

Is not the Lord God's (Word) of goodness and life? Does not it promise this unto the man who walks uprightly? Thy God is moving among His people! Awaken and see thy signs and hear that of the wind which sings of the miracles to come forth here. Hast not signs been given here? Warnings? Are you deaf? Doest (thou) not (see)? These warnings are from love and compassion. Awaken! Amend thy lives, for the reign of God is at hand! Repent, I say unto ye. Repent! For lo the Lord is at thy shoulder now and the earth trembles with fear! The Lord your God is a jealous God. Yea, I say unto ye, jealous and with vengeance. And with vengeance He shall strike ye! Is it not of the troubled multiplications upon the earth which (are) measured by your countless sins? Does a bride forget her sash? A Virgin her jewels? Yet thou hast forgotten the Lord God (for) days without number. My Heart (cries) out like that of the lone wolf. Lonely He beeth in His vastness. My Heart (cries) out like the mourning of the dove. Cooing of the great loss of My people...cooing for you to returnst unto Me. (August 1, 1988)

(Thou) stirrest about like a great torrent; yet that which is spoken be of sound lips! Doth ye not call Me "Father"...still the bridegroom in thy youth? You askes of the Lord God how long beeth His rage...the fury of His anger; yet (thou) continuest (thy) sins without remorse. Who can stand before the Lord God's wrath? Yea, I say unto ye: The Lord God (prepareth) a great chastisement upon the whole of mankind. Plead for peace, I say unto ye. Plead for thy mercy, for the Lord God hath (called) His people but, lo, they answer not. He seeketh for His people, but they turn their faces from (Him). (August 1, 1988)

Venerate the Blessed Virgin's Heart and My most Holy Son, Jesus' Heart together. For the

Lord has given unto the Queen of Heaven the effect of peace to the world. Pray for peace in this world. Yea, the Lord your God rules the earth and all that is in it; yet the prayers of veneration give great joy unto My being and stir Me to direct by (them). (August 1, 1988)

I say unto ye, My children: The stump of the tree-that of Jesse-is of the Tree of Life...a sweet blossom...the Fruit of Life. Partake of this fruit that ye (might) live and have eternal life. (August 1, 1988)

As it be of His kingdom; the lamb lies beside the lion, the bear (accompanies) the cow, and the hay is eaten by the leopard with the calf. The child shall lay his hand on the adder's web, but peace and no harm shall there be of this (reign). Yea, I say unto ye: Thy names shall reign in Him and your generations blessed. The world, I, the Lord God, shall make anew... a new moon...a new dawning and so forth. A new Sabbath. The old shall pass away as (will) their offenses against Me. Again the peoples will call Me their God and I shall have them as My people. It is in this that praise and glory shall be given unto Me again...and worship, once more. (August 1, 1988)

Oh, that ye might suck fully of the milk of (the) abundant breast, My children. That ye might be delighted and comforted as that of a young infant in the arms of its mother, receiving forth the love as of that which ye shalt receive from the Lord your God. A river of prosperity shall be overflowing unto ye and thy blessings multiplied. Abandon yourselves unto the Lord your God, for He knoweth of all thy needs and concerns.   **If ye (hast) the faith of a mustard seed, (thou) shalt receive that (for) which thou askest. Be not a part of this world any longer, for its very being is within the depths of hell itself.** (August 1, 1988)

Oh man, it is of your offenses against the Lord your God that comes forth your chastisements, your afflictions multiplied.   (dost) thou see thy bitterness in your turning away from your Father?...thine evil? The Lord God's vengeance shall be unveiled upon sinful men in thy deceit, bitterness, malice, murdering...in thy (lewd) conducts (all accounted for), in thy idolatry of (self), gossip... Oh, man, thou art inexcusable!... for (thou) seest the Lord God's glory magnified in all its splendor on earth and in the heavens! (August 8, 1988)

Fix this unto thine hearts...the Lord your God asketh of ye: Your forefathers were placed in a covenant with Me, honoring Me and giving Me unto Me homage. (But) for thou...with ye there be no thanksgivings! No honor unto Me do I find! Is it not so...? (August 8, 1988)

Love the Lord God with your whole mind, with your whole heart and with your whole strength. Instill in thy children the love of their Father. Attach it to your wrists, diadem thy foreheads, belt it about they waist...speak it in thy labors and in thy rest. Abroad and near, speak thy love for your God of hosts. For, lo, I am love and love I rightly claim! Paint it atop thy doors and post. Make firm thy covenant with the Lord your God.   And serve Me all the (days) that life's breath is within you. (August 8, 1988)

Your turmoils on this earth are at hand. Your savior saith: "I weep for you! Take My hand for I be gentle and humble of heart. My Heart (cries) out to you. How I long for you. I am merciful unto the sinner. Take thy cross up and follow after Me. My words are life...unto all men, unto the whole of the world!" (August 8, 1988

CHAPTER TEN

GEORGETTE FANIEL

The history of mystical theology is rich with stories of souls that God chooses to keep hidden from the world in order to better fulfill His mission through them. Many of these souls are in fact never revealed to the public, as God withholds any revelation of their meritorious service on His behalf to Himself and the Church Triumphant. In other cases, we often hear about the lives of chosen ones after their death, sometimes even centuries later, as God carefully engineers the timing of such affairs for the maximum benefit of souls. Finally, there are those hidden servants that God gradually moves from the invisible to the visible while still alive, choosing in His wisdom a blossoming of their life at a certain time and in specific situations that again are carefully designed to aid in the salvation of souls and in the expedition of bringing His Kingdom to greater reign on earth.

One such chosen instrument is a Canadian woman of Belgian extraction, whose life and revelations indicate that she holds, in God's eyes, great favor, high esteem and perhaps unparalleled merit in His service as a hidden victim. Most of all, she has been revealed to be a gem of the Eternal Father, chosen by Him as His instrument to bring peace to the world and spiritual assistance to the Church.

Georgette Faniel was born in 1915 and has resided in Montreal all of her life. As of this writing she is 84 years of age and residing in an elderly home in a suburb of the city. Regarded by many respected theologians as a mystic and victim soul of the highest order, Georgette Faniel's life in God began at the age of six when she first heard the voice of Jesus. However, it was not until 1985, almost seventy years later, that the world began to come to know of her life and special mission.

When Faniel first heard as a child Jesus speak to her, she said the voice resounded in the depth of her heart (inner locution) as well as in her ear (aural locution). This dialogue with Christ became clearer and clearer and she also then began to hear the voice of the Blessed Virgin Mary, the Holy Spirit (not heard as a voice but as an "inner light"), and eventually the Eternal Father. Over time, her heavenly conversations became a normal fact of life and her intimacy with God permitted her to spiritually grow in a way that is comparable to many mystics.

At the beginning of her spiritual experiences, Georgette thought that such divine favors were normal for all children and adults. But when she discovered they were not, she became fearful and withdrawn. Her nights became long episodes of prayer, with only an hour or two devoted to sleep. And like all such chosen souls, the devil would become her nemesis, often ridiculing and tormenting her unmercifully.

Over the years, Georgette's family also added to her cross, as they distanced themselves from her because of her experiences. A Jesuit priest, who believed in her spiritual experiences began to direct and advise her until she finally found a priest who would become her spiritual director. Father Joseph Gamache, S.J., operated in this role for twenty years until he died at the age of 84. After his passing, another Jesuit, Father Paul Mayer, took his place and served as her spiritual director for the next 20 years.

In 1981, Father Mayer asked Georgette to pray for a new spiritual director because of his age. (He was 81 years old.) After a five-day retreat, Georgette says that the Eternal Fathers instructed her that Fathers Armand and Guy Girard, twins and Canadian priests of the Society of the Holy Apostles of Montreal, were to now assist her. Fr. Armand Girard became her spiritual director while his brother, Father Guy, was to be her spiritual counselor and would have the responsibility of Georgette's spiritual notes. And it was with the advent of the Girard brothers' involvement that Georgette Faniel's life would soon move out from being hidden and into the public realm.

The Eternal Father

"Like My Son," the Eternal Father told her one day, "You will have a public life." At the time, Georgette did not understand the meaning of this revelation nor how it was to come about. For seventy-two years she had remained anonymous and if she had her way, she would refuse to give up her hidden life.

But in October 1984 the Girard brothers made a 10-day pilgrimage/retreat to Medjugorje for the first time and quickly events began to unfold which would reveal the life and mission of Georgette Faniel, especially her intimacy with the Eternal Father.

When the brothers returned to Montreal from Medjugorje, they discussed their spiritual experiences and convictions with Georgette. Her response was tempered, but careful and attentive. She revealed no enthusiasm and advised only prayer.

But on Good Friday of Holy Week in 1985, Georgette Faniel reported that the Eternal Father asked her if she would be willing to give her life in order to authenticate the apparitions in Medjugorje. **"Accept with love,"** the Eternal Father said to Georgette, **"that the testimony on Medjugorje be published so that the apparitions may be made known."** According to her spiritual director, she accepted this request with great faith and joy but knew her sufferings would be worse. Georgette then offered during the Holy Week of 1985 her life as a witness to the authenticity of the apparitions of the Blessed Virgin Mary in Medjugorje.

The following year (October, 1986) the two priests returned to Medjugorje after a seven-day retreat in Rome. There they shared with a Franciscan priest what was occurring with Georgette Faniel in regards to Medjugorje and sought to discern whether or not they were to do more, perhaps in the form of publishing the entire account and sending it to the Holy Father. A message from Mary through the Medjugorje visionary Maria Lunetti encouraged them. Upon returning to Montreal, they requested that Georgette Faniel ask Jesus during the celebration of a Mass in her apartment on November 16, 1985, if the events occurring in Montreal were to be published. **"Why would I have inspired you to offer your life to bear witness to the authenticity of the apparitions of the Blessed Virgin at Medjugorje?"** the Eternal Father responded with authority. With this confirmation, the two priests set about to write the book, *Mary Queen of Peace Stay with Us*. It was an account of testimonies in favor of Medjugorje, especially Georgette Faniel's words and mystical experiences in regards to the apparitions there.

The Girard brothers wrote their account with the interest that its contents were to remain confidential; only to be seen by two priests in Medjugorje. But the priests there, after having it translated into Croatian and reviewed by a few persons, wrote back to the Girard brothers that it seemed Georgette Faniel should not remain hidden anymore and the book needed to be published. When put in question by Georgette to the Father on whether or not the book, which contained so much about herself be published, the Father replied., **"Why should I have kept you in warm soil for years, if not so that you may produce much hurt?"** Faniel (now 71 years old) protested, "If the seed does not die in the soil it cannot bear fruit." To which the Father replied, **"I agree, but I want you to die to our own will".** He added **"I have already told you; Like My Son, you are to have a public life."** The Eternal Father also told Georgette Faniel why this was necessary:

> **Through the total gift of your life, you are the treasure of the Church where the lowly, the poor, the sick, of the Church, all of mankind will go to acquire riches in face of our espousals. You are the beloved daughter of the Virgin Mary, Queen of Peace, and you are the gem of the Holy Trinity. By accepting Our Will, you live with your beloved spouse the total gift of yourself as priest and victim, to glorify Me and to sustain the Holy Father, the consecrated souls and humanity. Accept with love that this testimony be published to make known the authenticity of the apparitions. Renounce your own will to accept only Our Holy and adorable Will on you. This act of surrender is the sublime act of your life as spouse of Christ, as mother of your spiritual children, as handmaid of the Blessed Trinity and as confidante of the Virgin Mary, Queen of Peace.**
>
> **We thank you and keep this peace of heart, soul and mind. The most beautiful gift you can offer Us is to surrender your will. You are living at this moment the beautiful prayer of the complete gift of yourself. Commend your will into my hands as my Son did on the cross through love. You must die as a victim of our love for the Church and for mankind which I have entrusted**

to you. Remain faithful to us to the end, then it will be the beginning of a new life with us for eternity.

A Bright Light on the Face of the Father

Indeed, the purpose of the Girard brothers' book can now be seen to have transcended its original intent–it shines a bright light on the face of the Father through the life of Georgette Faniel. Faniel's testimony in the book profoundly reveals our wonderful and omnipotent heavenly Father by offering the reader a glimpse of His intimate presence within all souls, and how, through chosen souls like Faniel, He desires that all souls come to love, honor, and serve Him in a special way.

The book especially reveals how the Eternal Father has come to embrace His servant Georgette Faniel in a special way through a series of mystical phenomena. On Georgette's body a mark in the shape of the number two was revealed in her flesh (lower abdomen). This mark, the Father told her, was to signify her "alliance" with God in the flesh. Received on July 15th, 1982, the Feast of the Precious Blood, Georgette heard Jesus then say to her **"Now we are two in one same flesh."** Medical doctors have marveled at this mystical phenomenon. Doctor Alain Farley examined it and describes what he saw and thought: "As a doctor, I have never seen a sign like this. It is unbelievable. This sign looks like a luminous neon whereby we can see the blood circulating, blood that is perfectly synthesized with the beating of the heart, and yet it is not like with any adjacent organ or blood vessels. I see it very well even if the number two is very small."

Another doctor took a photo of the mark with a hospital camera. The camera was equipped with a magnifying lens. The doctor had to take this photo while kneeling, therefore he obtained a perfect photo. Why did he have to kneel? According to Father Guy Girard, it was God who made it so that to see the miracle "one must kneel as a sign of a respect to the meaning of the sign." The number "2" on Georgette's body is made up of seven red dots depicting, the priest say, the seven gifts of the Holy Spirit. Several months after its appearance, Jesus said to Georgette, **"You must call this: 'the Alliance.'"**

A second mystical phenomenon that Georgette experiences is known as the transfixion or transverberation. This is an experience that causes her to feel a sensation "like a burning arrow of fire piercing her heart." The pain is extremely intense and increases when this arrow or "dart" is drawn out. Saint Teresa of Avila and St. John of the Cross have given a description of the transfixion. Said St. John of the Cross concerning this mystical gift, "Lord, wound me with a wound of love which may be healed only by being wounded again." When asked to describe the transfixion Georgette says, "I feel my soul must never cease giving thanks while Jesus is wounding my heart. I thank him for this suffering and I offer it to Him. At that moment, there is very great interior joy in my soul. The greatest joy of the world cannot compare with what I feel within myself."

According to Father Guy Girard, the Eternal Father asks Georgette to offer these sufferings for the needs of the Church and for the world. But very often, the Eternal Father asked her to offer these wounds for specific persons, such as the Holy Father, for the consecrated souls, for priests, for bishops, for those who need prayers and for visionaries in order that they will be protected from their enemies, visible and invisible.

Some of Georgette's suffering have been especially extraordinary, such as the time she offered to suffer for a young girl who was pregnant and wished to get an abortion. After meeting with Georgette and Georgette offering to accept her sufferings, the young woman experienced a flawless and painless pregnancy and delivery. Meanwhile, Georgette's abdomen gradually swelled over the nine months and she endured the pain of the delivery. A similar story is revealed by her spiritual director who complained of a swollen and painful knee that made it difficult to climb the steps of Georgette's apartment. Georgette apparently interceded on his behalf, unbeknownst to him after he disclosed his affliction. Upon his return the next day, his knee was fine. But when he met with Georgette, one of her knees was swollen and apparently painful, although she said nothing of the matter.

Devotion to the Father

But most of all it is Georgette Faniel's relationship with the Eternal Father that emerged from the Girard brother's book. As a child, Faniel says she heard the voice of Mary and Jesus, but it was not until much later in her life that she heard the voice of the Eternal Father. It was Mary, she says, that led her to the Father and taught her how to accept the Father's will on all occasions.

Through Mary, Georgette learned of the Father's love and mercy and came to understand his boundless tenderness and infinite patience, attributes that He wants all His children to know He possesses for them in His heart. "It is while contemplating the wounds of Jesus," says Faniel, "that I grasped the infinite love of the Father for each one of us, especially for the most abject, among whom I belong."

Georgette Faniel came to the devotion of the Eternal Father by listening to Him attentively: "I could see His great mercy in my life and so I began to know him better and to serve and love Him better. This is the purpose of our life on earth. One revelation concerning the Eternal Father through Georgette Faniel has especially been noted and has brought a response from around the world. In her spiritual notes, the Eternal Father, said to her in 1954, **"There is no chapel or church dedicated to me in the whole world."** This revelation has led to chapels being constructed or rededicated in the Father's name throughout the world. Likewise, some now seek to discern the building of a great shrine or shrines in honor of God Our Father, so that He may be better known and loved as our Creator, Our Father, Who is filled with love for all His children.

Georgette especially prays for the "arrival" of God's Kingdom:

> I pray that the Kingdom of God come. That it arrive. ...
> I pray that God the Father be known and loved as our
> Creator, our Father who is filled with love for all His
> children.

The following interview with Georgette Faniel gives us an intimate look at the mystical life of this chosen soul and how God Our Father is speaking to her, is really speaking to all mankind.

Q. *What were the first graces you received in your life?*

A. At about the age of six I began to hear the voice of Jesus in my heart. I thought that this constant dialogue with Jesus was normal for all children...

Q. *You must have been happy to hear that voice!*

A. Yes, but I have often wished not to hear that voice of Jesus anymore, for to remain faithful to Our Lord's requests is very demanding. Moreover, Satan would tell me that this was all fake (sheer invention)!

Q. *Did you speak of this to anyone?*

A. No, because I was afraid of being ridiculed and my soul as a child was often in anguish. At that time, Satan used to tell me that I was damned... He would tell me: "You have made a bad confession... You have committed a sacrilege." I was torn and I often wept at the thought of having lost my Blessed Jesus and my friendship with the Virgin Mary. Nevertheless, I always took refuge in Her. It was only later that my soul as a child was enlightened.

Q. *You have, therefore, spoken much to Jesus!*

A. Not only with Jesus, but also with the Father and the Holy Spirit and with the Most Blessed Virgin Mary as well.

Q. *You mean to say that you also hear the voice of the Eternal Father, the voice of the Holy Spirit...the voice of Mary.*

A. Yes, that is so...

Q. *But how can you tell them apart?*

A. The voice of the Divine Persons is sensed in the innermost depths of my heart, and also in my ear...

Q. *How do they address you?*

A. They communicate with me in different words and expression... The tone of the voice is also different.

Q. *How does the Eternal father speak to you?*

A. He speaks with more authority, but also with great love and great mercy. His voice is more solemn. I feel that a certain reverent but loving awe invades my heart, as the Father speaks to His child.

Q. *And the Holy Spirit?*

A. He especially helps me in the decision I have to make. I feel deep within me that it is the Holy Spirit who directs my prayer. He helps me in everything, even in material tasks.

Q. *Do you understand very well that the persons of the Trinity are distinct?*

A. Yes, I see it within me with a kind of evidence but I do not have the words to explain it. I also see that they make but one God.

Q. *You have told me that the Virgin Mary spoke to you. What role does She play in your life?*

A. She is my Mother! I am Her daughter. She is part of my intimacy with God.

Q. *What does She talk about to you?*

A. She speaks to me of the mercy of the Father towards mankind. She speaks to me of Her Son Jesus, of all He has suffered for me. She tells me to be very attentive to the graces of the Holy Spirit and to His inspirations. She is my confidante. She directs me to the Cross of Her Son as she shows me how to conform myself totally to the Will of the Father.

Q. *Does She do anything else for you?*

A. Yes, Mary is the one who guides me in my spiritual life. She is the one who gives me formative training.

Q. *What do you mean by formative training?*

A. She teaches me how to understand what God accomplishes in me. She teaches me humility; it is always with an infinite tact and a motherly gentleness that She admonishes me when I do not amend my failings.

Q. *Georgette, but do you believe that other people can hear this inner voice?*

A. Yes, I am convinced of that. I am not a person specifically set aside. We must be attentive to the inspirations of grace which we receive in prayer, and in silence be constantly asking the Blessed Virgin to lead us to the Father with Jesus. We must not seek the marvelous. It is in the simplicity of the heart, the soul and the spirit that God manifests himself. We must humbly ask the Virgin Mary to teach us how to love and serve the Father. The soul which asks with Faith and sincerity is always answered. Never does the Father reject a prayer! He chooses his hour! We must be ready to wait....

Q. *Georgette, do you have the wounds of Jesus's hands and feet?*

A. Yes, I have them. The Father gave them to me as a pure gift and I feel very unworthy of having them.

Q. *Precisely, where is the pain of the hands of Jesus located?*

A. The nails to support the body of Jesus on the cross were driven through the wrists. This is where the pains are the most acute and the most intense.

Q. *And the feet?*

A. No, it is a little different for the feet. When I am lying down, I always have my feet one on top of the other.

Q. *Where are the wounds in the feet?*

A. They are on the side, the left foot supports the right foot. When the Lord asks for much suffering, He is the One who places my feet.

Q. *And the crown of thorns?*

A. I received it on April 25, 1953. Jesus told me on the day: **"Today I am setting my crown of thorns on your head."**

Q. *Did you have difficulty in accepting it?*

A. No, I am not worthy of it, but I accepted that the Will of God be done.

Q. *Is it always more or less painful?*

A. It is much more painful on Fridays for two reasons: because it is the day of the Lord's death, and the other reason depends on what Jesus demands.

Q. *Did the medical doctors try to find where the pains come from?*

A. Yes, but the doctors found nothing! When the Lord chooses a victim for Himself, neither the doctors nor science can find the source and the intensity of the pains to nurse them. Jesus told me: **"It is only after your death that doctors will be able to know the pains that you have borne."**

Q. *What about the wound of the pierced heart of Jesus?*

A. The wound of the Heart of Jesus is a persistent pain which never stops, but the wound on the shoulder is the most painful.

Q. *People never speak of that wound on the shoulder.*

A. I know but, precisely, this sixth wound that Jesus has, is very painful. Jesus is the one who showed me that the wound of the shoulder was the most painful of all during the carrying of the cross. It was after considerable research that my spiritual director, Father Joseph Gamache, S.J., discovered that the existence of the sixth wound located on the shoulder had been revealed to Saint Bernard. **"While carrying the cross I had a wound threefingers deep and three bones were laid bare on my shoulder"**.

Q. *Did you ask on which shoulder was this wound?*

A. Yes, I asked Jesus and he told me: **"I was carrying the cross on my left shoulder (on the side of my heart) in order to keep my right hand free to bless my people a last time.**

Q. *Would you add anything else to these answers?*

A. Yes, I would say that the interior sufferings of Jesus were greater than His physical sufferings. *My soul is sad unto death,* He sighed. He was experiencing the agony of the soul, the heart and the spirit. The Heart of Jesus was wounded by the ingratitude of men. Jesus died of having loved too much! His Heart was opened by love even before the soldier pierced it to check if He was dead. This was but a symbolic gesture.

Q. *Are there any moments when these wounds are more painful and cause greater suffering?*

A. On Fridays, and when God the Father asks for more suffering for the needs of the Church.

Q. *Do you offer these wounds of the heart for any other intentions?*

A. Yes, I offer them so that the message of Mary, Queen of Peace, may be spread in all its authenticity throughout the whole world. Mary's message brings peace to souls and does not trouble them. The Most Blessed Virgin Mary never troubles souls. She always wants to lead them to the Heart of Jesus and to the Heart of the Father.

Q. *Georgette, we know from the Gospel that Jesus spent long hours in prayer in the intimacy of the Eternal Father. In my conversations with you, I became aware that there was a very strong emphasis placed on the Eternal Father in the spiritual life. Could you speak more to us about this hidden treasure? But, first, since when do you have this devotion?*

A. This devotion to the Eternal Father is central to my life. But it was not so in my childhood. This devotion came later.

Q. *Can you explain how this devotion developed?*

A. When I was preparing to make my first communion, I began to hear the voice of Jesus. I thought it was like this for all children.

Q. *And the voice of the Father, you could hear it?*

A. No, this came much later.

Q. *You were telling me, a few moments ago, that your devotion to the Eternal Father developed much later. Can you tell me what was Mary's role in this devotion?*

A. The Virgin Mary was leading me to the Eternal Father.

Q. *In what way?*

A. She made me accept the Father's Will on many occasions, among others, accept my illness, give up music lessons because of my ill health, and also trips with my parents for the same reason. She was preparing my soul for total detachment and liberating it for prayer and quiet recollection.

Q. *What else?*

A. She made me understand the Father's love and mercy, for I did not know Him well. It is thanks to Mary that I understood His boundless tenderness and His infinite patience. I have always asked the Blessed Virgin to lead me to the Father as She had done with Jesus.

Q. *Mary led you to the Heart of the Eternal Father. How did He reveal Himself to you?*

A. He revealed himself through His Son, Jesus crucified. It is while contemplating the wounds of Jesus that I grasped the infinite love of the Father for each one of us, especially for the most abject, among whom I belong.

Q. *Did you hear His voice?*

A. Yes, but not as distinctly as I do now.

Q. *So now, how do you hear it?*

A. I hear the voice of the Father like a voice which reprimands me with mercy, tenderness, being all the while firm as a father's would be.

Q. *What did He tell you?*

A. As soon as He presented himself, He spoke to me of His Son. He spoke to me as a Father does to his child. Then I would address Him: "Eternal Father" or "Most Holy Father".

Q. *How did you come to the devotion to the Eternal Father?*

A. By listening to Him attentively. I could see His great mercy in my life. And so, I began to know Him better and to serve and love Him better. This is the purpose of our existence on earth.

Q. *Tell us about the mercy and love of the Eternal Father?*

A. The Eternal Father, first, is a father. He comes to us filled with love and mercy, especially for those who suffer and those who need His mercy.

Q. *Have you anything else to add concerning your devotion to the Eternal Father?*

A. Yes. In fact, His love for us exceeds the love He has for His Son, because we need purification while His son gave His life to purify us. In the inmost part of His Heart as a Father, He loves us more in spite of our weaknesses and our sins. The more wretched we are, the nearer He is to us. The first step we take towards the Father, in spite of our sins, induces Him to shower us with His blessings. The least movement of repentance opens His heart to his boundless mercy, for He is always ready to receive us and to forgive us.

Q. *Concretely how should we approach the forgiveness of the Father?*

A. By going to Jesus, the divine Priest who gave those who represent Him the power to remit sins and, thereby, to confirm us in the Forgiveness of the Father.

Q. *What does the Eternal Father talk to you about the most?*

A. He speaks to me of the indifference of man to His creation which is destroyed and polluted in all its aspects. Man keeps trying to discover traces of his own works throughout the universe, unable to accept God as the Creator of all that exists. He also speaks of the indifference of man towards the Church and its teachings, as well as all those who abandon the Catholic Church in search of some other understanding which will never satisfy. Paganism has filtered into the Church, into its seminaries and convents and it is one of the causes for this indifference. God also speaks of the indifference of children towards their parents and their parents toward their children. As Jesus told us, God the Father will vomit from His mouth those who are tepid and indifferent.

Q. *What is the content of your prayer concerning Mary's apparitions?*

A. I speak to the Eternal Father about Mary, Queen of Peace. I am convinced the this pleases Him, for everything that concerns the Mother of Jesus consoles Him.

Q. *What led you to dedicate your place for prayer to the Eternal Father?*

A. It was because of the confidences of the Eternal Father that I wanted to offer Him this sanctuary. I knew that He would be consoled by the presence of Jesus and Mary. But it is a sanctuary on earth which is not made public.

Q. *Is there a public place dedicated to the Eternal Father?*

A. **No, the Father sadly told me one day: "There is nowhere on earth the least   chapel dedicated to My Name."**

Q. *What was your reaction?*

A. I was sorry and I prayed that someday there might be a public sanctuary dedicated to His Name.

Q. *And then?*

A. You know the answer to this better than I do. In May 1986, a chapel was dedicated to the glory of the Eternal Father. It is located in a hospital in Montreal. It was inaugurated on June 9, 1986.[1]

Q. *And so your wish and the Will of the Father have come true?*

A. Yes, thanks to the Lord.

Q. *One day, you said that you had asked the Eternal Father to send you an angel in addition to your Guardian Angel to help you in a difficult task. What did He answer?*

A. **"You have but to ask for help from the celestial court."** Surprised at this reply, I answered Him out loud: "Me?" *And* the Eternal Father replied: **"Yes, because if I ask them to help you, they will obey Me!"**

Q. *Did you speak of this to your spiritual director?*

A. Yes, and he told me: "My dear child, obey and especially do not hesitate to ask for help from the celestial court."

Q. *Do you believe we each have a guardian angel? Even the nonbelievers?*

A. Yes, I believe it, because we are all children of God. And God entrusts us all, believers and nonbelievers, to our guardian angel so that he may protect us and keep us in the love of God.

Q. *What makes you say that?*

A. Faith in what the Church teaches us, but also the experience of feeling that this guardian angel is close to me. This is difficult to describe, but it is certain that he is there. This is somewhat like a blind person being led by his guiding-dog; he does not see it, but he knows it is there. This presence is as evident as that.

Q. *Did you ever have a vision of your guardian angel?*

A. No, but I feel his presence; he is always with us, whereas we must ask for the "Celestial Court" with faith.

Q. *Have you seen heaven?*

A. Not as such. Once during a prayer vigil, I was lifted up to heaven by a vision where I saw Jesus and Mary, along with many different people who were offering gifts to the Eternal Father. I was very sad because my hands were empty. Then I saw our Heavenly Mother come near me and ask me why I was crying. I told her that my hands were empty and that I couldn't return to earth to fill them with gifts for the Eternal Father. Mary told me: **"I have a secret for you. Go and offer your heart filled with love to the Eternal Father and all will be well."** I did so after thanking her and awoke from the vision.

Q. *Describe the people in heaven.*

A. There were many people around as well as angels who were escorting Our Lady.

Q. *You've alluded to angels. What can you tell us about angels?*

A. I have a great devotion to angels, especially to my guardian angel whom I have sent on many occasions. He is dressed in white and his beauty is indescribable.

Q. *Have you ever seen purgatory?*

A. No.

Q. *Have you every seen hell?*

A. No. And I wouldn't like to.

Q. *Can you tell me what the celestial court has done for you?*

A. It helps me at the spiritual level. It accompanies me in my prayer especially at the time of the Eucharist during the offering. At the moment of the consecration, it prostrates itself and adores the thrice holy God.

Q. *Do you have more than your Guardian Angel near you?*

A. Yes, there are angels who watch over the Alliance; there are protecting angels who shield us from Satan.

Q. *Are there particular angels for the priests?*

A. Yes, they have their guardian angel, as creatures of God. But they also have a very special angel for their priesthood, for at their consecration they are identified with Christ.

Q. *Can you give me an example that could be verified when the celestial court helped you?*

A. When the Eternal Father asked me to kneel and to prostrate myself, I had the help of the celestial court. As you know, I have been an invalid for thirty-two years. This was an unwise move from the human point of view, but made it in faith to obey the Eternal Father.

Q. *What else can you tell us about the celestial court?*

A. The celestial court helps me greatly when I am experiencing a lot of difficulty. The Eternal Father taught me how to implore the help of the celestial court. At that time, I was working a lot with immigrants, preparing care packages and I couldn't tie the cords around the packages as my hands caused me to suffer so. I asked the Eternal Father to send my guardian-angel to help me. God the Father told me to ask for the celestial court to help me. I was so surprised! I said: "Me?" He said: **"Yes. If you obey Me, the angels obey me."** I have asked them to help me on many occasions, especially when I am in need of consolation. Everyday, I pray the celestial court to go throughout the world, protecting the children of God from the evil one who is seeking to destroy God's creation.

Q. *What can you tell us about this intercession?*

A. You have to have faith in the one you are involving. In my case, it's our Eternal Father. I don't pray for myself as such, but I pray for all souls that not one soul be lost because I didn't pray for it, to pray that no sin be committed because no one interceded for that soul. I offer prayers on intercession for those who do not offer their sufferings, either because they do not believe or because they are not in a condition to offer them. I pray prayers of intercession for those who hunger, for those who are without work, for priests and nuns who are confused or tormented and who hesitate in their mission. These souls chosen by God to shepherd His flock, need an emotional balance in their religious life. I pray for missionaries and for government leaders. I pray for teenagers, for married couples that are breaking up. Prayers of intercession are constantly present in my life. I beg God to forgive all those who neglect Him. I plead that He receive in heaven, all those children given to Mary at the foot of the Cross. That is my deepest prayer of intercession.

Q. *Mary's intercession?*

A. Mary prays to our Heavenly Father constantly, interceding for us, imploring God to grant us all the graces we need in order to remain faithful to His Will. Mary has accepted time and time again to visit us here on earth, teaching us and calling us back to her Son Jesus.

Our Lady's intercessions are precious to the Father. We need to heed her messages and to do our best to live these messages every moment of our life. How many times has she intervened in our life to protect us from harm without our being aware of it, even before the intervention of our guardian-angel? I am convinced that Mary holds the innocent victims of abortion close to her heart, just as she held the Child-Jesus. They are martyrs in every sense of the word. Our Lady's sorrow over these children is immense, especially when we consider her maternal instinct. She knows how much all her children need her love, protection and guidance.

Q. *Do you make a link between the Eucharist and the Celestial Court?*

A. Yes, during the Holy Eucharist, the Eternal Father sometimes allows me to see the whole multitude of angels and saints in a state of adoration around the altar! This is an invitation to the respect and to the dignity which must be given to the celebrant and to the participants. An attitude of respect is absolutely necessary before the Real Presence. We too often forget this and we hurt the Lord by these acts of disrespect.

Q. *Has the Eternal Father spoken to you about the world? How bad the world has become. Tell us about sin. What does it do to God?*

A. First of all, sin is an offense against God. Our Eternal Father gives us all the graces we need in order to avoid sin, to overcome our weaknesses, our tendencies. He gave us the sacrament of confession to cleanse us and heal us when we fall. He invites us to the Eucharist, that He might fortify us against those same weaknesses. Even now, Our Lord's Heart is wounded by our indifference, our ingratitude and our sins. Our values and our priorities are all mixed up. Not so long ago, our priorities were: God, the Church, our family, our work, our friends, comforts and finally entertainment. We don't have that vision any longer. Pleasure, money, entertainment seem to come first and God comes last. We must be aware of all that God does for us every day. Human beings today are convinced that they are due everything, that they are enlightened to everything, no matter that one's neighbor might be starving before our eyes.

Q. *What does sin do to us?*

A. Sin destroys us by separating us from God. It separates us from charity, the love and the mercy which God Almighty would like to bestow upon us. If after spending a lifetime nurturing, raising and loving your children, one of these children were to say to you: "You've never loved me. You've never done anything for me," wouldn't you be devastated?

Q. *What can you tell us concerning the Triumph of the Immaculate Heart of Mary?*

A. I pray for it with all my heart, because in that Triumph we will witness the Triumph of Jesus and of God the Father. I ask all souls to pray for that day of Triumph.

Q. *What can you tell us about Mary as Coredemptrix, Mediatrix and Advocate?*

A. I ask God the Father that everything be done in accordance to His Holy Will. It is God the Father who will decide by placing in the hearts of men His Great Plan of Love and His wish for all to recognize Mary as Co-Redemptrix, Mediatrix of all Graces and Advocate.

Q. *Has God talked to you about prayer?*

A. Jesus Himself taught us to pray the "*Our Father.*" If we pray the "*Our Father*" with faith and apply in our life everything that prayer teaches us and which unites all the souls in the universe until the ends of time, we would change the world. Prayer of the heart is very easy to do. It is the intimacy between our soul and God. We need to speak to our Heavenly Father as would a child who is suffering and who seeks solace and comfort from a parent. There are no secrets with God. He knows and sees all. We should hold nothing back from Him, secure in the knowledge that he will always hear our prayer. Sometimes a person tells me that God doesn't listen to his or her prayers. I tell that person, "you are wrong. You judge God severely. God answers all our prayers, but in His time, which is not our time." If our Eternal Father did not answer our prayers, He would act contrary to what Jesus taught us: "Ask and it shall be given. Knock and the door will be opened." God cannot refuse to ignore His Son's teachings. That is why God sent Jesus to earth, to teach us how to love and how to pray. Prayer doesn't have to be complicated. Invoke the Holy Spirit and ask Him to help you formulate your prayer to the Father.

Q. *How often and how much do you pray?*

A. I have no given hours. I often pray late into the night or awake in the middle of the night to pray. I am usually up by six and pray for an hour before I receive communion. Prayer is a really an elevation of our heart and soul to God in a communion of love and spirit. As such, I offer every heartbeat to the Eternal Father in love and thanksgiving. I offer up to God all the sorrows and sufferings that are not offered, either by unconsciousness by ignorance or by non-belief.

Q. *What do you pray for now?*

A. I pray that the Kingdom of God come. That it arrive. It is difficult for me to say "Thy Kingdom come." I prefer "Thy Kingdom arrive." To come seems so far off. If I say: "our friends are coming," even if it brings joy, it seems remote. But when I say: "They are arriving" I am more joyful. I pray that God change our hearts, that He purify our hearts by the Precious Blood of Jesus. I pray that the Precious Blood of Jesus be as powerful as it ever was, I pray that God the Father be known and loved as our Creator, our Father who is filled with love for all His children. I pray that we speak to others about Him that the whole world might have the same privilege of knowing God that we have. Believers or nonbelievers, we were all created by the Father's Hands and we will all stand before Him one day. Most of us tend to forget that basic truth.

CHAPTER ELEVEN

CHRISTINA GALLAGHER

Her name is Christina Gallagher and since 1985, she has received such incredible mystical experiences that her name has spread throughout the world as one of the most renown mystics of the latter-half of the 20th century. In fact, few such chosen souls in the annals of Catholic history present such a record of extraordinary experiences, causing people from all over the world to travel to Ireland in hopes of meeting with her.

Brigid Christina Ferguson Gallagher was born on June 4, 1953, in Calladashan, Knockmore, County Mayo, Ireland a small village of about ten families, two miles from her present home in Gortnadreda. Named after Saint Brigid of Ireland she has always gone by her middle name, Christina.

At about five feet tall, she looks and definitely sounds Irish. Her brogue is strong and clear, a textbook accent. Though fairly light-skinned, she has dark eyes and dark brown hair that is short and stylish. When she smiles her eyes seem to glimmer a momentary sigh of relief, perhaps from the pain she endures through the redemptive suffering she fully embraces.

Christina was married at age eighteen. Her husband Patrick, whom she refers to as "Paddy," is several years older than her and a plumber by trade. They have two children and for the better part of their marriage they have lived a quiet, routine life, that can best be described as "ordinary."

But what happened to her in 1985, was far from ordinary.

While visiting a grotto in County Sligo, Ireland, in the fall of that year, she unexpectedly witnessed with her eyes the Head of Jesus crowned with thorns. Unknown to her, it was this apparition that would actually begin the series of miraculous events in her life, events she could not have imagined.   From bilocations experiences to the stigmata, Christina Gallagher's mystical experiences mounted, but it was her visions and the accompanying revelations that drew the most attention.

Besides encounters with the Virgin Mary and apparitions of Christ, the simple Irish homemaker was soon being shown extraordinary, mystical, and heavenly sights. From awesome glimpses of the Face of the Eternal Father in Heaven to terrorizing experiences with the Prince of Darkness in her own home, her breathtaking accounts are numbing. Within a short time, a considerable number of messages for the Church and the world were conveyed to Christina. She was to be, God indicated, a "fearless witness" to a misguided and "sinful generation."

But her mystical experiences don't end there. God's plan through Christina continues to unfold. Although the Virgin Mary's apparitions to Christina began in 1988, apparitions, mystical experiences and heavenly messages continue with no end indicated. It is a generous outpouring of revelations. Revelations that deal with the urgent call for conversion of heart and the purifying events to come.

In 1995, Christina opened a "house of prayer" on Achill Sound, County Mayo. Tens of thousands have journeyed there and the miracles have continued, including healings and Eucharistic miracles.

The Eternal Father

But for our purposes, it is her experiences with the Eternal Father that need to be examined in detail. For these experiences add to the emerging picture of the face of the Father.

The following information and interview with Christina Gallagher is excerpted from the author's book, *The Sorrow, the Sacrifice, and the Triumph, The Visions, Apparitions and Prophecies of Christina Gallagher.* (Simon and Shuster NY, NY, 1995) It appeared in the chapter entitled "I, Your Father, Yahweh," and focuses specifically on her experiences with God the Father:

> Once when coming out of ecstasy, Saint Catherine espoused, "I have seen the secret things of God." These things the saint later admitted were not communicable by human words, for there were no words she could find.

Likewise, Christina Gallagher has also seen the secret things of God, yet more remarkably, even God Himself—God the Father. On more than one occasion, she received inner experiences of Him. These are mystical beyond words, beyond imagination. Like her other experiences, she struggles to describe these spiritual encounters. Yet they are a critical part of her revelations.

Over the years, Christina's relationship with God the Father deepened. On October 5, 1992, He spoke to her of His Son: **"Little one, to you I will reveal the opening of the heavens and the closing of the Gate. To all who desire to come to Me—come through the Mercy of Jesus My Son and by means of His Mother. Those whose desire is to disown My Son and His Mother, they will not find life. Only through Jesus My Son in His mercy will any soul find life. Those who desire to find life through Jesus, must drink of Him. There are many false gods. Man has returned to adoring all that is of the world. Man is raising up the antichrist through adoring false gods. Pray to her who is Wisdom. Only in her is Truth."**

According to Christina's spiritual director, Father McGinnity, this message was of significance, for it may contain profound meaning for our times. It was a message deserving more than just a glance. After praying and studying it closely, the theologian ventured his opinion:

*When the phrase **"the heavens opened"** occurs in Scripture, (at the Baptism of Jesus), we are told **"The Spirit came down"** and Jesus undergoes Baptism for the sake of saving the world. Now later, Jesus said, **"I have a Baptism to be baptized with and how eager I am till it is completed."** He meant His death, which would purify the world. The **"opening of the heavens"** which Christina is to see, would seem to be the cleansing of the world or purification. This is God's Spirit*

*descending in an act much, like our Baptism, like Christ's death.
It means dying to rise, letting go in order to gain, suffering to be
renewed.*

*The **"Closing of the Gate,"** when we return to Scripture, can
have a clear and definite meaning in the context of the messages.
Jesus in Saint John's Gospel remarks, **"I am the gate of the
sheepfold."** He makes this remark in the lovely discourse about
His tenderness and mercy as Good Shepherd. Now when the
Father says to Christina that to her will be revealed **"The
Closing of the Gate,"** He may mean that she will see the end
of this time of Mercy, when, as Jesus said in the Gospels, we have
to enter through Him to find life. In other words, the time will
come when, if we refuse His Mercy, we must face His Justice.*

*The phrase could mean the end of the time of Mercy, in which we
now find ourselves.*

*If people refuse this Mercy, then the cleansing of the world will
follow. The Father will determine those who will be allowed in
or kept out of the Gate; saved or lost at this important phase in the
history of Salvation.*

Fr. McGinnity further comments on the October 5, 1992
message:

*To understand this message, it is necessary to apply the rules of
Scriptural interpretation. In the interpretation of Scripture, one
goes to other parts where a similar message or similar words are
given. Now earlier on the same day (October 5) Jesus used similar
words and ideas. These throw light on the Heavenly Father's
message, e.g., when the Father says **"...must <u>drink of Him</u>,"**
He is speaking in a vein similar to Jesus earlier that day when He
declared, **"I am Peace, few come to <u>drink of Me</u>."** Now, that
message was directed towards behavior within the Church,
carelessness, desecration and **"the blind leading the blind"**
which is bad example and leadership. It seems then, that **"Who
is who?"** is a gentle way of saying "Be careful; people who lead*

may not be as trustworthy as you think they are." In other words
"Who is who?" *raises doubt about the genuineness of those we*
automatically and unquestioningly follow.

In the earlier message about the ***"blind leading the blind"***
resulting in the ***"trampling of the blood of the Lamb"*** *(the*
abuse of the Holy Sacrifice of the Mass), the question is asked
rhetorically by Jesus, ***"How can My little ones give glory to***
their Lord God?" *In other words, when the Sacrifice is*
dishonored through irreverence of malpractice, or more basically,
when it is not preached for what it is, then people who depend on
their spiritual leaders for the enlightenment of truth are deprived,
go ignorant and do not respond with reverence, adoration and
reparation. If they are not led to sorrow for sin, they will not
cleanse themselves in Confession. So the Sacrifice will be
profaned, for they are all given Holy Communion.

But the message implies that this is not primarily their fault.
They are led by the blind. So accordingly, as the true source of
Life, the merciful Jesus, is profaned and abandoned, the Church
moves to false means of fulfillment, and is thus raising up the
"false gods" *which God the Father then mentions. The*
Church is led in a worldly way. A great amount of time is then
spent on trivial, distracting programs and pursuits… all in the
name of religion, while less and less time is given to the ***Sacrifice***
of Jesus. *The Father then directs attention to Our Lady whom*
He describes as ***"Wisdom."*** *In other words, Our Holy Mother*
directs those who "pray to her" (as He desires) to the true source
of Grace.

But the Eternal Father had even more to say to Christina.
And a few weeks later, in late October, 1992, He again
addressed her. This time it was with an important message
for her own life, for her own cross.

To her surprise, He reminded her of a conversation she
clearly remembers having with Him as a child. At that
time, when she was five, the Eternal Father invited her to

come into His Kingdom. Not surprisingly, she declined.
But it was a choice, she felt at the time, the Eternal Father
accepted and blessed. Especially since she never heard
from Him again, and was still in her bed the next morning.
Now, over thirty years later, He talked to Christina about
that conversation's significance:

**My beloved daughter, I your Father reveal to you
what is hidden from the learned. To the little, will
My Kingdom belong. Jesus My Divine Son has
blessed you and called you in the womb of your
mother. To you I have spoken at the early age of
five years—your time. It was you who made your
choice. You chose the cross, for I your Father
Yahweh longed to draw you from the cross, as I
longed to draw My Divine Son. But Jesus My
beloved, My Son, He too chose the cross for My
people. You do not take the cross by yourself. For
you could not—only through My Divine Son.
Your share of it is little, yet it is great. Do you
now understand what you asked Me or when I
said, "So be it"?**

"Yes, my Father, I understand, but only a little," responded
Christina.

**"Oh, My little one, few have been chosen. All
have been called."**

"But my Father," she replied, *"I love You, though I am weak
and nothing. How could You have chosen me?"*

**"Out of the love of the Heart of My Divine Son.
Those of your generation, of your seed have
surrendered to the cross. To them, Jesus gave
glory, and rewarded them by calling forth one of
their generation of seed to be blessed and chosen.
That you are chosen is the fruit of their cross. For**

I am your God, and so be it."

Since that night, Christina has disclosed other personal conversations with the Eternal Father—conversations she holds dearly in her heart. Conversations that are not yet revealed. But they promise to be interesting. For God the Father, she says, has promised to **"reveal to her more of that which He has kept hidden from the learned and wise."**

From Christina's own words, we capture a little more of this unfathomable relationship, especially what our path to perfection should be like, since Jesus said that we should strive to be perfect as our Father in heaven is perfect.

Q. *Christina, you had a mystical experience of the Eternal Father and the Blessed Trinity according to a published account. Can you describe that experience?*

A. I was praying the Stations of the Cross, with the meditations out of a prayer book.

While doing the Stations of the Cross, I became totally aware of seeing, with my eyes, a beam of light going up. Then, I could see angels, and they were all like little babies. They were whiter than the light they were in. They ascended this beam of light, but they didn't fly up with their wings, although they had little wings. They seemed to move up the beam of light at will. At the top there was the most enormous area of white light. I've never seen anything like it.

Then I saw a man sitting in a big, wooden chair. This chair was very broad and powerful-looking. It was a chair of authority. This man Who sat in it had white hair. Although He looked "old," there wasn't a line or a blemish in His face. He was very beautiful. His face was identical to Jesus'; only Jesus had brown hair and He had white hair. But, Their faces were identical. When I saw them together, Jesus was on one side and the Blessed Mother was below Jesus on a step. I could see long steps, although they were nearly covered with light. And I remember saying, that is my Eternal Father, that is Jesus His Son and that's Our Blessed Mother. But I thought, where is the Holy Spirit? I then became aware, that very moment, that all of the light I could see was the Holy Spirit. Now during all of this there were clouds, white clouds of light. There were different clouds with angels on each of them. They floated over where the Eternal Father was sitting and Jesus and His Blessed Mother were standing. I could hear millions of little voices mingled together. They were singing, but their singing sounded like music. It was beautiful. It sounded as if the children were singing from a distance. I could hear a lot of children singing and their voices were coming across, as if on a breeze. It was like a beautiful sound from a distance. But it was more soft, like music. I didn't know what they were singing, but it was so beautiful, all mingled together. It sounded so soft, like the wind itself, yet a beautiful sound came from it.

Q. *On May 5, 1992, you were told the Holy Trinity dwells in you. Jesus said that you've found favor with God. Can you tell us about the meaning of this?*

A. I was trying to find out what it meant because I had realized that Jesus would live in me, but I didn't realize that the Holy Trinity could live in anyone. Then, Jesus said that He is One with His Father; that when a soul is chosen by God, they are one. He said, **'When your heart is open to receive God** (if I receive Him and He lives in me). When I asked to understand this, He said, **"When I sing in praise of Him, I sing in praise of the Father."** He said **"It's all through the Holy Spirit, through His actions."** This is the way of the Holy Spirit. However, that's not just for me. It is for many people who receive Jesus with an open heart. Jesus said, **"Everyone is called, but few are chosen."**

Q. *What did the Eternal Father say to you about being amongst the Chosen?*

A. When I asked about being chosen, He referred to the seed of my generation, that Jesus had glorified. It was through their cross that

Jesus gave them what they desired; which was a person of their generation to be chosen.

Q. *Does this mean you? Are you this chosen person?*

A. Yes, it just happened to be me.

Q. *In October of 1992, the Eternal Father said to you that He spoke to you at the age of five. Do you remember this?*

A. At that time, my mother was worried, because of the many illnesses I had. I had pneumonia and double pneumonia. And on this particular occasion, I was so weak that my heart was not beating. I was not breathing. My mother was investigating and she put her ear down on my heart. Then, my mother brought my father into the room. My mother believed the scream of crying from my father shocked my heart and it started beating again. It was at the same time that this experience with God happened. I remember I had an experience with God. I heard a voice and I knew it to be God, saying He was coming to take me to Heaven. I said, I didn't want to go to Heaven yet, that I wanted to remain on earth. I wanted to live and I wanted to grow up and be like Mommy and Daddy. I wanted to get married and have one or two children. As it turned out, I did get married. I have two beautiful children but because of complications, I can't have any more children. But now, going back over everything in my life, this conversation I had as a child with God and of hearing His voice is a realization more strongly, now.

Q. *Why do you think the Eternal Father spoke to you? What were the circumstances?*

A. As a child, I was often very sick. My parents didn't know for a number of nights whether I was going to live or die. I didn't realize that I was so ill. I wondered, "If God was going to take me to Heaven or not?" I would pull the blanket over me and say, "If You're going to take me, it'd be just like going on a holiday." I knew it was a holiday that would never end and that I wouldn't come back. Then this voice came again. The same words again were said to me about going to Heaven and I ended up saying the same thing to God. I told Him I wanted to live. At the end of this conversation with God, the second time around, I heard the words, **"SO BE IT."** And then, I knew that meant: "I can live! Now, everything will be all right"... I took it as meaning that I could live.

Q. *Christina, on October 5, 1992, you received a message from Jesus. He spoke to you about being a victim soul with Him. Then, the Eternal Father spoke to you. Can you tell us about Our Heavenly Father speaking to you?*

A. It's strange during these experiences because you instantly know the difference in the voice; although the voice may be the same. The Eternal Father to me has a stronger, more powerful something in His voice. He has a more firm tone, but yet, there is something very beautiful and gentle about His voice. It's more overpowering. I know when He's speaking to me, I know instantly it's our Eternal Father. He has spoken to me on a number of occasions—a number of occasions recently. He has given me other messages. He would say things like, **"My daughter, I am your Father."** One night, He repeated this a number of times. Then, He invited me to arise. I just said, "Precious Blood of Jesus cover me. In the name of God, if this is not of You, be gone in Jesus' Name." But this voice kept repeating, **"My daughter, I am your Father. Arise and pray."**

Q. *Did Jesus or the Virgin Mary tell you anything else about the Holy Spirit?*

A. I was told by our Holy Mother, **"The Word of God is alive, it is Spirit; the Light of God is Wisdom; the Light and Word of God is life, for those who receive it."**

Q. *Have you seen the Eternal Father when He speaks to you?*

A. Yes, I've seen Him on a number of occasions, like when I saw Him the time that I saw Heaven. And I saw Him on other occasions.

It's hard to describe Him. He can take many forms in His own right. I've become aware and I can inwardly see, on some occasions, where He's like immense light. I am conscious of the enormity of Him and the tininess of me. I see myself like a grain of sand in relation to Him. And yet, all the Eternal Father's greatness and enormity are impossible to describe. It's like being in an open space with the sky surrounding me. Yet, His pureness is beyond expression. Now these experiences, when they happen, are given me in a manner I cannot fully comprehend.

Q. *Have you seen how the people are dressed in Heaven?*

A. The only ones I saw in Heaven were the Eternal Father, Jesus and our Blessed Mother. They were all in white and a radiant light was everywhere.

Q. *So, you haven't seen any people in Heaven?*

A. No, no people in Heaven.

Q. *Tell us about the Eternal Father's love.*

A. It is an enormous love, yet there is—even though He's so great— no limit to the depth of His love where it will reach down to a tiny grain of sand, like myself, to raise me up to be united with Him in Jesus.
(Note: In 1994, Christina said, "My understanding of souls in Heaven (those who die in the state of grace), is that they are released into the Light and Spirit of God, from the degree to which God has drawn them in their openness of heart and response to His will in that Light and Spirit of God. The degree of their reward depends on their response to God while on earth. Some souls are drawn into the inner or higher degrees of the Light and Spirit of God depending on the reward God has given them for their sacrifices. The Light in the Spirit of God is like a million suns. The soul that is drawn into the inner or higher degrees must be as clear as a crystal that the light will reflect through the soul and they will radiate and bring greater joy to the Glory of God. Souls in Heaven

are aware of other souls in Heaven and on earth through the knowledge of God. In that knowledge they can only love as God loves.)

Q. *You have been told the meaning of the twenty-fifth day of each month is special for the Eternal Father. Can you tell us why?*

A. Our Blessed Mother told me: The two means the two hearts of Jesus and Mary. The united hearts of Jesus and Mary. The five represents the five major Wounds of Jesus, and the two and five added together represents the Seven Sorrows of our Blessed Mother. So, on the twenty-fifth of any month, it means that the sacrifices of Jesus and the Blessed Mother are offered in union with the prayers of Our Blessed Mother's children or the children of God to our Eternal Father in union with their hearts and their sacrifices.

Q. *So this means the twenty-fifth of any month of the year is a special day to be offered up to the Eternal Father?*

A. Yes. That's what I understand from what our Lady has given me on the meaning of the twenty-fifth. That's why it's so powerful because it's an offering of the major Wounds of Jesus and an offering of their two hearts suffering together. With the sacrifice of that, they're offering the Seven Sorrows of our Blessed Mother.

Q. *We know that Jesus was born on the twenty-fifth of December. Is this why?*

A. Yes, but again, it all represents the sorrow, the sacrifice and the triumph.

Q. *Your spiritual director reports that you were given knowledge from the Eternal Father concerning the Seven Degrees of the Spirit and how a soul moves toward holiness (perfection). Can you explain some of this?*

A. In January, 1994, I was given an awareness of the means whereby a soul advances in holiness. It concerned ascending the **SEVEN**

STEPS OF PERFECTION, which I had been shown sometime back, but did not really then understand. I was given that God desires the Seven Degrees of His Spirit to permeate the person who is being perfected in the seven faculties of <u>heart</u>, <u>soul</u>, <u>mind</u>, <u>body</u>, <u>will</u>, <u>intellect</u> and <u>memory</u>.

THE SEVEN STEPS TO PERFECTION

Christina has been given the gift of knowledge from Almighty God to understand how there are seven steps, stages, or degrees on the path to perfection, or the path of purification:

I saw seven steps, and the more we respond, surrendering to the Cross for the love of Christ, the more we are drawn into the degrees of His Spirit with God raising the soul to a higher degree.

The heart of the Holy Trinity is the Godhead and from the heart of the Godhead comes the beacon of light which is the Holy Spirit. Through this beacon God desires to radiate His Spirit and to draw the soul to a higher level of union with Himself.

From the unity and love of the heart of the Godhead, the desire of God is to draw each soul in a deeper way into Himself.

Every soul is redeemed by Jesus and in that way is part of the Mystical Body of Jesus.

By the person decreasing in self and allowing God to increase in his or her soul, God desires to draw each one to a level of mystical union or marriage with Christ. Many however, do not achieve this union because they will not decrease in self to allow God to increase within them.

WHAT OUR LADY ASKS

When our Blessed Mother asks through her message for prayer, sacrifice and fast, these teach us to decrease in self in childlike humility before God by depriving the flesh and so opening the heart to permit the Spirit to freely flow in the seven areas of our being, that is, heart (which is the main channel or entrance leading to the), will, mind, intellect, memory, body and lastly, the soul.

These first six areas depending on their response can lead the soul into light or darkness. Everything is first of all desired in the heart and the heart then requires the will, the mind, the intellect, the memory and the body to respond in an open channel to permit the seven degrees of the Spirit to purify and strengthen the six areas of our being, whose response will leave the soul in either light or darkness.

THE HEART, because it is the main channel leading to the other faculties, and is itself the source of desire which leaves the other channels open or closed in willing, choosing or action, needs to be purified of its weakness, because the heart can be open or closed to God.

THE WILL can become so unyielding to God's will that it stubbornly resists the prompting of God and becomes shaped in a pattern of self-interest and self-concern and can become too weak to decide for God.

THE MIND can be molded more and more by the thinking of the world, the expectations of people and the standards of earthly judgment.

THE INTELLECT can lose its realization of God's Wisdom being supreme, a greater treasure than all human expertise and greatness. It can even rationalize what suits itself and begin even to justify as right what is objectively wrong. A loss of humility before God leads us to trust in ourselves and less in Him: more in our personal potential and less in Him Who is indeed the source and giver of every talent we possess. God may need then to prevent pride from building up and taking us over for then we would lose the greatest gift, God Himself. But as he removes our securities we are made to feel vulnerable and helpless of ourselves.

THE MEMORY can be clouded from consciousness of the merciful deeds of God in our past and need a purifying and a strengthening from the clutter of personal concerns that accumulate and block our loving dependence on the God Who loves us with an everlasting love. To make us realize this, He will have to bring us down to a realization that we are nothing and that we draw all from Him Who is the giver of life itself.

OUR BODY through its weaknesses as a result of original sin and because of constant temptations from the other deadly spirits—apart from pride—who can gain many influences over the bodily appetites and temperament of a person through their attacks of greed, lust, anger, gluttony, envy and sloth, will need strengthening for the mastery over self which is imparted by the Spirit's gift of self-control. This spiritual reinforcement of our higher faculties over our lower appetites will shatter our composure the more dependent on the flesh we have permitted ourselves to become.

THE SOUL through failure of the other faculties to respond to God can experience only light or darkness. Although this work of purifying is not the release of the Holy Spirit as in the Sacrament of Confirmation, it will inevitably result in a freedom of movement for the Spirit already received through the Sacrament for He is hindered and hampered by our imperfections and impurities and the residue of past sins already forgiven.

PURIFICATION CAN BE PAINFUL

The seven degrees of the Spirit of God can be a work at any given moment, or there can be three or four, or any number of degrees of the Spirit at work at any time.

For instance, if the heart is open and the mind is weak and Jesus wants to purify the mind, sometimes the darkness experienced feels like abandonment. The mind is not able to understand, and thinks God has abandoned it until God can, in His degree, penetrate sufficiently to purify that particular area of the mind, and then one can receive the Light and gain the understanding of the Spirit of God.

If somebody is living with bad thoughts, and God is purifying and strengthening the mind, it has the ability then to overcome the bad thoughts, but when God withdraws that degree of the Spirit from the mind, the mind is in shock, as it were. It feels like a depression, a feeling of distress, while the purifying is taking place.

As the Spirit of God progresses and works through each area, it is a painful procedure, and the key to everything is surrender; surrender everything for the love of God.

Until God purifies a particular area, it is like being in a darkness, depending on how open or how blocked the particular area is, and depending which degree of the Spirit of God is at work. The higher degree of the Spirit, the more powerful it will be and the greater will be the shock caused.

God might bring a person to a particular level and that level can be purified and doing well, but that person can, of their own free will, fall to the temptation of Satan in sin and darkness. The memory, for instance, can forget the mercy of God, and the truth. Then God may have to repeat, in His mercy and goodness, His purification of that person's memory again and re-awaken it's faculty.

If the will is weak, God will have to work on the will. It is the temptation of the flesh in our free will to decide against the desire God has given in the heart. And if God is working on the will in any degree of His Spirit, the will can get shaky, feel fragile, and even seem about to collapse.

SURRENDER IS THE KEY

The key is surrender. Everything has to be surrendered. As we get to know ourselves we get to realize our own nothingness, that without God we are nothing and the will more than any other faculty is instructed and taught by this. We realize that we depend on God for absolutely everything, for His gifts of Light, Wisdom and Mercy and the degrees of the Holy Spirit in every area of our lives.

The Holy Spirit wants to strengthen all the areas of our being, and since all these areas work together, if there is something blocking any one area, the other areas suffer. The quicker we surrender everything to God, for love of Him, the better; and understand ourselves and our nothingness in the sight of God; and come with hearts totally open and bent on receiving everything from God in humility.

WHEN THINGS GO WRONG

It is easy to surrender when everything is going right. But when things go wrong for us, when a person may wonder where God is in all this, we find excuses and have negative thoughts and feel as if we've had enough, then we can fall back to where we were previously. But if we can surrender out of love of God, and not even be interested in questioning, then it is as if the heart is allowed to open up to a greater extent, and the Spirit can flow freely, through this channel, into the soul.

PRIESTS

Whereas consolations of soul follow the process of purification for those God is drawing to perfection through the seven steps, with priests it is generally different. The meaning of the priesthood is to be a victim in union with Jesus: priests share in a special way in the victimhood of Christ, the Great High Priest Who is sacrificed for the sins of the world. The priests who are enduring the purification process will therefore experience emptiness during and following it because the benefits will be applied by God to the souls whom they pasture in their shepherding of God's flock. Jesus pastures His sheep by means of the priest's ministry. So priests will be benefitting the flock in their charge in a deeply spiritual way as they themselves are led closer to perfection by means of the seven steps.

It would be nothing strange for a priest to go through his entire priestly life feeling no spiritual consolation, a prey to many temptations, emotional loneliness, inner emptiness and as if abandoned by God. In addition, they suffer the lack of knowledge to understand the spiritual fruitfulness God draws from their victimhood—a wealth of spiritual riches to lavish on His little lambs.

But God also expects the people (His little lambs) to respond to the greatness of spiritual wealth in the sacraments which He provides for them through the victimhood of His priests, by their response in prayer and sacrifice to keep holy the anointed ones of God.

As in the Scriptures, Jesus questioned Peter three times: **"Do you love Me?"** And each time Peter replied, "I do," Jesus desired that he feed the sheep. He was to fulfill this in the suffering and death Jesus immediately prophesied for him. So Jesus' intention in saying **"Feed My sheep"** is **"suffer for My sheep."** The cross is the pasture!

THE GRACE OF GOD
AND HOW WE RECEIVE IT

The highest degree of grace is received through receiving the Holy Eucharist at the Sacrifice of the Mass for the person who is in the state of grace. This requirement of being in the state of grace shows the importance of the Sacrament of Penance.

Through the Sacrament of Penance comes the second highest degree of grace we can receive.

The third highest degree of grace comes through prayer and our good deeds for fellow-members of the Mystical Body. This grace comes as an outpouring from the enormous beacon of Light, the Spirit of God, in unity with every soul, through its higher degrees.

HOLINESS

Holiness is not, therefore, to be equated merely with health of mind or well-being of body. To be holy means to be wholly in union with the Spirit of God. In this union we draw upon the living source of the everlasting Spring of the Spirit of God.

WHAT HAPPENS AT DEATH

When released from the body each soul is destined for immortal life and its future in eternity is determined by its state when death takes place, and the soul is released from the body. When the body dies and the soul is released, it suddenly finds itself in the full light of awareness, able to see itself as it stands in the sight of God. It then realizes the darkness to which the body's actions condemned it. The sensitivity of the soul to the enormity of Light of God is like the naked eye before the brilliance of a thousand suns and the soul in darkness quivers in pain. It plunges itself into the sea of Hell to avoid the pain of the enormity of the Light.

PURGATORY

The soul destined for Purgatory seeks shade at the level in Purgatory appropriate to its own imperfection. It will automatically plunge itself into Purgatory to be cleansed and purified, aware of all the sins for which it failed to atone sufficiently; it will gladly go to whatever level of Purgatory is necessary, and it will be eternally grateful to God, in the knowledge that it will one day gain His Presence in Heaven.

THE REALITY OF HELL

During life, if a soul gets deeper and deeper into sin and darkness and blindness, God will call and call that soul, time after time, urging it to respond to the Light.

But if a person does not want to hear and does not want to see and refuses to respond, the body will make of that soul a living hell, in all the faculties of that person, and it responds only to the temptation of the Devil.

If the person dies in that state, his soul, on being released from its mortality, realizes that it cannot come before the greatness and Light of God in that state, because it just could not bear it. The pain would be too great, because if that soul had been prepared for Hell by the life lived by the body on earth, and it came before the greatness of God—everything is total love and goodness—in the enormity of that Light and Goodness, the soul would suffer enormous agony.

So it is not so much God condemning it or casting it into Hell, as the soul itself, unable to bear the pain of the enormity of the Light of God casting itself into Hell. (The reality of Hell shows us the importance of

Confession, and of true repentance for our sins.)

HEAVEN

The soul when it dies and is purified for Heaven according to the degree of its response to the Spirit and grace of God, will be drawn to an outer level of that Light of God in Heaven. It will be totally fulfilled according to the completion of its own capacity for God. To the extent of the decrease of self on earth, thereby permitting the increase of the Spirit of God, this capacity is increased in the souls who receive a high degree of God's calling in life. They will be drawn into the deeper areas of the Godhead. Such a soul could be described as a shining crystal allowing the Light of God to radiate or reflect through it, bringing greater glory to God.

SAINTS

Hence, to pray through our Lady does not distract from the glory of God but actually enhance God's glory for she is what she is in the Blessed Trinity, being the only person at freedom in the Spirit of God to go to the Godhead of the Holy Trinity.

To pray through the saints glorifies God for they are all united in the Spirit of God at whatever level to which they have been drawn. Because they have been drawn into Heaven through the action of their response to His Spirit during their earthly life, God would joyfully permit His Spirit to respond to the earthly soul seeking help through them.

THE CALL TO LIFE
IN THE HOLY TRINITY

In the Holy Trinity, we have the Father and Jesus, and uniting Jesus and the Father, the Holy Spirit, tremendous

Light and Wisdom, with all His Gifts, and together with the awe and greatness, love and union between the Father and the Son, God's infinite Mercy and Justice. The Father created the World, the Son redeemed it, and the Holy Spirit purifies and draws it to Himself. God desires to draw to Himself those who have been redeemed, and are loved, but through sin they experience darkness and are unable to respond to the Light and the Truth.

God created us to love and adore Him, but being in the world and responding to the darkness of sin, we start to love and serve self. That is the temptation of the world and the flesh that will lead us into a darkness that will blind us from perceiving the Light of God. Although the world is the creation of God, it is the Devil's kingdom which tempts the flesh. Because it is redeemed, the soul can choose through free will the desires of the flesh and the world or the eternal home God has prepared by following Jesus. Jesus is the Way, the Truth and the Life.

GOD DESIRES TO SAVE ALL

God wants all souls to be saved, and Jesus died for all of mankind, but God has given each created person free will, and our Lady has emphasized over and over again, that all a person has to do is stop sinning and to turn back. She is pleading all over the world with her children to come back to her Son, before it is too late, while they still have time. And this is why our Blessed Mother even weeps tears of blood, because so many souls are being lost.

FREE WILL

I saw from the Tree of Light many white roots going in every direction, and there were larger black roots on the Tree of Darkness and all these roots were intertwined with the narrower roots of the Tree of Light.

Then it was as if there were little ants running along on the roots, representing people, and each of those on the white roots of the Tree of Light had a little white dot of light on them. And they would be going grand until they met a place where the roots intertwined, and then they would halt at the crossroads and not know which way to go. And they might then drift off on the other black root of the Tree of Darkness, and then their light would go out. Then they might come again to another meeting place of the two sets of roots, and some would go back on to the white roots of the Tree of Light and their light would be seen again.

As they came nearer to the trunks of the two trees, those who reached the Tree of Light just disappeared into the Light while those on the black roots coming nearer to the Tree of Darkness seemed to go at great speed, as if rushing into Hell. That is how it was given to me, and I was shown no in-between.

As I understood it, this was a representation of how free will and the grace of God works, how we receive it, and then reject it, and how God is always forgiving us, through Confession throughout our lifetime, but He has given us free will and He does not force us to accept it.

THE ROLE OF A VICTIM SOUL IN THE MYSTICAL BODY OF CHRIST TO CIRCULATE GOD'S GRACE OF CONVERSION

The more a person surrenders to God, the more the Lord will invite that person to surrender, and the more the person will be enabled by God to receive and respond to His Spirit, Love, and Grace, surrendering in total abandonment and trust.

What this means is that God wills the sins of others to be purified through the victim or suffering soul who surrenders and offers his or her sacrifice to God to be purified in its uniting with the sacrifice of Jesus, thus permitting God to draw many other souls to Himself. Look at the crucifix, and see the outstretched arms of Jesus. He went on the cross to redeem us. He was born in a stable, to show us He wanted nothing of the world. He had no roof over His Head, showing us the unimportance of everything of the world. Yet He was the Son of God, teaching us as He said, what He had been taught by His Father through the Spirit. So everything that Jesus knew was through the Spirit and He was teaching us the way, the way home—how to gain Eternal Life. He was teaching us that to be nothing in the eyes of the world, is the way home through Him.

That is why, if we see self as important, or see our progress in the world's eyes, see anything of the flesh, as important, then we have gained nothing. It is only if we gain it through God's Love and Spirit that we gain anything and that we permit God to develop in us, to grow in us. Our souls, then, will be more and more transformed into the likeness and Image of Christ. The more we permit our souls to be transformed, the more will the radiance of God's Spirit and Light reach out and touch others, by the decrease of self and the increase of the Spirit of God.

This is how the accepted sufferings and sacrifices of one person who trusts and surrenders, are used by God to help others in the Mystical Body, who are in darkness and sorely in need of His grace. This is how, through the purifying action of God's Spirit in a victim soul, others too can be drawn back to God. This work of purification, then, in individuals is not intended to benefit themselves only. God in His love is drawing good out of it for the conversion of lost souls.

THE PARALYZED HAND
AND THE WORKING HAND

If a person has a paralyzed hand and cannot use it, then that person must compensate by using the other hand much more.

The paralyzed hand represents the person who cannot be bothered with God, and is without God's enlightenment and the other hand is the other person in the Mystical Body who is prepared to suffer and to cooperate with the Spirit of God in order to convert the other. What Jesus wants to do is to flow His grace of conversion from the working hand to the paralyzed hand and so renew His life in that soul.

When we hear about a "conversion," the grace for the renewal of life in that soul comes from the suffering of someone else. With the Mystical Body, God will use the victim soul, to help those who are in the darkness of sin. He will take the victim soul to Himself, and give it His gifts and graces in a greater way, and will nourish it, and give the victim soul the strength and ability to surrender in all things to Him, to be crushed like a grape.

The victim soul is the working hand, and the soul in darkness which does not want to know about the Light, is the paralyzed hand... It hasn't got the ability, because of darkness and sin, to draw on the Light and ask for the forgiveness of God. When someone is far away from God, in deep sin, that person does not recognize the truth, or the reality of the true presence of God, so Jesus will use the victim soul, and crush it, and the grace and the Light of His Spirit can then flow freely to the person in darkness, giving the soul his life anew—renewing God's life in that person.

So when we hear about a person being converted, that "conversion" has come about through the surrender of a victim soul. God does not interfere with the person's free will, but He will use the victim soul's efforts united with His Divine Life and Mercy to help the soul in need.

MESSAGE

The dialogue in a personal message dated September 24, 1988, sheds more light on this teaching:

Our Lady: **"My dear child, if only you were to know what good my dear Son has permitted, with your acceptance of pain. I cry tears of joy."**

Christina: "My dear Mother, my pain is but nothing. I long so much for God to save souls, including my own."

Our Lady: **"If you accept all God permits you in suffering, many will be saved."** (Our Blessed Lady then promised Christina that she would later understand the mystery of God ("what was hidden from the learned and given to the little ones"): **"I know you do not understand what is becoming of your body. When you accept the cross my Son Jesus permits you to carry, you are purified in soul and body and save many others. My child, your cross will be heavy, and your pain greater at times. Be at peace. Accept, with all the love in your heart.... My tears of joy and sorrow will fall on you to comfort and console you. You are surrendering your body and soul to God. I ask you to try to pray more. Keep your heart with Jesus my Son, asking Him to save souls. My Son will grant you what you ask in prayer....Tell my Son it is because you love Him that you accept it with love...."**

CHAPTER TWELVE

MATTHEW KELLY

Matthew Kelly is now 25, tall and handsome. He is personable and energetic. He possesses humility and charisma. He has charm and intelligence. Most importantly, he possesses wisdom—not just human wisdom, but supernatural wisdom. It is a gift, the young man says, that the Eternal Father gave him.

At his age, with his looks and intelligence, Matthew Kelly could now be making the world his oyster—if not, he says, for what occurred on that special night of April 7, 1993.

That evening, Matthew was preparing for bed. He had been up since 5 a.m. and was exhausted. But it had been worth it because his life at that time seemed perfect.

"Everything was going brilliantly in my life," he recalled, "work-wise, study-wise, family-wise, friendship-wise. Everything was going brilliantly."

Born in Sydney, Matthew Kelly grew up in a large family of eight brothers, of which he was the fourth. His mother, Jenny, managed the home while his father, Bernard, supplied catering equipment to restaurants and bakeries. By 1993, Matthew was on a path to success. He was studying commerce and majoring in marketing at the University of Western Sydney. He enjoyed sports and music. He liked all the things people his age everywhere like. Thus, perhaps it is revealing that on that first night, the voice he heard intervened only after Matthew reluctantly removed the radio headset from his head.

It all began that night with a feeling, an intense feeling. Matthew says he had planned to listen to music before falling asleep, but moments after putting on his headphones, a strong sensation overcame him. It was an uncontrollable urge. After a few moments, he fell to his knees in prayer by his bed. It was something he wasn't prone to do.

Then, as he knelt in the darkness slightly before midnight, the feeling intensified. Suddenly, he says, there was a voice, a clear voice. Even though it wasn't audible, Matthew remembers that he could "hear" it.

"Keep doing what you are doing and believe in yourself and in me, " he says the voice commanded.

With that, the incident ended. The voice said no more, and the urgent feeling disappeared. The next morning, Matthew was not sure what had happened. However, something started to erase his anxiety. It was a "peace," he says. "A tremendous peace had filled me at that moment, and it remained with me," he said.

The supernatural events in Matthew Kelly's life began during Holy Week. Four days later, on Easter Sunday, April 11, 1993, something happened while he was at Mass. At the moment of the consecration of the bread and wine, he says the voice spoke to him again.

"Listen to me, hear my words, and do my will."
Now, Matthew knew. He says he knew the voice was real beyond a doubt. And he knew the events of the first night had been genuine. Two days later, the voice revealed its identity: **"I am your heavenly Father."**

After that, Matthew Kelly's life would never be the same. He began to receive locutions and messages from the Eternal Father, an extraordinary number of them, sometimes 10 a day.

He says the Eternal Father made it clear to him that he was to keep his mind open and trust God. The Father requested he visit a church three times a day; morning, afternoon, and evening. He was to write down everything he received because the messages God the Father would give him were not just for him—they were for the world.

During the dictation process, Matthew says he would hear the Eternal Father's voice only as long as he wrote. When he stopped writing, the voice would cease. When the Eternal Father began a message, His voice would repeat it three or four times, until Matthew realized he was to record it:

> The first night it was engraved in my mind. I was very tired. I wrote it down, and then the next ensuing days, as the messages got longer, He, (God the Father) started saying just the first three or four words and He would

repeat them over and over until I would start writing. And then He told me that I had to write them; if I didn't write them, He wouldn't continue the message. And He would repeat the three or four words, and as I would write, He would then dictate. If I'd stop, He'd stop. If I'd run out of ink, if I'd run out of paper, have to blow my nose, He'd stop and repeat the next three or four words over and over.

The Message of the Father

According to some Marian writers, the Eternal Father's messages to Matthew Kelly were profound in their simplicity and filled with a wisdom that revealed their divine authorship. The messages revealed God's ways during lessons that covered many subjects, ranging from the Virgin Mary to life itself. Matthew reported that Christ also began to speak to him. Overall, the revelations presented a mosaic of divine knowledge:

May is Mary's month. The Mother of God, the most beautiful creature I ever created. In Mary, you will find care and concern for even the smallest details. Mary is a mother; she knows what you need. You are her son; she loves you as she loved Jesus. When she wept for Jesus, she also wept for you. She is the 'Mother of the World' and is greatly disturbed that her household has strayed.

But in any household, there is one or two that keep the faith and in time bring the rest of the family back to My love. ... Bringing her family, the world, back to your Heavenly Father's love, little by little.

She has revealed to others the way in which this should be done: prayer, the Mass, the Rosary, and fasting. Her love is stronger than all the love and attention you have ever been shown put together.

All this love will come to you every moment of every day if you open yourself to her.

In this month of May, try especially in the area of devotion to Mary. ... Love, Love, Love is the answer.

Mary is your mother, and she loves you dearly; consecrate yourself to her each day, and the graces of love will flow through your work, prayer, and relationships. (May 14, 1993)

On Saturday, May 15, 1993, Matthew said that God told him he needed to trust in Him alone: **"You, My son, have a path to follow. You don't know where the path is going; that is one of the major parts of your faith journey. You must trust in Me, your Heavenly Father."**

The following day, a message from the Eternal Father revealed how important the family was to civilization and the future of the world:

Family. Family. Family. You must push and emphasize the importance of family. If the family unit and family morals had not been broken down by Western Society, the world would not be in the dark pit of sin which it is.

The return of family importance and family values and morality are the secret to bringing the world out of this pit, the secret to the world's finding the light, My Son, Jesus Christ. You must touch people by your deep concern for them, especially your family; you must show them that they are precious and very important in your life. Other people may or may not see your love for your family, but they will not be able to help feel it by the way you live your life, doing the little things well.

Work endlessly and untiringly at this task of family. You tell Me that you encounter opposition to your love for Me. ... and I tell you, wasn't it written that no prophet, no one that loves Me and keeps My Son's way, will be loved in his home town? Love them and their hearts will

melt, and they will find Me.

Your family is important; even if you feel you are getting nowhere, don't be discouraged, be patient. You must be careful never to tire in loving them because one tired moment could cost you a month's work; if you are tired say nothing, it is too dangerous.

Love all, but especially love your family selflessly, and you will bring My love to them without their even recognizing it. (May 16, 1993)

Matthew says that Jesus also imparted to him messages that were deeply profound and revealing, and confirmed that Mary was appearing in Australia:

Today, you must tell the world that time is short. Before long, I will be with you again. ... You, My brother, carry My cross and do My work, prepare My way. My mother has specially formed and selected Pope John Paul II for this time in the world. The evil one is not happy at this. The Pope is a great instrument of your Father in Heaven and in a single day, in a single address, can return many hundreds, even thousands of hearts, to a fuller love of Me. You must pray for the Pope.

In these times, persecution will occur. Throughout time since I left the earth, Christians have been persecuted, but it will become worse than ever. People will shed blood, people will lose their lives. Share My cross. No servant is greater than his master. I, your Lord, Jesus Christ, suffered. As My servant, how do you expect you will escape this suffering? But more than this, you must suffer lovingly. Do it for love and suffer acceptingly.

Many who are close to Me don't understand these times. There are many manifestations of the Holy Spirit taking place to

warn you, but due to the increasing level of
apostasy in the world, many of the faithful are not
interested in these many warnings and won't be
until the Church approves them.   Mary is
appearing to many and speaking to many more.
She is appearing right here in Australia. If you are
relying on people to believe you, I'm sorry; you
will be sadly disappointed. You must seek refuge
in the Immaculate Heart of Mary from the attack
and pain that will come from nonbelievers.

On your own, you are dust, but I have
taken you and done great things for you; I have
led you through a conversion. Your love for Me
has never been stronger or more complete, but be
wary that you don't become lazy or lukewarm. I
will vomit the lukewarm from My mouth. You
must continue to pray, especially the Rosary, go
to Mass daily, go to confession regularly (at least
once a month), fast, and work on bringing your
friends to a greater love of Me.

Above all, trust. Do My will and all will be
provided. You will have all you need and more.
You will have peace and love.

Most importantly, Matthew reveals that the Eternal Father
confirmed reports about the coming times, revealing that great warnings
and miracles were to come:

The mini-judgment is a reality. People no longer
realize that they offend Me. Out of My infinite
Mercy, I will provide a mini-judgment. It will be
painful, very painful, but short. You will see your
sins; you will see how much you offend Me every
day.

I know that you think this sounds like a
very good thing, but unfortunately even this
won't bring the whole world into My love. Some
people will turn even further away from Me; they

will be proud and stubborn. Satan is working hard against me.

Poor souls, all of you, robbed of the knowledge of My love. Be ready for this judgment of Mine. 'Judgment' is the best word you humans have to describe it, but it will be more like this: You will see your own personal darkness contrasted against the pure light of My love.

Those who repent will be given an unquenchable thirst for this light. Their love for Me then will be so strong that united with Mary's Immaculate Heart and the Sacred Heart of Jesus, the head of Satan shall be crushed, and he will be detained in hell forever. All those who love Me will join to help form the heel that crushes Satan.

Then, as you all die naturally, your thirst for this light will be quenched; you shall see Me, your God. You shall live in My love; you will be in Heaven.

Now, do you see how important these times are? Don't wait for this mini-judgment; you must start to look at yourselves more closely so that you can see your faults and repent. You are fortunate to have the faith needed to believe. Read and accept this message; you must not go away indifferent to it. You must examine yourself more every day and pray in reparation.

All of you, be like the blind man. Each day you should cry, 'Lord, open My eyes,' and My son will open your eyes so that you can see your wretchedness and repent.

Pray now more than ever, and remember the world's standards are a false indication of My justice. I am your God, and while I am perfectly merciful to those who repent, I am perfectly just to those who do not.

Many people think that I, your God, won't mind; it's only little, they say. But it's not a matter of minding. I want people to love Me. Love respects little things as well as the big things, and in the most cases, these little things are not so little.

Do not judge your actions or other's actions; you are unable to judge; you are incapable of judging because you cannot read a man's heart.

You must love Me with your whole heart, with your whole mind, with your whole soul, and with your whole strength.

Today is the day; do your best to renounce yourself and let Christ reign in your lives. You will never be ready for the mini-judgment, but some will be more prepared than others. You must aim to be one of those and bring as many others as you can to be prepared, or as prepared as possible.

Above all, do not fear; I don't tell you all of this to become scared. No, simply try to become better people each day; more than this I could not ask. I am your God; I am perfectly just and perfectly merciful. You are sons and daughters of Mine; does not a father look after his children? I send this message to spare you from any pain I can, but the pain that you experience by seeing the darkness of your soul is an act of love on My behalf. Do you not see that this will return many, many souls to a fuller love of Me? This will save many souls from the fires of hell.

This is the most important of all My messages: I am the Lord, your God; you are My sons and daughters whom I love very much, and My greatest delight is in being with you, and I want to be with you for eternity. Anything I do is done out of love for you, My children. Trust in Me, your Heavenly Father.

Although Matthew Kelly reveals the messages he receives, he

does not discuss visions, apparitions, or other gifts he may have been given. His personal mystical experiences are not part of his mission, he explains. He says the Eternal Father made this clear to him. "The purity of the messages is only *infected* when I get involved," Matthew said.

By early 1998, the events in this young man's life were attracting incredible attention. Over 100,000 copies of a book that contained the revelations to Matthew Kelly were distributed and Matthew Kelly was traveling around the world, bringing the Eternal Father's messages to all who invited him. He was on an urgent mission because like the others, he was aware of a divine schedule.

Indeed, the revelations to Matthew especially confirmed that all was to be fulfilled. Formally announced at Fatima more than 75 years ago, Mary's work throughout the world, was now, with all her chosen messengers of the 1980's and 1990's, approaching its climax.

Moreover, the Eternal Father explained to Matthew that soon His justice would come upon humanity:

> **You are called today to accept My words and live in My love; many have rejected My love, and many will. They will feel the whole force of heaven against them when fires come from heaven, when My justice comes to those who abuse their freedom, which has been entrusted to them by Me, your Heavenly Father, so that they may pursue eternal happiness for their souls and assist others in doing the same.** (June 21, 1993)

And like Mary reportedly has revealed so often, God the Father told him that this was the world's call to change:

> **This is the only preparation for the times that await at the doorstep of the world.**
>
> **My son, tell the world to pray and return to the Sacraments. I am the Lord your God; I come to you out of My infinite mercy in these words, but before long I will come to you out of My infinite justice, and the world will feel the wrath of My justice through natural disasters worse than**

those ever experienced. Now is the time to respond, My children.

Seek My Will in each moment and live not for pleasure in this life but in hope of Heaven.

Seek first the Kingdom of God and His justice and all else will be given in addition.

My children, spread these messages; deny no one the opportunity to heed My warning one more time.

I have spoken to this young boy, but I speak to you all; he is merely the instrument I have chosen to use.

These messages are to each and every one of My children throughout the world. These messages will show you how to live My Will in the midst of these times. (July, 1993)

A Call to Joy

Over the years, the heavenly messages have added up. They are a treasure of divine instructions. But equally noted is the understanding Matthew Kelly has brought to the communication of the messages. For in many ways, he demonstrates an uncanny grasp of the profound, yet simple meaning of what has been told to Him. He can explain the truth of what God has taught him. And his book, *Call to Joy*, which reveals his infused wisdom, is a measurable achievement on its own.

Kelly's message is simple. If we truly learn to live in the presence of God, and listen to prompting of the Holy Spirit, along with accepting the Church's valuable role in guiding us, we will experience a true call to joy in our lives. To simplify this message, is not to do it justice. But a summary here is necessary.

Matthew Kelly says that God the Father has taught him that life is a journey of the soul seeking to discover and live truth and that the joy comes from the struggle. The struggle, in simple terms, is for one to better one's self, to change and to grow with courage and patience and to secure salvation.

In our world today, we are all headed down different paths with uncertainty. But if we stop and look to find God, we will discover that our paths are part of His plan. This plan, says Kelly, can then be better fulfilled through prayer, which is what God wants from us. It is His call to each of us. To not pray causes paralysis in our journey and possibly misery. Each path, says Kelly, is different. And many of the paths do not seem fair but if we do the little things each day, we can make it the way God wants us to.

These little things include living for the moment, and using each moment to grow. By keeping our minds off the past and future, and recognizing no certain happiness or sadness need come from such thoughts, we then allow God to make us a better person according to His plan, and that this gives glory to God.

We need to smile more, say less, listen more and especially to pray and trust more. We especially need to trust God more. The voice of God, says Kelly never ceases in our life but it does use different channels to communicate. Silence, he insists, is especially important to discover how God is trying to speak to you. Silence he says is sacred. "Noise is the mouthpiece of the natural world. Silence is the mouthpiece of the supernatural realm." Kelly says that God the Father told him that, "You can learn more in a hour of silence than you can in a year of books." Says Kelly "For the soul to be nourished adequately, we must spend time each day in silence. In this silence, God leads, heals, renews, refreshes, directs, discloses, enlightens and teaches us. As Scripture notes, "Be still and know I am God." "God," says Kelly, "bestows His wisdom on men and women in the classroom of silence. May silence become a great friend of ours."

Kelly also confronts the difficulty of uncertainty in our lives. This is best handled her says, by giving up control, by resolving to let God control and consequently, this permits suffering and sacrifice to mean more. In turn, we also then form strong commitments to the ones we love.

Once more, Kelly emphasizes that God, our Father, is with us every step of the way. He speaks to us to encourage us. He is just like a human father. He loves us and has wonderful plans for us, the greatest plans we could ever imagine. But we must ask him to reveal His plans and this means we must persevere in listening for them.

Finally, Kelly says that God has taught him that we must confront our fears in order to trust Him more. We need to focus on God, and on good and noble desires. We must focus on the positive and we must reject sin. This calls us to humility and surrender and to being honest with ourselves. All of these character building strengths, he says, come from prayer and the Sacraments. Together, they heal and unite us and allow spiritual laws to assist us in achieving joy in our life.

"God is love", says Kelly. "When a man loves, he expresses himself with virtue. Virtue is truth, and truth begets love. The greatest act available to man is to be like God. When you love, you become like God."

Everyone can learn this, says Kelly. All they need is faith which will lead them to holiness. And nothing, he argues, is more attractive than holiness. To act in faith, is to act in Christ. Christ is the way, the example the Father has given us. Thus, little by little, we can grow in humility, in fortitude and love. The voice of the Father he says, calls us along the ways of truth and love: "Love is truth lived. Joy is the result of truth lived. Misery is the result of lies lived." Truth gives but joy and lies give but misery in this life and the next, says Kelly.

Kelly's wisdom in this matter is perhaps nothing new. But his strong advice on prayer and imitating Christ is extraordinary in its style and simplistic approach.

Finally, Kelly argues that we must read the Gospels to understand how simplicity leads to perfection and how consistent prayer can transform our lives. The end result: peace. Peace, he says, is the proof that God is present in one's plans.

The following interview with Matthew Kelly permits us to gain greater insight into his understanding of the Father from his experiences, and to absorb the wisdom God has shared with him and seeks to share with us all.

Q. *Tell me how your experiences began?*

A. I'm twenty-five, (25) years old. I was born in Sydney, Australia. I was brought up in a large family. I have seven 7 brothers. I'm the fourth in the lot of eight 8 boys. Up until part way through last year, I was studying at University of Western Sydney, studying commerce majoring in marketing. I guess, more than anything else, I considered myself a fairly normal young person. You know, lots of interest, in sports, in music, etc. On the 7th of April in 1993, I was getting ready to go to bed. I'd been up since about five o'clock in the morning and as I got into bed, I reached for my walkman (radio) on my side table to listen to some music before I went to sleep. As I did, I had a strong feeling not to put the walkman on. I ignored the feeling and put the walkman on. I turned the music on but the feeling continued to intensify till I found myself getting out of bed, taking the walkman off and kneeling down beside my bed and doing a sign of the cross as if to pray.

Q. *How was your prayer life before that moment?*

A. I would go to Mass on Sundays. My parents would always insist on that. And, about three months before that date, I had started dropping into church every day before I went to the university for about ten minutes.

Q. *Can you remember what compelled you to do that?*

A. Everything was going brilliantly in my life, socially, work-wise, study-wise, family-wise, friendship-wise. Everything was going brilliantly. But I hungered, I felt empty in some way, something was missing. I remember one day going for a long walk and looking at my life and thinking. "Well, the only thing that it could really be was that I needed God, because everything else was going to well. Everything else is going so well. And it can't go better, so it must be something else." So I started going there and I didn't really pray. But I would sit in the church for ten minutes a day and I'd just think about what I was going to do that day. And it just seemed to bring me a "new peace" sitting before the Tabernacle. I was aware that Jesus was in the Tabernacle. I think that was just a "grace" given to me because it wasn't something that I was taught in school. But I was aware and I believed that Jesus was in the Tabernacle. I would sit there before the tabernacle for ten minutes on the way to the university. That was, so to speak, my prayer life.

Q. *So, on that first night, what else happened?*

A. I got out of bed and I knelt down beside my bed and I did the Sign of the Cross. Now at that point of my life, it was very unusual for me to be kneeling or praying at any point of the day, never mind, just before midnight. But I knelt there somewhat confused, I guess in the darkness.

Q. *How would you describe those feelings you had physically?*

A. This urge, I wouldn't describe it as something physical. It's impossible to describe. Just like the messages are impossible to describe. Because it's supernatural event and I can only describe in it natural terms. The difference of what actually happens and what I describe only misleads people.

Q. *In what kind of natural terms can you describe what you were feeling?*

A. I don't think that I've ever experienced such an urge, in a physical way. It was just a "knowing" that you had to do something. It almost wasn't a free action, but it was a free action. And so, it's obviously become something very confusing once you start to try to describe it.

Q. *This was April, 1990?*

A. April 7th, 1993. So any how, in the silence, darkness and confusion, all in an instant, I heard a voice speak to me. And I heard later that the voice was to be called the "Voice of God the Father," and I've been receiving the messages almost daily since.

Q. *How did you know it was the Voice of God the Father?*

A. At that point, I didn't. It was at least six days later before I knew that is was God the Father.

Q. *Did you hear the voice in your heart or in your ears?*

A. It was as clear as you speaking to me now, as clear as what you speak to me now.

Q. *Okay.*

A. But I, once again, can't describe it in natural terms, because I'll only mislead you, because it's a supernatural event.

Q. *It's not auricular?*

A. If you were sitting next to me, you wouldn't hear it.

Q. *But you would hear it?*

A. But the closest way for me to describe it is exactly what I have said to you now. If I don't hear it with my ear, I wouldn't know how to say, "I hear it".

Q. *Some locutions are internal, some locutions can be auricular, though, so I'm just trying to see if I understand.*

A. Well, I would describe it as being something material. When people have asked me, I've described it as a voice that starts in my ear.

Q. *But six days later you knew it was the voice of the Eternal Father?*

A. Yes, Because He described Himself as God the Father.

Q. *What did He say?*

A. Well, the last sentence of the message that first day was: **"I AM YOUR HEAVENLY FATHER."**

Q. *Tell me what this voice sounded like?*

A. It's impossible to describe. The difference between what actually happened and what I describe is enormous. So I only mislead people if I try to describe it. More than anything, what I am being asked of is not to speak about what happens, not to speak about the event. The purity of the message is only infected when I get involved.

Q. *How many times a day did this continue after the first day?*

A. Many times a day. Sometimes up to 10–11 times a day for the first six days. On the sixth day, or around there, He addressed me as being God the Father. He then made it clear to me that He wanted me to visit a church three times a day once in the morning, once in the day and once in the evening and that He would address the messages to me three times a day. This went on for a month or so. And then, He told me only to come in the morning and the evening. He asked me to come for longer periods of time and that he would give me two messages a day. Some months after that, it came to only one message a day. And now it's not always every day.

Q. *Did He tell you to write these messages down?*

A. It was always a dictation.

Q. *How soon after this began did you know to write the messages down. Did He instruct you to write them or you just knew to write it?*

A. The first night it was engraved in my mind. I was very tired. I wrote it down then the next ensuing days, as messages got longer. He started saying just the first three or four words and he would repeat them over and over until I would start writing. Then He told me that I had to write them, if I didn't write them, He wouldn't continue the message. He would repeat the three or four words, and as I would write, He would then dictate. If I'd stop, He would stop. If I'd run out of ink, if I'd run out of paper, if I had to blow my nose, He'd stop and repeat the next three or four words over and over until I'd start writing again. So it's a dictation just like when you were in class and the teacher dictated to you. And also, you know, sometimes you can be writing what the teacher's saying, but thinking about something else. That's the same here. Very often the messages are that long. I'm writing what He's saying, but thinking about something completely different. This is because you're listening to Him, and you're sort of writing it, but you can think about something else because the thought process is not my own. And so that was one of the things that really, really confounded it for me. You know obviously the devil's in there and he wants to attack too. On that first day, I'd been up since five, as I said, and I had been that physically tired so I sort of woke up in the morning and thought, "Well, what did happen?" I knew that it was something I'd never, ever experienced before. But equally, I was that physically tired, you know. I thought anything could have happened.

Q. *Did you doubt it at that point?*

A. I didn't doubt it. But I didn't know it was God. So I didn't count it as God. All that I had to go on was that tremendous peace that had filled me at that moment. And that still remained in me, that peace when I woke up in the morning. That was a Wednesday night. I had the first message before Easter Sunday. On Thursday I woke up and nothing happened. On Friday nothing happened, on Saturday nothing happened. But on Easter Sunday morning I went to mass, and as the priest consecrated the bread and wine, I got my second message.

Q. *What did the voice say on the second message?*

A. It was a personal message, that's one of the messages that's left out of the book. It was here that I knew, without a doubt.

Q. *But, that wasn't the moment that you discovered it was God the Father?*

A. No, it wasn't. But, I knew it was without a doubt, coming from God.

Q. *And a couple of days later, you discovered it was God the Father?*

A. Yes.

Q. *Did you tell anybody in your family?*

A. No.

Q. *How long did you go before you told anyone in your family?*

A. Three months.

Q. *After three months then who did you finally decide to first tell?*

A. Well, I told someone after a week or so. Ten days later or so, I told a close friend of mine. And I come from a particularly religious family. But I didn't really know who to turn to. I hadn't had much Catholic influence in my life. But I knew a doctor. He was a very good man, and he struck me as being a holy man. I knew I could trust him. So I went to him and I showed him the message. I told him the whole story. He was surprised. But he said, "Look this is too much for me. I don't know what to say. I don't know what to do. But, I know this priest and I'll make an appointment for you to see him. You tell him everything you've told me and he'll work all this out." So he did and that priest is now my spiritual director.

Q. *What's his name?*

A. Fr. Anthony Bernal.

Q. *What was the priest's reaction when you first told him?*

A. He listened. I talked to him for about three hours. He said, "You know, everything that you said sounded like it was from God." And he said that he had no reason to doubt that it was from God.

Q. *When did you finally tell your family?*

A. During this time I was having a conversion. This was my time to change, my time to get my act together. I got this peace this joy, this happiness. And people are thinking, "What's happened to Kelly?" You know? What's going on here? Is he in love or something? So my family was wondering what was happening. But then God had other plans and started talking about sharing the messages. This is when, probably out of the whole time, I really hesitated. Because, I thought, what were people going to say?

What were people going to think? I was set in the conversion. But now it cost something. You know? So, he then asked me to print the book. He gave me criteria to select the messages to put in the book. I did that.

Q. *God the Father did or your priest did?*

A. No, No, God the Father did. I took them to my spiritual director. He went through the messages with me and then we went through the messages and we went picked them out. Then we made suggestions to each other and he said, "Well this is the reason." So we came up with the book and took the book to the publisher.

Q. *Let's get into the message then. What is the heart of the message? What's God asking through you?*

A. The heart of the message is a message of encouragement for the people of these times. My job as a chosen instrument, is to encourage people to resist the ever present pressures to dilute the Christian ideal that surround us at every level of society. The pressures are there. They're in every environment or just about every environment. The Christian ideal is our call to holiness–God calls each and every one of us to holiness. The problem is that people don't understand what holiness really is today. People think to be holy you have to run away from the world and find a cave to live in. People think to be holy you have to be on your knees in church for fifteen hours a day praying. People think to be holy, you have to walk around with a halo on.

You're not allowed to smile or have any fun or enjoy yourself at all. These are all the very unnatural and unattractive ideas that the world proclaims about holiness. When the reality is there is nothing more attractive than holiness. There is nothing more attractive than virtue. There is nothing more attractive than Christ. So when Christ truly comes to live in you and I, there will be nothing more attractive than that. And people will be attracted to us, just as people were attracted to Christ. Wherever Christ was, people wanted to be with him. When He was eating, when He was drinking, when He was walking, when He was talking, people wanted to be with Him. Why? Because He brought them peace and understanding, gentleness, compassion, forgiveness, and healing. And when we, through our words and actions, bring people those same things, we will bring to those people Christ. They will be attracted to us, not because we're anything special but because it's no longer us that lives but Christ that lives in us. And in that humility, people will continue to be attracted to us. And so, that is the holiness that God is calling us to. And that opportunity that God gives us to obtain His holiness is in every moment of the day. Every person that comes into our lives, every circumstance or event in our lives, is an opportunity to be holy.

Holiness is measured by how we respond to the people and events and circumstances of our lives. How lovingly we grasp the moments of the day, one by one, for God. So, in this way, every moment of our day can be transformed into prayer. And many of the moments of the day, many of the sacrifices of the day, should be transformed into prayer–thus, making every moment of our day prayer. You know, St. Paul said "pray constantly." We all can't pack up shop and go into the churches and pray twenty-four hours a day. So, what did he mean when he said, "Pray constantly?" He meant transform everything in the day into prayer. I speak to students a lot, particularly to students lately here in the United States, and I tell them to imagine the mountain of work that's before you in this one academic year. And to recognize that work had an enormous value in the eyes of God. The challenge that is presented to the students today, for the next year, is to transform that mountain of work into a mountain of prayer. And one of the things that I really say to them is: you're going to read hundreds of pages this year, you're going to write hundreds of pages of notes, take a pencil with you, and at the top of each page, place the initials of somebody you know who needs prayers, and offer the work on that page for that person as a prayer. It's simple; it's beautiful. They can transform each page of work. By that way, our attention is turned to God.

But more importantly than that, the individual grows closer to God because of the recognition of the person's presence. And beyond that, prayer demands excellence. Prayer encourages excellence. Prayer creates excellence, because you're no longer doing the work just for the marks. You're no longer doing the work for the exam. You're no longer doing the work just to impress the teacher or just so you don't get into trouble. You're no longer doing your work for money or for a boss. Rather, you're doing your work for God. And because you're doing it for God, you'll work that much harder. And because you'll work that much harder, you'll pay attention to detail, as attention to detail makes people stand out. Most people, during these times, don't pay attention to detail. So, the personal holiness, by transforming their things into prayer, have been transformed into excellence.

But more than that, people begin to notice that you're different. People begin to say "Well, what makes you different? Why do you do this? Why do you pay attention to your details? You're such a hard worker. You're a good worker." The response: Christ makes me different. And so, what was just work had been transformed into prayer and has now created excellence, has created an opportunity to do a personal apostolate. And to bring someone else in the workplace closer to Christ. Beyond this and the overall perspective of society, is that you and I in every different occupation, in every vocation, in every state of life, at every age become an injection into the bloodstream of society. And, because we're doing it for God, we're doing it well, we become the best in our field. We become the best we can in our field. And so, we rise slowly to the top of every honest human occupations and professions. And then we become politicians, and leaders, and teachers and university chancellors. We begin as Christians to have the highest positions within society, politically, culturally, socially and then we begin to form society in a Christian way.

Q. *Has the Eternal Father explained all this to you?*

A. Well, everything I've been taught has come through the messages or through silence. Now obviously, a lot of things haven't been told to me directly through messages, but one of the things He pointed out to me very early on was that He wanted to use me. He said that the way people would know He was working in me, was because he would give me a tremendous gift of wisdom, a gift well beyond the age of twenty-one, and he said, if He was to give me this wisdom, then, I had to make silence one of my greatest friends. He said, God bestows His wisdom on men and women in the classroom of silence. And so, it is through silence that He would give me light. It is through silence that He would teach me. It is in silence that he would lead me and show me things that many people sit down and study for many, many years to learn. He said, "You can learn more in an hour of silence than you can in a year from a book."

Q. *What else has He the Eternal Father told you about silence?*

A. One of the things that is robbed in the world during these times is silence. As you know, young people, wake up in the morning to a clock radio. They go down, they shower, they turn a radio on in the bathroom. They come down to have breakfast and they watch T.V. while they're having breakfast. They go out to a university or to school and they put a walkman on and listen on the way. Or they get in their car and they turn their radio on. So there's always noise, always noise. And the noise influences us. What you hear, what you read today, walks and talks with you tomorrow. And so the influences, the noises that surround us, influence us. We surrender three quarters of ourselves to be like someone else. Because we don't know who we are. Because we don't know silence. It's in silence that we discover ourselves and it's in silence we discover God. And in discovering ourselves, and in discovering our God, we discover how great God is and how little we are. And how we need to grow to be more like that. And so it's at that point, in that silence, that you have the decision. Well, I am here—God is here. I am here, the image of Christ is here. Do I want to grow in that image because, if I do, it's going to cost. And that's why people are scared of silence because we discover the need to change in silence. And people, the reality is, don't want to change. We're happy doing that we're doing, when we're doing it, how we're doing it, and where we're doing it. God calls us to silence. So may God give us the wisdom to pray and to make silence a friend. But may God also give us the wisdom and the strength to live what we discover. It's in the latter of the two that most of us have the problem in hearing God.

Q. *Has God talked to you about this awareness of when to be silent? Has He taught you to be silent when you first meet somebody? Has He taught you to be silent when you first enter a new place? Has he taught you a schematic approach to applying the virtue of silence?*

A. I think, more than anything, He's calling people to spend a period of time in silence, every day, preferably before the Blessed Sacrament, preferably in front of a tabernacle where Jesus is present or before a monstrance where Jesus is present. The other practical applications throughout relationships and work are really the application of the virtue of humility. That's something He has spoken about very often.

Q. *What has He taught you about prayer and how has He taught you to pray?*

A. Firstly, partaking in any activity, you have to know what you're doing, what you're trying to achieve. You know, you have to understand the practice, of it. To understand prayer, and certainty, to understand Catholic spirituality, you also have to understand the Sacraments and the Church. And so humanity is walking the path of salvation to get to heaven, but it's more than that. It's the growth of the individual towards the completion that God created the individual for. It's the growth, in the image of Christ. Humanity is walking the path of salvation. Prayer is a gift from God to assist us along the path of salvation, to assist us in that personal growth.

The Sacraments are God's ultimate gift to humanity to assist and accelerate us along the path of salvation, to assist and accelerate us in that personal individual growth towards the completion that God created us for, to assist us in our growth in the image of Christ and likeness of Christ. St. Thomas Aquinas wrote, "The glory of God is the fulfillment of the creature." We are asked to grow to our fulfillment, to grow to the completion that God created us for. The role of the Church is to direct each of us individually toward that fulfillment, along the path of salvation. And when the Church says "this is the rule" or "this is a sin and this is not a sin," it is not saying "don't do this, don't do that, because we don't want you to." The Church is not saying, "Don't do this because we don't want you to have any fun." The Church is saying, "You shouldn't do this, because it offends God." And why does it offend God? Because it stifles our individual growth towards God. And ultimately, we kill a part of ourselves as a creation of God and we stifle the growth that we have towards God, the growth that takes us to our fulfillment. The growth that takes us to our completion. The growth that takes us to the fulfillment that brings us peace, joy, and happiness, which we all desire.

Until we understand the Church, as directing us in this very positive way towards God and our fulfillment and happiness, until we understand prayer, the Sacraments, and the Church in this very positive light, we will never witness the richness and beauty that they were designed to achieve in our lives. Too many people would have us believe that the perfume of God is pain and suffering. It Is not. God's perfume is happiness and it is that which He wants to share with us. And it is for that which He calls us to prayer. One thing is certain, and that is that we all yearn for happiness. Our yearning for happiness is a yearning for God. Unfortunately, for too long we've confused this yearning for happiness, this yearning for God with a yearning for money, a yearning for possessions, a yearning for comfort, a yearning for pleasure of the flesh, a yearning for power. Our yearning for happiness is a yearning for God.

Jesus said, "The Kingdom of God is within you." Surely, the Kingdom of God contains happiness. Surely, the Kingdom of God is a happy Kingdom. But, we're forever looking for our happiness outside of ourselves. This is particularly true with young people, who think "if only I could find the right guy or the right girl, then I'll be happy." They are looking for their completion outside of themselves, as if they themselves were created incomplete. Or you hear people say, "When I have this much money or this car or this boat or this new house, then 'I'll be happy.' They are looking for happiness outside themselves, looking for their completion outside of themselves, as if they themselves were created incomplete.

Jesus said, "The Kingdom of God is within you." And happiness is within the Kingdom of God. But our happiness, this happiness that we yearn for, this happiness that is God is only a by-product of something else, and that is the seeking, discovering, and struggling to live the truth. And so, our spiritual growth is dependent on how much we seek, how much we discover and how much we struggle to live the truth. We're forever looking for the truth also in the wrong places. I'll tell you just a quick little story. When God was creating the universe, a few angels got together and they decided that they would have a meeting to discuss where God should hide the truth. One of the angels said, "I think God should hide the truth on the summit of the very highest mountain." Another angel said, "No, I think God should hide the truth in the very depths of the ocean." Then, a third angel came along and said, "No I think God should hide the truth on the very furthest star. Finally, God came along and God said, "I will hide the truth in none of these places. I will hide the truth in the very depths of every man's and every women's heart. Therefore, those that search humbly and sincerely and deserve to find it will find it very easily. And those that do not will have to search the whole universe before they do."

This is what's happening. We're searching the whole universe and God is calling us to go within. It's through going within, through prayer that will lead us to this truth. By struggling to live this truth, by searching part of that within, is the happiness that we all desire. And that is the call of prayer. But unless, we understand this as being something positive, then men and women will continue to think that prayer, the Sacraments, the Church are a burden on the shoulder of mankind.

Q. *In a practical sense, how should we pray?*

A. There are many practices of prayer. The way that He has lead me most in prayer, with the understanding of the importance that He's placed on silence, is to come each day and sit before the Tabernacle. Now, the first thing to understand when we come to pray, is that we have a body and a soul. The spirit within us, the soul, is very still. Let's pretend that our right hand is the soul. The soul is always very still and when we live in the state of grace God dwells within the soul. Obviously, the soul has no physical characteristics. With the other hand, you have the concise mind that is always being distracted, by the things we see, the things we hear, the things we do, the things we watch, the things people say to us. The first thing we have to do when we come to prayer is to recollect ourselves, to slow this down, so that the two can meet, which is union with God. This is when the soul sings for joy, overflows. It flows out into our conscious mind. It flows out in through our words, through our actions.

So we have to recollect ourselves so these two, the soul and the conscious mind, can meet. The union with God can then be achieved, so God can work through us more and His happiness can flow, which is the by-product of this union with God. Now, I can sit here and wave my hands around, but it's not very practical. So, how do we achieve this recollection? Well, the way I've been lead is to come and sit before the Tabernacle, to adopt a comfortable position, and then to hold that position and not to move. Then, I close my eyes. By doing this, I cut myself off to the sensory world. Okay? Because when you sit still, in this little way, you overcome the body. And you rise to the level of the spirit a little more. By closing your eyes, you cut yourself off to the visual senses. Hopefully, it's silent. Cut yourself off to the audible senses, so you can rise above the sensory world in a little way. With my eyes closed then, I've been led to imagine an image before me. An image I very often use now is the image of a single red rose. A single red rose has been a symbol for Christ throughout the centuries. It's been an image of Christ, who we are all trying to grow to be like. Now, closing my eyes, I imagine this single red rose before me and I focus on this single red rose. Now, everything that's happened before in the day, these are going to be distractions in my mind.

And so, as these distractions come one by one, I kick them out. I kick them out of my mind, focusing of this single red rose, which I am imagining before me. After doing this for five or six, seven minutes, maybe ten minutes, the distractions will still very often be coming, but you will have slowed your self down a lot. You will be brought to a calm and a peace. But more than that, what's been achieved in this time of recollection is that we've placed our energies, we've directed our energies towards God and placed our attention on God. Rather than on all the other distractions. This recollection will bring us to this union with God. It is then that we have prepared our hearts, our minds, our souls, to engage in some communication through prayer with God. Then I will go into a mental dialogue with God. Sometimes after this period of sitting very still, I will then take a book, Holy Scripture, or the messages, which is exactly what they've been given to me for and read them.

Q. *When you say a mental dialogue, is this then when you start to just talk to God about what is on your mind?*

A. I start to talk to God about what's happening in my life. And many of the messages speak about it. God says, "Come and speak to Me about your worries, your fears, and Jesus will take away the anxieties. Speak about your problems, but speak about your joys. And one of the most powerful lines He said to me about prayer was, "Too many of you only tell me of problems." You know, I was always telling Him, "God fix this, do this, do this." You know? This is your prayer? A little kid wrote a letter one day, saying, "Dear God, if you bring me a bicycle for Christmas, I'll be a good boy for a whole year. Love, Tommy." He looks at the letter, thinks that's too hard, and rips it up and throws it in the bin. He starts again, "Dear God, if you bring me a bicycle for Christmas, I'll be a good boy for a month. Love Tommy." He looks at the note and thinks this is too hard, so he throws it in the bin. "Dear God, if you bring me a bicycle for Christmas, I'll do the dishes for three months. Love, Tommy." He looks at it again. It's still too hard, so he rips it up and throws it in the bin. Then He goes to Mass on Sunday and sees a statue of Our Lady on the side altar. When everyone's left the church, he goes up there. He takes the statue and he takes it home. "Dear God, I've got your mother, bring me my bicycle! It wouldn't be much of a Christmas without your mother!"

You know, our prayer is like that. Very often, we're trying to make a deal with God. There's no deals with God. And so, do we only tell Him our problems or are we only trying to make a deal? Are we only trying to use Him? Because when you have a friend, your friend is the first person you tell about your good news. You know, a friend is not just someone you tell your problems to and say, "Listen, I've got this problem. This is the situation. These are the circumstances. What do you think I should do?" No, you also share the good with your friend.

Q. *Do you wait for an answer? Do you wait in the sense that you would hear an answer like you hear it? How do you know what answer you get? I mean excluding the locutions.*

A. Firstly, I don't have a personal conversation with God. I don't have the extraordinary relationship that people expect me to have. I get the messages but that's it. That's it. I'm in prayer like you. One of the things, you know is that people expect me to be told by God what to do in my personal life. But God says to me, "Pray, discern." Otherwise, you're a hypocrite. You go out there and you tell everyone to pray and discern and you expect Me to tell you everything. Well, how can it work that way? You can't lead people in something that you haven't been led in yourself." God expects me to sit there, speak to Him, and then spend some time with Him. But that's what He's calling us to, the silence, the stillness. In one of the messages, it was very short, He said, "In your heart, you know." And I think if you come to silence, and you sit there and you discuss an issue with God, He will place the answer in your heart. He always has for me. I don't think that's an extraordinary gift. I think that's a gift that God will give every person who approaches Him humbly and sincerely and says, "Listen Lord, this is how it is, you know, I understand I am nothing. I understand You are everything. I am nothing. I can do nothing. I am worth nothing. I have nothing. I know nothing.

You are everything. And in Your Son, Jesus Christ, You have made Yourself mine."

Q. *What did the Father say to you about suffering?*

A. The value of suffering is obviously enormous. Why do angels envy human beings? Firstly, because they can't receive the Blessed Sacrament. Secondly, because they can't suffer. So they can't share in the redemption in humanity. They can't cooperate in the redemption of humanity with Jesus's suffering on the Cross. It's easy to talk about suffering. It's hard to suffer. I've never really suffered. And so it's easy, much easier for me to talk about suffering. But, when I find people are suffering, I find that I am a beggar. And I come to them begging them to offer their sufferings for my work, for the work I do.

Q. *How about your Guardian Angel? Do you know him?*

A. My Guardian Angel has always been a great help to me and is spoken about very often in the messages. The power of Guardian Angels and how many Guardian Angels there are employed up there in heaven and surrounding us I'm aware of. When I come to speak to people, I'm aware that the Guardian Angels are there. And I'll be addressing their Guardian Angels before I'm addressing them. You know, even just day to day, when you come to meet with someone and you want to have a fruitful meeting, speak to their Guardian Angel. Get your Guardian Angel to speak to their Guardian Angel.

Q. *Has the Eternal Father spoken to you about the future "Era of Peace?*

A. He's spoken to me about something like that. But I don't know whether you can count off history and the future into set periods of time. But certainly, we will experience a time of peace.

Q. *Many say the Church and the Pope must suffer much? Has He talked to you about the suffering of the Pope?*

A. He has talked to me very much about the Pope. The Pope is here
    with a mission. He has a job to do. And you can be assured that,
    the minute the Pope leaves the earth, God intended him to leave
    the earth. God has a plan for him. He has a mission for him and
    the Pope is not going anywhere until He has finished that mission.
    We're talking about a man who's come through communism,
    who's come through assassination attempts and many other much
    greater problems than perhaps people could have imagined before
    the turn of the century. We're talking about a man who does an
    enormous amount of prayer. Who is a man of God! And, we're
    talking about a man who is much stronger than a lot of people
    recognize. Yes, he is a lone voice out there. Yes, he has the support
    of God. And, I guess, as Catholics, we have to support him more
    than we do. You know, we hear people talking about the Pope
    saying this and that. If they spoke about your father like that, if they
    spoke about my father like that, I wouldn't tolerate it. Nor should
    we when they speak about the Pope like that. He has a job to do
    and I think when he does die, people will be shocked. People will
    think, "Ah, the forces of darkness snatched him from the earth."
    They will be wrong. His job will be done.

Q. *Has Mary talked to you about any future hard times coming? Has the
    Eternal Father talked to you about that?*

A. Certainly, I'm given an enormous amount of information of our
    future events. But my message is not about these future events.
    My message is not about these things that are told to me. So it is
    not for me to proclaim these things, these things that are told to me.
    I understand what's being asked of me. My job merely is to
    encourage people in a very positive way and, in a small way, try to
    lead people in education and understanding of prayer, the
    Sacraments, of the value of human work as prayer and the richness
    and beauty of the Church.

Q. *Has the Eternal Father talked to you about the "Triumph of the
    Immaculate Heart?"*

A. He has. Obviously, it's a prophecy that goes back all the way to the earliest Scriptures, that our Lady would crush the serpent's head. The misunderstanding of this during these times has been pointed out to me. And that is that people think when our Lady crushes the head (of the serpent), that automatically, in the click of the fingers, we're going to have a "new" time. That all evil will be taken away. No. Because, we're tempted by three things. Firstly, the flesh ourselves. Secondly, the environment. And thirdly, Satan. We will eliminate one. But there will still be a struggle. St. Paul wrote, "The good that I would, I do not. The evil that I would not, it is that I do." You know, the things we don't want to do are evil. It seems to be that this struggle, because of our holiness must occur. St. Peter said, "The spirit is willing, but the flesh is weak." This is a struggle that will remain with humanity in every moment of our life until the end of time.

Q. *But won't the fruits of the Triumph appear?*

A. The fruits of the "Triumph" are dependent upon you and I. And this is where these people are really missing the point. Because if they don't understand this point, they can't play the role that's being asked of them. Why do you and I know what we know today? So we can use it in a way that will help God. And the reason people are having these experiences, are being awakened prior to, say an "illumination of conscience" is because once that does happen, they can help God. We need to be able to lead them. There are not going to be enough priests. There are not going to be enough nuns. There are not going to be enough bishops. And lot of them are going to need their own help. So you and I have been called to, not only to study Marian apparitions or the messages, or what's happening in the world, but to study our faith. So that we can bring people to study their faith. So we can bring people to understand their faith.

Q. *Does the Eternal Father want us to go to Mass every day?*

A. It's not something that's been mentioned, but I think God leads people to that.

Q. *Have you been taught about any great signs that are going to appear?*

A. There will be a great sign in these times and closer than people perhaps think. But the times and the history and the future is not going to fall into the logic that some people have sat down and said.

Q. *Has the Eternal Father talked to you about the value of children praying, the change that children can bring in the world?*

A. Certainly, the power, the beauty of purity and innocence in prayer in children is enormous. Children do what they see. And so, obviously the richness of family life, is very important. The Father speaks about the importance of family life as being the most basic structure within society. If we get the family right we get the world right. Why? Because every person comes from a family. But we have political structures that support immoral family activity through welfare payments etc., etc., etc... What are we doing? We're promoting immoral family activity. We're promoting immoral family structures. This only leads to even greater problems.

Q. *Can you tell me about the love of the Eternal Father?*

A. If I would describe God the Father from how I know Him through the messages and through the prayer, I would say He's very gentle. He's very gentle, but very, very firm. And this gentleness and this firmness creates a trust. And this gentleness and this firmness and this trust creates a self-assurance in each of His children. This trust and self-assurance are the two things that lead to happiness. Yet, the very things that we kill in society— trust, self assurance—are the most basic Christian principles. If someone cannot trust someone, if someone doesn't understand the value of themselves, someone cannot be a Christian. Yet, we're forever killing people's trust. We're forever killing people's self assurance.

CHAPTER THIRTEEN

BARBARA ROSE CENTILLI

A t the age of 44, Barbara Rose Centilli began to record what she believed to be the voice of the Eternal Father speaking to her in prayer. Since then, a body of revelations has emerged that many believe to be of the most extraordinary nature, perhaps adding new insight on the First Person of the Holy Trinity.

Barbara Rose was born and raised in Michigan. Except for a few special experiences that she believed to be from God, her life as a mother, grandmother, teacher, and wife were typical of the average American woman of her generation. She received degrees from universities in Michigan and New England, and later taught communications courses and worked as a corporate consultant. But a generous portion of her time was devoted to being a mother to four children and a grandmother to three more.

In the mid 1980's Barbara went from being almost indifferent about her faith to a firm, practicing Catholic who joined a prayer group, taught Catechism, and even became a Eucharistic minister. She also began to develop a silent, steady prayer life that gradually led to her writing prayerful conversations with God the Father in a journal. These conversations took the form of a dialogue, and while she felt God was moving and inspiring her, she believed there was nothing supernatural. However, these journals were eventually destroyed when a retreat director told her God does not work in this way.

However, in 1996, Barbara again began to record her conversations with the Father. By this time, she noticed the Father's responses to her in prayer were becoming very clear and distinct within her. She could recognize His voice "in her heart and mind."

Furthermore, as she reconciled and confronted what was happening to her, she became certain her experiences were not self-induced or imaginative but rather something she had no control over within herself.

The Revelations of the Father

It would not be possible to fully address the extraordinary contents of the revelations given to this soul. Like many revelations, they cover a range of topics and are rich in detail concerning Barbara's interior life with God. However, the essence of the revelations is unmistakable. God the Father was again requesting, as He did with Mother Eugenia Ravasio in 1932, that through His Church all mankind be returned to Him. His children, He told her, must begin to come home to Him at this time. The Father told her that she was to be a special instrument for His messages, a seed to be planted, that would now bring His Kingdom "on earth as it is in heaven." His children must abandon any fear of Him, He told Barbara, and must know that He is all Love and all Mercy. Most of all, His plan for the times was at hand and was soon to be fulfilled, and that she had to accept that she had been chosen by Him for this work:

> **Though it may seem that you are alone and abandoned, you are not. The best is yet to come. I have plans for you....Demonstrate your trust by coming to Me in faith, trust, and humility. There is no shame in this. Only a wealth of graces—graces, unbound and untethered. That is what grieves you, is that you must let go of the ground beneath you and come to Me in trust. I will catch you in My Arms—and never leave you—because you are Mine. Delivered to Me by My Son and Your Mother—to do My Will. There is no escape from this, daughter. My Will. Embrace it and do not let it frighten you. Remember, you are Mine always and forever; you are dear to Me.**
> (August 15, 1996)

Later, she wrote another extraordinary message in her journal:

Remember, child, all is well within My Heart....stop, listen. The crashing of the waves. The pounding of the sea, sound breaking over rocks....THE TIME HAS COME FOR THE RECKONING OF MANKIND -A REUNION WITH ITS FATHER. You have all been away a very long time. The call is on, the crashing and the calling–but to hear the call, broken over the rocks, the hard, hard rocks, you must be in the silence and dark of the night. You've always known this.

I have shown you this symbolism and have shared this with you in our dialogues for many months now. The time has come for you to explain this to My other children. Help them understand that this is the GREATEST HOUR OF MY MERCY. This is the Triumph long awaited for. But so many will be lost without the Light of this loving message.

I am the Father of all mankind. I love each and every one of My children. My heart desires that I live in My children and they in Me. I long to live among My children. The Great Sun amidst so many stars—all glowing with the Love of God. Such glory. Such power. Such wonders await those children who choose to return home now.

Night falls and the storm approaches. My children need to convert, turn toward their Father, and come home. And when they arrive at the threshold of My loving Arms, they must say "Yes, Father, I will dance with You in the rhythm and harmony of Your divine Will." In this way they will remain with Me always— with and in Me. Not outside Me, separated from Me.

It is all quite simple. Before you took refuge in your Mother's Immaculate Heart. She was truly in My Divine Will and so in Me and I in her. Now it is time to recognize that in being safely in her Heart, you are in Me, your Father. The process, a roadway leading to Me. Mary, your Mother, is in the Heart of My Son Who is in My Heart—One contained in the Other. How is this possible? Through My Holy Spirit. (Sept. 30, 1997)

On November 30, 1997, the Eternal Father revealed to Barbara the meaning of a dream He had given her and why Our Lady communicated to her about this dream in another message:

Where you lay your head is on a bed of roses— each sweet and pure. This pillow of roses is made up of the souls that have sacrificed themselves for the good of all. They have given themselves for this holy purpose. Here you will find your rest, little one.

Roses, roses all, who give themselves to the Father. Each blossoming on the Spring of My Merciful Water. My Water of Love. Each rose watered by My life-giving water. The water which proceeds through Me, through the Heart of My Son and the hands of Your Loving Mother—graces to bring you home. This is important. Little time remains before I will come and visit My Children. I will come to make My abode with them. Prepare them. Make them ready.

A rose must be watered and opens to the Sun. Be beautiful as the rose, My children. Open up to your Father. Be all that you were intended to be. Without My Saving Water, without the warmth and radiance of My Sun, you will wither and perish, never to realize what you could have been—My heirs. Now do you understand, Barbara?

The rose on your pillow was for you—it

was your own soul. Opened and blossoming in
the Sun, which is the Father. Yes, daughter, even
the rose that has bloomed will soon die, and so
with all My children. But this is the way it must
be. You and so many others will send the sweet
scent of your offering and consecration to Me—
especially on My Feast Day—to the very heavens.
Draw Me with this scent. For soon I will come,
as I have planned. Draw down My Mercy,
Barbara. Teach all My Children to draw down
My Mercy. And I will surely, come. Soon, very
soon. Time is but a pane of glass that we look
through. It is like a transparent sheet of glass.
See Me through it." (Nov. 30, 1997)

Through a series of messages, the Eternal Father communicated
to Barbara that the end of an era will dawn upon the world and that these
are truly prophetic times. Most significantly, the long awaited Triumph
of the Church is about to be fulfilled. This is the "Triumph" Mary
promised at Fatima in 1917. And according to the Father's Words to
Barbara Centilli, it will be completely fulfilled in accordance with His
Will through two means: *individual consecration to God the Father and by the
Catholic Church proclaiming a Feast Day in His Name.*

Like the revelations to Mother Eugenia Ravasio, the Father
revealed to Barbara that this request needed to be addressed at this time in
salvation history, before the end of the 20th century:

There is not much time, little one. Draw this
world into the heavenly paradise of My Divine
Will. Heaven and earth will touch. Bid Me
come, and I will come—followed by My Son and
the Power of My Holy Spirit—to renew the face
of the earth. To begin again as in the old ways,
I will be present again. And My Presence will
remain for all times, in all places. I will be present
with and in My children, as I have willed from the
beginning of all time.

Come to Me, My little ones. Come back

to Your Father Who loves you.   Night
approaches and surely you will be lost. Approach
now while there is light. Come by the Light.
Follow My Son home.   He gathers up My
children. The sheep are being gathered in—as
we speak. Do you understand little one?

The Consecration and Feast Day are the
beacon and the means by which My children may
approach Me and by which I will come to My
children.   "THY KINGDOM COME, THY
WILL BE DONE ON EARTH AS IT IS IN
HEAVEN." Your Mother has prepared for this
long and many years. Now is the time. Rest in
this knowledge.   Your offering has been
accepted. In opening the invitation and reading,
you have offered it back to Me. Work for the
restoration of My children.

FATIMA leads to this time. Fatima leads
to Me. The time of the revelry is over. The time
of rebellion is over. Make My presence known
through the Consecration and Feast Day. I am
coming. Prepare yourselves. (November 13, 1997)

On January 12, 1998, the Eternal Father revealed to Barbara more
about the meaning of the Miracle of the Sun at Fatima and how the miracle
illustrated the consequences of choices, choices mankind must make at
this time:

Be at peace, daughter. You have suffered much
for this work I have given you. Put the pen to
paper and write. All around you is in the blaze of
a recovery from sin. The wind blows but the
motion of My Spirit goes undetected. See it in
the workings and phenomenon which surround
you—and the world at large. These are times
steeped in treachery and intrigue.   Much is
transpiring which My children cannot and may
not see. For it is cloaked behind a veil of secrecy

and sin. There will be a reprieve, a brief time more before the knowledge of this can no longer be denied. Pray, pray. Pray with your whole heart—given to Me in reparation—and for solace. Understand the gravity of what I say. Much is transpiring—even now. This time is decisive. My children must choose; they must respond now. I weep for them—all the missed opportunities. Fortify them, daughter, with My Consecration and Feast Day.

All is foretold in the Miracle of the Sun (at Fatima) — The pattern of the fabric I have woven is drawn tighter and the image clearer. Do you understand? All the colored threads of the tapestry which is the story of mankind's salvation history, their journey home to Me, is played out on the diorama that is before you. All the answers are there....Help My children see the grand tapestry which is before them. Watch the threads as they are woven more tightly together. The image comes into clearer focus. The analogy is greater than you thought. Meditate on this. Ponder it in your heart. It (the Miracle of the Sun at Fatima) was more simple than they [My children] thought. A graphic illustration. You were correct in your assumptions about the sun—now follow through on the thought. Why was this shown to My children at that particular time? Meditate on the effects. Harnessing the sun. Harnessing God. For I am energy and light. Consequences–response. Now is the time for choices. Wisely made, based on love. Know Me, My children, before it is too late! I come and I come soon. Know this and be ready. Forgive all those who have offended you. Time is short. And soon petty annoyances, slights, and irritations will no longer matter. I will come to My children in a new way, a powerful way. Sleep

now and remain close to My Fatherly Heart. (Jan. 12, 1998)

Several months later, the Father revealed to Barbara how all of Mary's work has been leading to this moment in time, His return, and how all can be symbolically understood in the Miracle of the Sun on October 13th, 1917, at Fatima:

> **My daughter, you must realize by now the tightly woven bond which exists between this devotion to Me and the immediate steps leading up to the Triumph of your Mother's Immaculate Heart. Laid out in the scheme of mankind's Salvation History is the end, the ultimate completion of this journey. Through your Mother's Fiat, her "Yes," My Son Jesus came into the world to redeem My children, all. Now, the time approaches when this final Triumph will be realized....**
>
> **Only when I am recognized, loved, and honored by My children—all—will this triumph be completed. Do you understand?**
>
> **The return of My children is your Mother's triumph. All My children must return unhindered to their one True God and Father. Then My kingdom will have come on earth as it is in heaven.**
>
> **This process will be gradual, but IT MUST BEGIN NOW....Each of My children has their role to play in My Plan for Mankind....Yours to present to the world—now in this time.**
>
> **I come to My children as was shown in the MIRACLE OF THE SUN. [at Fatima] I come so close to warm you and fill you with My Light. Why does this frighten My children? Because they are not ready; they are not prepared. They are not able to see beyond their own preconceptions—their constructions of Truth.**

And the approach of your God without proper preparation as outlined by your Mother is folly indeed. Purification must take place. A cleansing of hearts, bodies, and minds. [I see an image of the Miracle of the Sun—the way the sun's rays seem to color and permeate everything they touch.]

See how I effused all that I touched. See how I chased away the gloom and discomfort. I am Light and Love. And I bring with Me a power that will transform. All will be transformed in the Lord. I WAS PRESENT AT THE MIRACLE OF FATIMA—in graphic depiction of what could have been and what will be yet.

St. Joseph, My good and tender son, represented the Fatherly Arms that hold and behold My Son Jesus—as I desire to hold all of you. The Spirit, My Spirit, was represented in the rays of the sun penetrating all My Creation. The miracle was not as great as it could have been. I withdrew from My children as they shrank away in terror from the power and glory of their God. Even then many forget the impact of this experience. Yes, daughter, I am represented in the sun as you see clearly in Holy Scripture, My Word. The power of the sun gives life, but it has also been harnessed by man, in aping God, to take life away. LIFE OR CHASTISEMENT. HOW WILL THE POWER OF GOD BE USED?

I wait patiently, oh, so patiently, to enter you and warm your souls in My Love. But as with all My gifts, even this has been abused and will be again in chastisement if My little ones do not find their way back home to their Father. At Fatima you saw the options and reactions played out. Approach Me in love and trust and you have nothing to fear. I showed you this at Fatima. See and believe.

I wish mightily for this devotion to be

spread swiftly and without hindrance — this Holy
Octave of Consecration to God the Father. Be at
peace and know that your Father guides you in
your efforts. All you need will be provided in My
own way, in My own time. Delight in this gift I
give the world. Understand this priceless gift I
have placed in your hands. This is what your
mother Mary has prepared you so diligently. The
precipice is closer than you think, mankind.
Approach your Father who will save you as I have
written in 1 Sm 3:21. (March 23, 1998)

  *[1 Sm 3:21— "And the Lord appeared again at
Shiloh for the Lord revealed himself to Samuel at Shiloh by the
word of God." (Shiloh was a central shrine to God, sanctified
by the presence of the Ark of the Covenant.)]*

The Holy Octave of Consecration and its Feast Day, the Father
revealed to Barbara, was significant in His plan for the new era. Over a
period of months, the Father explained the concept of the "Octave" to
Barbara, its relevance to the Old Testament times, and its relevance to the
future of the Church and all mankind. Barbara came to understand that
Christmas and Easter were once celebrated as Octaves and that this Feast
would be, in that same tradition.

Indeed, the Father told Barbara how Scripture clearly revealed the
concept of an 8-day preparation:

The time is ripe! Your purpose will bloom forth
with power and My Glory. I will work through
you. You are very sensitive to My Will. You are
not comfortable in the world because you were
not made for this world....You will fully realize
your mission in time. For now, ponder My
requests for re-consecration of My Temple.
THIS PROCESS TAKES 8 DAYS. Yes, you are
right. I am not speaking only of a physical
Church, but My Living Church and My people
individually.   LOOK TO SCRIPTURE TO
BEGIN PREPARATION.

Barbara, the 8 days is significant because
it is a purification process. My Tabernacle, My
Church, My People have been contaminated.
Where darkness is, I cannot be. The darkness
must be displaced, swept clean, sunshine and
fresh air—housecleaning. TO DO THIS TAKES
8 DAYS OF PREPARATION. ONLY THEN
WILL I COME—only then....Look to the
Psalms, Jeremiah, Hosea, Wisdom,
Revelations....(October 10, 1996)

On February 2, 1997, the Father explained what would be
accomplished over the 8-day period:

EIGHT DAYS SIGNIFIES A PERIOD OF TIME
MAN LIVES THROUGH AND THEN A
TRANSFORMATION OR NEW PERIOD
BEGINS. Through these periods, I have saved
man many, many times.

Scripture starts out with Noah and the
EIGHT on the Ark. Because of those "EIGHT"
safely carried in My Ark, mankind was saved, and
so it was again and again.

After EIGHT days, through My
circumcision covenant, you became My children
and were saved. Even My Son Jesus underwent
this ritual. Then He became the sign of My
Covenant. Through the purification rituals, you
were healed and saved from sin.

Through EIGHT days of prayer,
purification, and dedication, I came to be in and
with My children.

My Son, on the Feast of Dedication (8-day
feast), announced that He and I were One, that I
was with you and among you—in Him.

After EIGHT days, I revealed to Peter,
James, and John on Mount Tabor who My Son
Jesus was—God, My Son. This was

transformation and the beginning of a new period.

After EIGHT days, My Son was victorious in saving My children—He conquered sin and death by rising on the EIGHTH day of His Passion Week.

After EIGHT days, Jesus came to His frightened, doubting Apostles to show His Risen Self.

Always, a revelation, a transformation after a period of time. To you, My little one, EIGHT is important. IT POINTS TO A NEW TIME, A NEW TRANSFORMATION WHEN I WILL BE WITH YOU ALL IN A NEW WAY.

You must prepare yourselves for Me to come. YOU MUST PURIFY AND DEDICATE YOUR TEMPLES.

SEE THE "8:—TWO CIRCLES: They are continuous, Barbara. Two perfect circles joined—the beginning and the end, the Alpha and the Omega joined with My children. It is through this Octave that My children are joined with Me. Speak this, Barbara. Show them how this is so. The 8—it is more than a concept, but a visual aid! You are Mine, little one. Be one with Me. I love you as you do Me. Bring souls, My dearest daughter. This is no light matter. WAKE UP! See Me! I am with you, little one. The "EIGHT"—a perfect harmony of the influx of the Holy Spirit. So be it!!! (March 16, 1997)

As in former times, the Holy Octave of Consecration to God Our Father is an eight-day consecration to be celebrated as a whole, culminating with a special feast day in the Church to honor the Father of All Mankind. The actual consecration involves a series of daily prayers, including meditations, a litany, and the praying of a chaplet, all directed to God the Father.

It must be especially noted that the Father emphasizes to Barbara Centilli that there is to be no separation of the two–the Consecration and its Feast Day. This is because, He says, the **"practical purpose of the Feast (Day) is for My children to consecrate themselves to Me."** The Father further states that **"the Feast does not exist for the purpose of providing Me with a Feast Day on the Church Calender. It is what the Feast accomplishes–the return of My children to their Father! This cannot be accomplished with limited and temporary honor given Me at one Mass on one Sunday a year. No, this is much greater than one act....this is the final step toward the new era, a new relationship with their Father and God."**

While much more could be noted, one final point is emphasized. Through the Holy Octave of Consecration and Feast Day, the Father declared to Barbara that this is the fulfillment of what was meant from the beginning. This, He states to her, is to a degree the meaning of the profound words in the Lord's prayer, **"Thy will be done....Thy kingdom come on earth as it is in Heaven."** It is the long awaited Triumph of God, promised by so many visionaries.

The Virgin Mary also told Barbara about the coming of her triumph:

> **Your Father is with you. From His hands comes my Triumph. Through me all the children of God are beckoned and led back home. See the events around you? Do you doubt that the drama unfolds? Each is to play their own part. Truly let it be known that the passing of an era is upon us. As surely as the sun sets, it will also rise. My Son's Passion is seen and felt more clearly in these times. All must carry their cross. Bear up, child. Know that I am always with you. Through the grace of God all will be well for those who bear the light of my Son's Cross.** [She points to the sun and I see a cross embedded in its center.] **See, the earth is left barren, rocky and dry, bones lay bare and scattered. I hold you, daughter, and I promise you this—cherish Me as I have cherished you. Soon the darkness and struggle that separate us**

will be chased away in the dawning of a new era.

The Father then added to her some more insight:

Barbara, the horn has been sounded. Let those who have ears hear. Yes, there is much clatter and noise that drowns out the music alerting My children and leading them home. They must stop and listen—quietly. And they will hear. It is the Cry of the Father for His children. Landless and lost they wander. Allow yourselves to be led by your tender mother. Come to Me—only Me—your Father and your God. The drum beat sounds to the rhythm and harmony of My Will. Feel the intensity and power of this time. Gather yourselves together to await the coming of your Father. CONSECRATE YOURSELVES TO ME. HONOR ME WITH A FEAST DAY. SHARE WHAT I HAVE GIVEN TO YOU WITH THE WORLD....

Never hesitate when you believe it is My Will. Never. Proceed. Move forward always toward Me, your Father. There is no fault or danger in this, only My Fatherly embrace. Come to Me, My children. And watch as My Glory ascends in this new day. The presence of your God is with you. Of this there will be no doubt. Faith and confidence, My little ones. Your trials will soon be over and we shall begin again. Approach Me. Choose Me in these times.

The Father spoke to Barbara about many other subjects. These revelations were also extraordinary, especially a message and vision given concerning what the world will be like after a certain, terrible but purifying event of God's justice:

[I saw a flat area on the far side of the mountains. There are buildings. They seem to be in ruins and smoldering.

I ask My Father where all the people are.]

They have fled the ruins of what once was, as will you all, once at a time in the not too distant future. The ruins are uninhabitable, little one. My children can no longer survive where they once lived, how they once lived. The choice will no longer be theirs. Where they once lived, how they once lived can be no more. My children can no longer survive in the culture "they" have created. (April 6, 1998)

Just as fascinating was the Father's word's to Barbara concerning Judith and her times in ancient Israel. It is a story the Father told her that foreshadows the coming Triumph:

It is Mother's Day. I love and honor my mother Mary and my own mother and grandmothers.

Father, I just read the story of Judith. The people of Israel were going to be destroyed by a stronger pagan power. They gave God five days to save them or they were going to surrender to survive. Judith, a chaste widow, prayed to God and said they should not try God with limits. She also said they must be patient and humble and that God sometimes chastises His children for their own good and this is how they should look at it. Judith cuts Holofernes' head off and then when the "sun rises," the Hebrews dress for battle so the enemy will react (but the enemy panics after discovering that their leader has been decapitated). The sun rising is the signal to begin the deceptive offensive—after Judith had laid the groundwork for victory. The sun rising was the sign, the time, to begin their offensive.

Father, what do You wish to tell me on this night? I love You; I adore You; I worship You, my Father.

Be at peace, my little one. Oh, my daughter, look to Judith for a true picture of what will be in

the world and for each of My children. What did
you learn?

I see the symbolism of the rising sun as a signal or catalyst
for action by Your children—in their fight against their
adversary. I believe I see Judith prefiguring Our Lady in
"crushing the head" of the adversary.

**Man's ways are not My ways, daughter.
Judith knew this. She remained close to Me in
the quiet and seclusion of her upper chamber.
Did she not caution My children against testing
Me—setting time limits for my action or
response? She knew My children can approach
Me only in humility and that I chastise those I
love—allowing them to be overtaken and
defeated when they wander outside My Will.
And do I not come to their defense when they
choose to remain in My Will? Such a simple
formula for Peace, is it not? Humble submission
to My Will. And the defeat of the adversary
comes through the hands of a woman. She went
stealthily into the enemy's camp, adorned in all
her beauty and splendor, feigning betrayal of her
own people, using wiles to combat wiles, and
committing the fatal act of removing the head of
the enemy.**

**Think on this, little one. The enemy's
head must be crushed and My children must act
when the sun rises—and I will do the rest. The
enemy will flee in disorder and great distress. For
the head of their initiative is no more, has been
crushed, beheaded, separated from the body—by
the woman. A woman beautiful and chaste—a
woman given solely to the Creator—her God and
Father.**

**She knew what was needed and so should
you all. Your Mother comes in these times to tell**

you over and over, calling you unceasingly. But still, so many do not listen. Who will be ready to put on their armor when the sun rises? It is I, your Father and your God. And I will come on the heels of your Mother's great Triumph. Who will be ready? Who will be awake to see the sun rising in a new dawn, a new day?

The prodigal son spent his inheritance on harlots—lust, a counterfeit of love. The wedding feast of the Lamb and His bride awaits all those who wish to return home and who can overcome those things outlined in the revelation of the apostle John. Look to those things, daughter.

The chaplet encapsulates the response of the prodigal son. This is good. Now what must be overcome on the journey home?

Suit up for the battle. There must be charity between My children and love between each child and Me, your Father. False doctrine and prophets must be rejected. My children must feel passion in their love of their Father, and they must complete all the necessary work needed for their journey home.

What awaits them? Life! I am Life. And that is where it all began and where it all must return. Do you understand, little one? No death, no lies, no counterfeits. Only the Truth of Life in God your Father. I await you all patiently. I see you yet far off and I am beginning to run toward you, arms outstretched and a heart that beats out a song of great relief and tremendous rejoicing. My children are returning home.

They are being restored to their Father and their God. Your Mother acts to protect and defend you in these times. Be at peace and know that all will be well in the Lord!

Raphael says: **Praise His Holy Name!**

Our Mother Mary says: **Through their**

prayers, my children can draw down the mercy of God. Tell them. Through your prayers and in conforming to God's Will—you remain in the Heart of Our Father. Protected and cherished always. Choose, my children! I cajole and nudge, but you must make the choice of your own free will. All has been laid out in Holy Scripture. Open your eyes, ears, and heart—and believe! The Day of the Lord is at hand. The Peace of the Lord is with you—remember that always. Now you, too, must be about your Father's business.

Reading: Is 13—"...Howl ye, for the day of the Lord is near: it shall come as destruction from the Lord....For this I will trouble the heaven: and the earth shall be moved out of her place, for the indignation of the Lord of hosts, and for the day of his fierce wrath...."

Reading: Judith 8—"...This is not a word that may draw down mercy, but rather that may stir up wrath and enkindle indignation....You have set a time for the mercy of the Lord, and you have appointed him a day, according to your pleasure...." (May 11, 1998)

On May 12, 1988, The Father explained to Barbara about what it really means for a king to have a Kingdom, and how the world needs to be for "His Kingdom to come." Again, the following entry is from her journal:

Dearest Father:

Father, if it is Your Will, would You offer us some insight on Acts 1:6-7: "Lord wilt thou at this time restore again the kingdom to Israel? But he said to them: It is not for you to know the times or moments, which the Father hath put in his own power." Jesus said it is not for us to know the time or moment of the restoration of the Kingdom.   Is there any connection between the restoration of the Kingdom to Israel and the Holy Octave of Consecration? If it pleases You to respond to this, Father, your daughter is listening.

Be at Peace, My daughter: Let the gentle calm of the day's end settle over you. My Kingdom. What is My Kingdom? A Kingdom is something a King reigns over. But it is more. It is a place where he lives. A place that he protects. A place where he maintains peace and dispenses justice. A good king is just and fair and is loved by his people. Ideally, a kingdom exists in harmony and affords the people security and happiness. A king should be honored and respected by his people. All these things are true of a kingdom, are they not, Barbara Rose?

Yes, ideally, Father.

You ask Me if the restoration of the Kingdom to Israel is somehow connected to the Holy Octave of Consecration. First of all, a king should be present to his people, not only to afford them protection but to give them hope and heart. Do I truly dwell with My children? Do they see and hear Me in their lives? Secondly, do My children honor and respect Me? How so, My daughter? Thirdly, do My children feel security and happiness in the realm they now live in? Perhaps on a superficial level.

For a kingdom to come, My children must acknowledge their king. They must recognize that there is indeed a kingdom. The Kingdom of God is not forced upon My children. They must choose to enter it. They must choose to return home to their Father.

So many images: Father and Paradise, King and Kingdom, the New Jerusalem. What does all this mean?

Expressed in simple terms, I speak of My children returning home to Me. Where I am, so is heaven, so is Paradise, so is the New Jerusalem.

As I have explained to you before, little one, the Kingdom will not come from without but from within.

How can it ever come if My children refuse to see it, acknowledge it? Even more, they must want it.

How many of My children acknowledge that it exists? How many bid it come? How can they? They have no knowledge or belief in it.

When the cutting edge of Truth slices through the illusion that is the world, those who are not prepared will have difficulty in adjusting to the light which will penetrate powerfully into each and every soul.

Who will welcome this kingdom? Who will embrace this kingdom? Who will battle and overcome for this kingdom?

Remember what I have told you—the children of God can have no kingdom restored to them, O Israel, until they know, love, and honor their Creator and Father. Then and only then will the Kingdom truly settle into the hearts of My children and My Kingdom will be realized on earth.

Stages and degrees have been involved in the coming of this Kingdom—the restoration of the children of God to their Father. Now is the time that it comes into clearer and clearer relief—toward final realization.

Do you need to ask, Barbara Rose? Truly, in your heart you know the answer. You have outlined the path of My children's journey home—culminating in an Octave Consecration and Feast Day. Can you not see? The prodigal children will at last have found their Father. They will celebrate with joy. For in finding Him, they are no longer lost. Having been dead, they are now come to life.

As I requested an 8-day feast in Old Testament times, so now My children respond to My desire to be known, loved, and honored at this time, in this way. And as with the final day of assembly, this consecration feast day will serve to regather ALL My children. The spirit will move mightily in this effort.

My children's response—so sweet and simple: "I love You, Father, and I give myself to You." And I will come to dwell with you and I will be your God and you will be my people—I am your Father and you are My children. And once you have found your way home, you will look around you and realize that you are loved and protected for all time. For you are now in the Kingdom. The Kingdom has come and it dwells in you as you dwell in it. Do you comprehend what I am saying to you, daughter?

My children must acknowledge My existence. They must see that I am truly their Father. They must choose to leave the world of sin and disobedience and come to Me—in humility and trust. And I will shower them with such tender love as they have never before experienced or imagined.

Do you see now how the Holy Octave of Consecration to God Your Father leads to the restoration of the Kingdom to Israel—My children?

I believe so, Father.

There should be joy and celebration. As in the return of the prodigal son!

[Reading: Gal 4:1-7—"Now I say, as long as the heir is a child, he differeth nothing from a servant, though he be lord of all; but is under tutors and governors until the time appointed by the father: so we also, when we were children, were

*serving under the elements of the world. But when the fullness
of the time was come, God sent his son, made of a woman, made
under the law: that he might redeem them who were under the
law: that we might receive the adoption of sons. And because
you are sons, God hath sent the Spirit of his Son into your hearts,
crying: Abba, Father. Therefore now he is not a servant, but a
son. And if a son, an heir also through God."]*

**And so, daughter, from servitude to sonship—
and now is time for the children of God to return
home.   Thus will the Kingdom of God be
restored to Israel—My children, all.**

**A parting thought, daughter.   The
prodigal son, by choice, returned to his father.
By choice, always by choice.**

Sleep in My Peace, little one. (May 12,
1998)

The Father also explained to Barbara how Abraham's sacrifice of
Isaac and Christ's sacrifice on the Cross are mystically connected, and how
He, the Father of All Mankind, suffers daily in this manner still:

**Now as to your question regarding Abraham and
these times you live in—these precarious times.
Have I not shown you how My Fatherly Heart
breaks from My children's suffering? Each one,
daughter, is in a sense offered on the pyre of
sacrificial offering to Me. And in their sacrificial
offering I am united with them in a way that goes
beyond compassion or pity. Yes, it is true, that
I feel ALL that My children feel. But do I not also
feel, in addition to the pain, the anguish of a
Father who must witness the sacrificial pain and
suffering of each and every one of My little ones?
Comprehend what this means.   I cannot
eradicate the suffering. I cannot take away the
sacrifice. Each must follow in the steps of their
Brother and Lord God—My Son Jesus.**

So I have ordained it. Did I Myself not suffer, die, and be buried in and with My Son? I was the agent and victim, Father and child.

But, Father, why is this necessary? If it grieves you so, why must Your children suffer to be reunited and restored to You? Couldn't there have been any other way?

No, little one, My rose, because each human life is precious and bestowed with free will. Only in this way can My children be FREE to choose their Father, to love their Father.

And to draw the human spirit back toward its origin, its Creator, its Father, there must be a path of purgation and purification. And so the sacrificial wood of suffering, whether it be the flames of offering or the suffering of the Cross, all leads to Me, the Father.

Now, how is this related to these times and the Holy Octave of Consecration to God Our Father? I am providing the wood of sacrifice, the means of sacrificial offering through the eight days of consecration and My feast day. In this way all is subsumed back into the Father. All is brought back into My Fatherly Heart which is torn asunder until all is restored. Do you understand?

Yes, I think so, Father. So *The Holy Octave of Consecration to God Our Father* is like the pyre in Abraham's Old Testament story and the Cross of Jesus in the New Testament.

Daughter, this gift to My children in this time will send sacrificial smoke ascending to heaven— a final connection between the Father and His children. In this way, all will eventually be completed, restored to Me—the Father of All

Fathers. Through the example of My sacrificial offering, My children resemble their Father in all things.

The eight flames upon the Cross, daughter! Remember this image. [I see the Cross with eight candles lit and the smoke from the flames ascending into heaven.] The offering on the wood of My Son's Cross—the bridge home to Me, your One True God and Father, sacrificial smoke ascending to heaven.

Be with Me as I am with you. Be in Me as I am in you. This is how I will come to My little ones, all. I await the response of My children, given in offering to Me, as I have offered Myself for them.

Now go in My gentle and merciful peace played out so powerfully in these times.

Reading: Gen 42:33-38: ...*You will bring down my gray hairs with sorrow to hell*" [Jacob's lament over possibly losing another child.]

The Father's explicit revelations of all that is unfolding in both the spiritual and physical realms is especially revealing. The Eternal Father told Barbara on July 23, 1998, that the culture we live in is toxic to our souls and leading us to ruin. Only He, He told Barbara, can save mankind:

Everyone I know is having serious problems—especially with their children. Lord, why can't people see that the culture is destroying the children?

The culture has become toxic, daughter.

Father, if we agree that the culture is toxic, what is the answer? What can we do? Please tell me, Father. I know You want us to come home to You and You want us to know, love, and honor You—but there is something still lacking in what You ask of us—those children who say "Yes" to this. Father, do we stay in and fight or do we separate and leave. This is not entirely clear. But please help me understand.

I am with You, Father, and I am listening.

Barbara, My Daughter:
The result of My children's choices is indeed the culture you are now living in. It is replete with every kind of menace and defilement imaginable. And what was unacceptable, unthinkable, even one generation ago, is now commonplace, has now been legislated into law. The law, little one. Laws that legalize corruption and sin. Laws that violate the laws of God—My Truth, My Will.

How can this be? Because My children have abandoned Me. They think of Me no more. To them, I am nothing more than a legend, a myth. That is why, Barbara Rose, My Presence is no longer perceived or desired by My children. Why? Because for them I no longer exist. I never did. I have been explained away and banished to the past.

But some yet remain in My Truth, in My Will. And for these, existence has become very difficult, if not impossible. The disease of your culture has spread and is out of control—its victims most often are the children.

This you know, child. But your question was "what are we to do, Father?"

I repeat to you again: know, love, and honor Me. By raising up this standard, many [of My children]—more than you imagined—will rally toward it. And here is your strength for what yet lies ahead. There is strength in My little remnant, the ranks of which will swell as more and more children are awakened from their sleep. Anaesthetized so long. Not conscious of

**the state of darkness that has developed subtly,
but, oh, so swiftly. But it is here, the darkness I
speak of, and it is time to move toward the Light.
The Light of your Lord God and Father.**

**Follow where the Light of God leads you,
daughter. Follow My Light and you will find
Me—waiting to welcome you home.**

Now sleep in My Peace.

Reading: Dn 7:25— *"And he [the antichrist] shall
think himself able to change times and laws."*   (April 11,
1998)

The following is an in-depth, extensive and revealing interview
with Barbara Centilli. It's candor and insight are most revealing of who
our Father is and how He awaits our return to His protective arms.

Q. *Barbara, tell us how your devotion to God Our Father began?*

A. The first real memory I have of devotion to our Father took place
when I was a child. I came home from school one day and I was
very sick. Both my parents worked, and on this particular day, my
dad came home first. He took me to the doctor who gave me a
shot of penicillin. The next memory I have is looking up at my
dad and telling Him I couldn't breathe. I felt as if I was dying. I
realized in that instant that he (my earthly father) couldn't save
me—only my heavenly Father could. This was quite an epiphany
for me. I learned later that I had gone into anaphylactic shock and
could have died.

After that, as I was growing up, the Catholic school I attended
focused primarily on Jesus and Mary. As an adult, I never really
thought about or prayed to God Our Father until I read Mother
Eugenia's Church-approved messages several years ago.   I
remember that they seemed too good to be true. For the first
time, God Our Father seemed like a real person—an
extraordinarily wonderful and approachable person. From that
time on, I felt close to our Father. It was an invitation to love Him
and be loved by Him that I couldn't resist.

Later, I became involved with an Apostolate that was distributing Mother Eugenia's messages. I was asked to edit the Messages from British to American spelling and punctuation. During this period, I would regularly walk around our neighborhood block and say the Rosary. One particular day at dusk (which I realized later was seven days before the first Sunday of August that year), I heard a voice say, "Look up!" After arguing with myself that this must be my imagination, I heard it again. When I finally looked up, I didn't see anything out of the ordinary. It was a normal neighborhood with houses and cars, etc. The only thing that caught my eye were footlights leading up a pathway. I couldn't imagine why anyone would be telling me to look at footpath lights. Then I heard, "Count the lights." I counted eight lights.

I had no knowledge of what this meant or why this would be important. I had no affinity for numbers nor did I attach any special significance to them. I didn't know what to do or where to go for answers. When I got home I went to the Holy Scriptures (which I was only superficially familiar with) and I began to read from beginning to end. Almost immediately, I began to recognize the significance of the number eight (or octave). It was for me a startling revelation. After that, one thing providentially happened after another and I began writing my conversations with our Father down in my prayer journal. From this experience and the dialogues came *The Holy Octave of Consecration to God Our Father.*

Q. *Why do you think you were being called by the Father?*

A. If we were chosen to do God's work based on uncommon sanctity, I would not be a likely candidate. If anything, I am a typical woman who was born at the mid-point of this century, grew up in America in the 50's and 60's, went to college and had a family. I have the same weaknesses as everyone else and have made many of the poor choices and mistakes common to every human being. Sometimes I think of myself as the "poster child for prodigal children."

Perhaps our Father called me to this particular work because He has graced me with skills in writing, researching, and teaching. I also have a longstanding interest in culture and how it affects our relationship with God—particularly in the areas of media, science, medicine, technology, etc. My life also seems to have been touched by many of the major issues of our present-day culture.

Q. *Has God the Father ever appeared to you, as in an apparition?*

A. I have never seen any corporeal visions. I see our Father in prayer, in my heart. These experiences are very real, very touching, very powerful, and very memorable.

Q. *How long have these experiences been going on?*

A. I began hearing the voice of our Father interiorly while I was writing a prayer journal during an Ignatian retreat in the mid-1990's. I was advised to stop listening to the voice of God by the retreat director, but experienced the voice again strongly on that July day when I was told to "Look up!" After, I learned that this experience occurred on the feast of St. Ignatius. I again began writing down my dialogues with our Father in my prayer journal.

Q. *Tell us how you hear His voice? In your heart or ears?*

A. I do not hear our Father's voice audibly through my physical senses, my ears. Rather, I hear His voice in my heart. It is different than an imaginative voice. Sometimes it comes unexpectantly. Sometimes I hear His voice while I am actively involved with my own thought processes. In other words, the two things can occur simultaneously. Often, He will repeat things if I hesitate to write them down. But He never forces me. The dialogue is always consensual.

Q. *Were you afraid at first?*

A. I was not "afraid." Our Father's voice is never frightening. I would better describe my reaction as confused and concerned. I never wanted to be mislead or to mislead others. This was my constant prayer to our Father. For a long time, I questioned what was happening to me. I agonized over it. But so many providential things happened related to the dialogue. And the Scripture readings our Father gave me were so closely related to the dialogues. The content was so far beyond anything I could have imagined. In fact, if I try to replicate our Father's words, I cannot. I am unable to simulate His content and style.

I think it is human to doubt this type of experience. And certainly I did. I needed to have our Father demonstrate their authenticity and reassure me over and over again—which He did.

Q. *How often does He speak to you? Where at?*

A. My spiritual experiences include epiphanies and dialogue. Epiphanies come as powerful and unexpected insight—any time and any place. Usually, they occur during the day when I am active and take me totally by surprise. These are communicated to me as ideas rather than as a voice. The dialogues usually occur in a much more structured environment. I pray the rosary or chaplet and follow this with an entry in my prayer journal. Our Father then speaks to me and a dialogue occurs. When I dialogue, I take time to quiet myself, usually when my family is gone during the day or when they are asleep at night.

These dialogues would take place whenever I sat down to pray and journal. Sometimes when my life was unusually hectic, several days would pass between dialogues. Sometimes, when I felt the need, I would dialogue more than once a day.

I felt that our Father was always with me—especially during dialogues. At times, I would just sit in the Presence of our Father; other times I was lead only to a reading. There were several times of crisis or illness when I spoke to our Father and I heard His voice separate from the more formal prayer journaling.

I feel our Father is always with me and all His children and that He is available to us whenever we need Him or He needs to communicate something to us. I find myself thinking of and talking to our Father throughout the day.

Q. *Do you record all your conversations?*

A. I record only the dialogues in my formal prayer journal. If there is something our Father wants to speak to me about, I will feel a strong prompting to do this. It usually occurs when I have gone several days without journaling due to family obligations. When this happens, I try to journal so that it is written down. I also attempt to include epiphanies in the journal.

I often find myself talking to our Father throughout my busy day, asking Him to help me, commenting on something that has happened, etc. Many times our Father will tell me to have peace or that He loves me and He is with Me. This happens outside formal journaling, usually when I am having some sort of difficulty. This is not recorded in the journal.

Q. *You once said you were advised that God doesn't speak to His children like that. Tell us what happened with the priest who told you this and why you destroyed the original messages.*

A. Several years ago, during a retreat, I was instructed by a priest to begin writing a meditative prayer journal. During this journaling process, I began to hear what I believed to be the voice of our Father within me and to experience interior visions. When I spoke to the priest about this, he told me that God doesn't communicate with us this way, He explained that we should operate by faith only, be highly suspicious of experiences like this, and that we shouldn't desire to hear God's voice or to have visions. This advice disturbed and concerned me so much that I destroyed all my journals.

This saddened me because for the first time in my life, I had felt very, very close to God. The dialogues created an intimacy between myself and God that hadn't existed before. I found that

I was relating to Him in a personal, not impersonal manner. I found that I missed Him and felt a tremendous loss. Our Father became the focus of My Life, and after destroying the journals and feeling that I could never dialogue with our Father again, I felt desolate and very empty.

After the retreat, I continued to recite formal prayers, but I felt our Father drawing me back to Himself—He didn't seem to want an impersonal, superficial relationship, He wanted something different. I felt that He wanted me to speak directly to Him and that, likewise, He wanted to speak directly to me.

After the experience with the eight lights, I began journaling again. I felt our Father wanted an intimate relationship not only with me—but with all of us. I have come to understand that our Father doesn't want one-way communication, with us talking "at" Him. Rather, He wants us to listen for His voice and see Him in His Creation (especially in each other)—to see and hear Him in our soul.

Q. *How would you describe the voice of God the Father?*

A. Our Father's voice is the voice of a man—not old, not young, but at the prime of life. It has energy and power—but extraordinary tenderness and compassion. His voice elicits love, not fear. Sometimes His voice is commanding, but never angry. It is not flat and sterile, but lyrical and passionate—passionate with love for His children.

Q. *Have you seen the Father in visions? Tell us about the most extraordinary vision you have had.*

A. Yes, frequently during dialoguing and sometimes after Communion I see our Father interiorly. I don't believe I can single out one vision. What is most memorable is that I am in the intimate Presence of our Father. It may be on a mountaintop watching the sun rise, in a meadow as He calls His children home, near a campfire telling me we must prepare for a battle, or in a place deep in my heart. But the theme is always the same. He greatly desires that all His children come home to Him and that this time is important—we must choose.

Q. *What exactly does He look like? Does He look old? Does He have a long white beard? How was He dressed?*

A. As with His voice, our Father is neither young nor old. He is in the prime of Life. His hair is dark, slightly wavy, and slightly longer than shoulder length. He has no beard or mustache. His eyes are brilliant blue. His clothing has never really seemed important to me. His eyes and smile are what draws my attention.

Q. *Does God the Father seem happy or harsh?*

A. Our Father has never seemed harsh. He seems serious and concerned, sometimes even sad about His children. This causes Him great suffering. Many times, though, He smiles, very, very gently and lovingly. He also has a sense of humor and when I've been terribly sad, He has tried to make me laugh or smile.

When I was working on *The Holy Octave of Consecration to God Our Father*, I would occasionally have uncertainties and He would show me the "8" in the most unexpected places. And I would smile and even laugh at the strange, mysterious, and even sometime humorous ways of our Father.

Q. *Does God the Father ever get angry in your conversations with Him?*

A. No, I can't say "angry." Concerned, serious, and powerful are how I would describe it—like a parent who has lost their children and is frantically looking for them.

Q. *What message is the most significant one, in your opinion, that really revealed Him to you?*

A. I don't really view the dialogues as separate messages but the ongoing unfolding of one unified message. The message is this—

God is our one true Father and we are His true children. Our Father has been waiting for His prodigal children to return home. These are critical times and we must make a free-will choice—to choose God Our Father and His Love, Mercy, and Holy Will. This period is special, and soon this time of tremendous grace will be over. It is God's Plan that His children know, love, and honor Him by consecrating themselves to Him and by celebrating His feast day (*The Holy Octave of Consecration to God Our Father*).

This is directly tied into our Lady's Triumph and the coming of our Father's Kingdom on earth as it is in heaven. We have not begun to understand yet our inheritance as the children of God.

Q. *Have you experienced any miracles with Him?*

A. There have been, what I consider, private miracles and ongoing providential occurrences. But my love for our Father, the work that has been done, and His Presence with me are more miraculous than anything I could ever ask for.

Q. *Have you seen Mary?*

A. Yes. To me, she looks very much as she is represented in the Fatima statue. She is very loving and maternal. There is nothing to fear from her. Our Lady comes to me when I am sick or weary—she is our true Mother. In fact, she seems more my mother than my earthly mother, whom I love dearly.

Q. *Have you seen Jesus?*

A. Yes. Often, I see Him on the Cross. He is always with our Lady.

Q. *What role has Mary played in this plan?*

A. Our Lady has always appeared as a comforter and one who gives advice. My understanding is that she will triumph when the children of God return to their Father. This will occur when she crushes the head of the seducer who wants nothing more than to separate us from our Father.

Q. *Has He spoken about the sacraments?*

A. Yes, I have come to understand and appreciate our Father's true
   Presence in the Holy Sacraments. He as said that we should
   approach Him through the Sacraments and the devotion He has
   given us. Our Father has explained that the Church with its
   Sacraments was designed so that we could become "real"
   children of God, of His own being and image. Mary shapes and
   leads us, so Jesus may dwell in us. In this way, our Father is with
   us. This is His most fervent desire. I was also told that the "Day
   of the Lord" approaches and that we must all prepare ourselves in
   body, mind, and soul. We need to purify ourselves, availing
   ourselves of the Holy Sacraments and preaching the good news.
   Our Father explained that a time would come when the
   Sacraments would be administered by a scant few, but that the
   Church would not die....a new time and new traditions were
   coming.

Q. *The Father speaks to you of "Mercy with Justice." Tell us what you
   believe this means.*

A. My understanding is that the words "mercy" and "justice" are
   not antithetical—they are not oppositional or contradictory.
   Instead, because of the condition of the world, our Father's
   justice—in correcting what's wrong, making things right,
   placing us back in sync with His Will—is, in fact, merciful.
   Without His "merciful justice," we would completely destroy
   ourselves and separate ourselves from God eternally.

Q. *The Father said to you, "The time has come for a reunion with Him."
   What will be this reunion? How will it occur?*

A. Our Father wants all His children to come together in peace. He
   wants us all to come home to Him. The only way these two
   things can and will occur is when we individually and collectively
   embrace God as our true Father and we recognize our inheritance

as the children of God. Only then will we have the Peace of God. I also believe He is giving us a means for this reunion through *The Holy Octave of Consecration to God Our Father.*

Q. *Are these events in Scripture? Are prophecies being fulfilled here, in your opinion?*

A. Yes, I believe they are being fulfilled. From the early days of the dialogue, our Father has always drawn me to particular readings in Holy Scripture which I believe highlight, support, or clarify the dialogue. Many of the readings have come from the Old Testament, especially the prophetic books.

   The selected passages many times deal with chastisement. But they also promise restoration. Several dialogues and readings have specifically referred to the antichrist and end times—especially how they relate to our breaking God's laws and creating our own laws and idols.

Q. *This plan, can it also be delayed, canceled, or mitigated?*

A. Our Father has always said this is a special time of "choice." Our choices are directly related to consequences. Recently, He said we can "tremble in fear or tremble with love of Him." I also understand that when He does come to us, the state of our preparedness (based on our choices) will have a great deal to do with how we undergo the transformation that will take place.

Q. *How are we, as the Father said it to you, all prodigal children? Tell us about your vision of the passage in the Bible on this subject.*

A. One day while dialoguing, I saw the Holy Scriptures opened to the middle—to the Parable of the Prodigal Son. Then I saw the Book of Genesis at the Beginning of the Bible and the Book of Revelation at the end. Our Father helped me understand that the entire Bible and our salvation history were about this one parable and it has to do with each and every one of us—individually and collectively.

From the time of our first parents, every single human being (with the exception of Jesus and Mary) has left the home of our Father through choice. Our only purpose for existing is to find our way back home to our Father through our free-will choice to return and by saying "Yes" to His Holy Will.

Q. *Has the Father spoken to you about the Pope? Have you had any visions of the Pope? Will the Pope be martyred or go into exile?*

A. I have had visions of the Holy Father being in danger.

Q. *Has the Father spoken about His son, Jesus, and the Redemption?*

A. My understanding is that our Father loves us so much, He wants us home with Him forever. Since we left His house (Paradise) to wander, lost, He sent His Son Jesus to redeem us so that we could return and then lead us back home. Jesus shows us the way home and reveals the Truth that God is our Father. Through, with, and in Him, we find our inheritance—eternal Life with our Father.

Q. *Your messages are often accompanied by Scripture quotes. Why is this? Tell us about the meaning of the verses given to you to read.*

A. In the early days of the dialogue, I reasonably questioned the authenticity of what was happening to me. I asked our Father for a sign. Each time I did this, He would draw me to a Scripture passage. For me, this was miraculous because I am not a Biblical expert, nor have I memorized the Bible chapter and verse. I would either hear the biblical citation, see it visually, or I would be lead to open Scripture, lay my hands on the open page and "feel" the passage.

These quotes almost always compliment, support, and clarify what I have been given in dialogue. Sometimes, however, they deal with preceding or succeeding dialogue. This can only be appreciated by reading and studying the dialogue as a whole. The Scripture readings, when taken as a whole, focus primarily on God's children rebelling, turning away from Him, and leaving home, as well as our Father's merciful chastisements, the restoration of the Temple, and the coming of the New Jerusalem. The theme of vigilance and preparedness for battle are also included.

Q. *We are, the Father said, "Living in a grace-filled period." Is this the same as Divine Mercy?*

A. I believe Jesus told Sr. Faustina that a period of Mercy would proceed a period of Justice. And that it was important to respond now, during this period of Mercy. Similarly, in what our Father is relating to me, I understand that this is a special and critical period in mankind's salvation history. This is a time of choice. How is it grace-filled? I believe that through our Lady, our Father is releasing untold graces to soften our hearts and enlighten us so that we accept the Truth that God is our Father, we are His children, and that ultimately we need to be reunited with Him.

Finally, based on the dialogues, I do not believe that this period will last forever—it will eventually end. Our Father has used the word "soon" several times in reference to this. He has said that after the Light has been withdrawn, it will be very, very difficult for those children who are still lost and wandering to find their way home. He is very insistent on this point, and this seems to concern Him very much.

Q. *The Father has spoken to you about the Divine Family. What is the Divine Family?*

A. Our Father has used this term several times during the dialogue. I don't think any human can fully grasp what this means. But my understanding is that the Holy Trinity is relational; it is a family: the Father, His Son, and the Spirit of Love that flows between them. By virtue of Jesus' human and divine nature, His mother Mary is drawn into this Divine Family—she is the Mother of God. Through Mary and in Jesus, we, likewise, are brought into the Heart of our Father. We have the overwhelming privilege of being children of God.

This is not to say that Mary or mankind are part of the Trinity. Rather, we are children of God through Mary and in Jesus and the Holy Spirit. This, I believe, is what our Father means when he refers to the Divine Family.

Q. *The Father has spoken to you about chapels that are 8X8X8. Can you tell what He wants? Can anyone build them? Will the Father be there in a special way?*

A. I believe the reference to chapels is both symbolic and literal. 8X8X8 would typically designate height, width, and depth. We can only assume, then, that the chapels are intended to be built physically. However, no exact measurement is given (feet, inches, etc.). Therefore, the proportions would remain constant but the actual size could vary.

Our Father mentioned "chapels" (plural), and so we can also assume that there is to be more than one huge Church. These chapels would, I believe, be places where we could better know, love, and honor our Father. Most importantly, however, I see these chapels symbolizing a new way of life centered around our Father. In other words, our Father would be the central figure in our lives, in our culture, in our world. These chapels represent a new relationship between God and His children. In a sense, they represent our own souls–temples of the Holy Spirit.

Lastly, I see the chapels as symbolic of the "Church" as a whole. I believe it is our Father's desire that all His children be reunited and that they know, love, and honor Him. Then He will be with us in a truly new way.

Interestingly, 8X8X8, provides us with three numbers of eight. Three signifies the Holy Trinity, but it also refers to the triad of knowing, loving, and honoring our Father. And the number eight itself represents the Holy Octave of Consecration to God Our Father and the coming of a new era.

Q. *What is the meaning behind the ejaculation, "I love you, Father, and I give myself to You?" This seems to be a prayer that is a shift from "reparation" to "restoration."*

A. This ejaculation accomplishes several things. First, in saying it from the heart, we are addressing and, thereby, acknowledging God as our Father. Secondly, we are expressing our love for our Father. Thirdly, we are offering ourselves totally to Him. We are giving ourselves back to the One who made us. And in this act of surrender, we are acceding to His Holy Will. It is a short ejaculation, but it says so much. It is, in essence, the most basic and direct form of consecration.

Q. *Tell us about the Octaves in the Chaplet and the Consecration. Tell us about each of the themes. What do they mean?*

A. The chaplet of *The Holy Octave of Consecration to God Our Father* is made up of a Major Octave outlining Mankind's Salvation History and a Minor Octave detailing our approach to God Our Father:

MAJOR OCTAVES

The Disobedience and Exile of God's Children

God Our Father was with us at the beginning in the Paradise He created for us—the Paradise of His Divine Will. Seduced by Satan, Adam and Eve chose not to do the Will of God and were, therefore, expelled from this Paradise and denied God's intimate presence. However, our Father promised that "the woman" would ultimately defeat the evil that had caused this separation—the evil of saying "No" to God's Will.

The Presence of God With His Children
During Old Testament Times

Although God's children were expelled from Paradise by their choice not to do God's Will, God never abandoned them. He was present with them from the beginning. In Old Testament times, He manifested His presence through His own voice, the words of His Prophets, in the burning bush, in a pillar of smoke, and in the Ark of the Covenant. After God rescued His children from the bondage of Egypt, He requested that they celebrate the Feast of Tabernacles for eight days each year. He wanted them to remember that He loved them, He saved them, and He was present with them. Later when God was present in the Ark of the Covenant, Solomon built a magnificent Temple to house it. He then celebrated an eight-day Feast of Dedication in preparation for God's presence in the Temple. And God responded by manifesting His presence in a tangible and powerful way. At the close of the Old Testament, the Maccabees's re-instituted this eight-day feast to purify and re-dedicate the Temple that had been defiled through pagan influence, so the Presence of God would dwell with them once more.

The Fiat of Mary Our Mother

Mary gave her "Yes" when the angel Gabriel came to her and asked her to be the mother of the Son of God. The Holy Spirit came upon her and the power of God our Father overshadowed her. In saying "Yes" to God's Will, Mary (the "woman") allowed God to be present with His children in a new way. She actually became the "New Ark," a living tabernacle of Jesus, the Second Person of the Holy Trinity—mankind's Savior—who with His Mother's cooperation, would restore the exiled children of God to their Father.

The Fiat of Jesus Our Savior

Jesus offered His "Yes" to God our Father during His Passion in the Garden of Gethsemani. Through His Passion, Death, and Resurrection, Jesus redeemed us, defeating the sin (saying "No" to God's Will) and death (separation and exile from God) which Satan introduced into the world. Through Jesus, His Church, and His Sacraments, we could now return to God our Father and have eternal life.

The Sending of the Holy Spirit

Before ascending to His Father, Jesus promised that He would not leave us as orphans. He asked God our Father to send the Holy Spirit. In doing this, God could again be present with us in a new way. It was now "possible" for God not only to be "with" us (as in Old Testament times), but "in" us.

The Choice of God's Children to Return to Their Father

As prodigal children of God our Father, we are given the

opportunity (individually and collectively) to make a sincere, free-will decision to return to our Father's House. This means deciding to turn away from our own will, our own sinfulness, our own worldliness, and "convert" or turn back toward the presence of God our Father.

The Fiat of God's Children

In giving our "Yes" to God our Father, in agreeing to do His Will in all things, in giving ourselves completely to Him, He comes to dwell in us and we dwell in Him—we are home with our Father. We become temples of the Living God. In a sense, heaven and earth are joined: "Thy Kingdom come. Thy will be done on earth as it is in heaven."

The Coming of the New Jerusalem

The New Jerusalem is the eventual conclusion of our Salvation History—when heaven and earth will be transformed, when mankind will finally be fully restored to God our Father, and when God will manifest His presence and dwell with His children forever in a new way.

MINOR OCTAVES

Praise: Praise God Our Father and His Creation.
Thanksgiving: Thank Him for all that He has done for you.
Offering: Offer Him all that He has given you.
Repentance: Ask for His forgiveness when you offend Him.
Inheritance: Acknowledge and celebrate that you are truly a child of God; embrace the joys and responsibilities.
Fiat: Say "Yes" to God's Will in all things.
Fidelity: Be loyal and persevering.
Consecration: Give yourself to God Our Father.

Q   *How often should we pray the chaplet?*

A   I believe our Father gave us the chaplet as a means of knowing, loving, and honoring Him. Our Father wants us to have a loving, intimate relationship with us. To have a loving, intimate relationship with Him, we need to spend time with Him on a regular basis. Ideally, we should pray the chaplet each day. And, certainly, we should pray the formal chaplet during the *Holy*

Octave of Consecration to God Our Father.

Q. *Have you seen angels?*

A. During prayer I have seen angels as I see our Father—in my heart. Raphael, especially, has played an important role in this work.

Q. *Have you been to heaven, hell, or purgatory? Have you been told about these eternal destinations?*

A. I believe that wherever our Father is, that is heaven. So in that sense, I have experienced heaven. I have not, however, seen purgatory or hell. In the dialogues, our Father primarily stresses His desire that all His children return to Him. I know the possibility of His children not finding their way home exists, though, because our Father is extremely concerned that they do find their way home. He tells me that it will be very difficult when His Light is withdrawn—when this special period of grace ends. I don't believe I needed to "see" the actual suffering of purgatory or the horror of hell to believe that they exist. His loving and passionate concern that none of His children be separated from Him is what thoroughly convinced me.

Q. *Have any saints come to you?*

A. During the dialogues I have seen young David several times. He has always beckoned me to follow him up a hill or mountain. At the top was a new church or temple. I wasn't allowed to go in yet, but we admired it from the outside. David seemed very excited. Our Father has spoken to me about Abraham, Isaac, Mary Magdalene, Ruth, Judith, etc. I have also had a recurring vision during the dialogues which involves Peter and the apostles.

Q. *Have you seen Satan? Demons?*

A. At the beginning of my spiritual experiences in the late 1980's, I had a dream that was more real than if I had been awake. In that dream, I was in a courtyard. Across the courtyard was a man—a very attractive man. I was drawn to him and seemed to run toward him. But as I got closer, he became more and more horrid looking, uglier and more hideous than anything I could describe. He was so horrifying that my heart seized up and I began to experience what I feel was a heart attack and death. I didn't know what to do and so I prayed the Hail Mary. I had to pray very slowly, as I could barely breathe or move from the crushing pain. But the pain remained and I frantically grasped for something to save me. I then began to say the *Our Father* prayer. Each word came out agonizingly slow. By the time I got to the last word, the pain eased up enough that I could breathe better, and I woke up. I was shaking and terrified for hours after that.

At first, I was confused about why I wasn't able to stop with the Hail Mary, and I had to go on to the *Our Father* prayer. I believe now that the hideous being I experienced was Satan, and I was being shown that our Lady always takes us to our Father who ultimately "delivers us from evil."

Q. *Tell us about the love God the Father has for His people.*

A. How can I begin to explain how much our Father loves us? That has been the primary focus of all my dialogues with Him. And it is not an impersonal, intellectual love. It is a real love—very personal, intimate, and intense. His love for us is very protective, very tender, very involved, very vigilant. His loving Presence is with us always. He may at times "feel" far away, but this is how we "feel." It is our perception, not the truth and reality of God.

Q. *Tell us about the Father and each soul He creates.*

A. Because of His intense, passionate love for us, He desires that not one child be lost to Him. He wants every single one of us to come home. His love is illustrated in the parable of the shepherd who goes off to find the one lost sheep. Our Father wants us all.

It is difficult for us to realize that God made us, knows everything about us, has counted every hair on our heads, and knitted our very bones in our mother's womb. He knows us better than we know ourselves. We are His children, in the most real and total sense of the word.

He cares about everything that happens to us. He wants to be close to us. He wants to be part of our lives. He wants us to love Him as He loves us. Most importantly, He loves us in all times, in all places, in all situations—He loves us unconditionally.

Q. *Why do you think people are afraid of the Father?*

A. We are not born with fear or terror of our Creator, our Father. Instead, we learn to be afraid of Him. The word "fear" is used in Holy Scripture to describe how we should feel about our Father, but I do not believe the word is used in quite the same way we use it today. Most of us today think of fear as meaning that we are afraid of something that could hurt or kill us. I do not understand the use of the word in Scripture quite this way. I understand that the fear we should feel as God's children is twofold: (1) tremendous "awe" of our Father, (2) extreme apprehension over being separated from our Father. But we have somehow absorbed a mentality of fearing our own true Father. And this "fear" causes us to avoid Him.

This unfair and inaccurate picture of our Father has made if difficult, if not impossible, for His children to know and love Him—and it stands to reason that honoring someone we don't know or love would not be a priority for us. Because the true face of our Father has been hidden for so long, most of mankind has forgotten Him, put Him aside, or denied His very existence.

Q. *Why do most people only pray to Jesus? Has He spoken of this?*

A. I believe that if we could all climb to the top of a mountain and look down on mankind's salvation history, we would have a much better perspective of God's relationship with His children. We need to remember that our Father created us for His own Heart to be with Him forever, and that since man chose not to do

God's Will and separate himself from eternal Life with God, our Father has grieved and been actively with us until we are one day restored to Him.

In this effort, our Father sent His Son Jesus to ransom us so we could return, to show us the way home, and to reveal the Truth that we are God's children. Jesus is also present with us and sustains us on our journey home to our Father. Jesus asked our Father to send the Holy Spirit to purify and refine us so that the Presence of God could dwell in us.

We must understand, then, that our Father sent Jesus and the Holy Spirit to us for the sole purpose of bringing us back home to Him. For some reason, however, we have confused the "way" with the end or goal of our journey. We misguidedly refuse to look beyond Jesus, forgetting that His mission was to shepherd and lead the prodigal children back home to their Father.

If we read the Gospels with a fresh perspective and highlight everything Jesus ever said, we would clearly see that He knows, loves, and honors His Father, and that He came to teach us to do the same. Jesus would be the first one to direct us to our Father. That is why our Father sent Him to us. We need only read the words of Jesus.

Yes, Jesus is also God and part of the Holy Trinity. But the Holy Trinity is relational. The three persons are not identical, nor are they one faceless entity. They are three distinct Persons. The mission of Jesus the Son and the Holy Spirit is to restore us to our Father. Because Jesus and the Holy Spirit are God, part of the Holy Trinity, we should also know, love, and honor Them. But we must not neglect our Father, nor should we forget that our only purpose for existing is to return to Him.

Q. *Has the Father spoken to you about the fact that no churches are in His name? That His honor is not very visible?*

A. This is related to the previous question. We are a very Christ-centered Church, to the disadvantage of our Father and the Holy Spirit. I don't believe we can have a Trinitarian God and unequally focus on one member of that Trinity. We need to re-look at this as a relational process in the Holy Trinity. Jesus and the Holy Spirit moving us always toward our Father. We must remember that all things proceed from the Source, God our Father.

But because the Catholic Church focuses almost exclusively on Jesus, we see this reflected in the names of our churches, paintings, statues, prayers, hymns, devotions, etc.

God our Father wants us to honor Jesus, Mary, and the saints in this way. However, I believe He is saddened that we have forgotten Him—and surely we have. Ask yourself how we honor God our Father in the Church. This glaring oversight should serve as an unsettling epiphany.

Q. *You said that the Father is desirous of consecration to Him using an 8-day (octave) consecration. Tell us about this consecration.*

A. The most compelling precedent for consecrating ourselves to God Our Father over an eight-day feast, or octave, is found in John 10:22-39. This passage describes how Jesus, during the eight-day Feast of Dedication, revealed that He was consecrated to God our Father. Jesus further explains that He consecrated Himself to our Father so we, too, could be consecrated in truth (Jn 17:19-21). The concept of "Consecration to God our Father" is crucial because, as Jesus tells us, "the hour is coming, and now is, when the true worshipers will worship the Father in spirit and truth, for such the Father seeks to worship him. God is a spirit, and those who worship him must worship in spirit and truth" (Jn 4:23-24). If we follow Jesus, if we model ourselves after Him, shouldn't we also consecrate ourselves to God our Father during an eight-day feast, so that we, too, can adore Him "in spirit and in truth?"

Q. *Why 8 days? Is there some meaning to this? Is it Scriptural?*

A. The concept of an "octave," or 8-day feast, has been significant in our relationship with God since the beginning of our Salvation History. It is not by coincidence that Jesus chose to reveal His consecration to God our Father on the eight-day Feast of Dedication. Clearly, the octave symbolizes a designated period of time when God's children grow and God's relationship with them changes or is transformed.

Unlike other feasts and consecration methods, *The Holy Octave of Consecration to God Our Father* views the "big picture" of our Salvation History. It involves the entire process of our spiritual journey which includes Mary, our Mother; Jesus, our God and our Savior; and the Holy Spirit, our God and our Sanctifier—with progression always toward God our Father.

God's Word in both the Old and New Testaments provides us with extensive Scriptural support for an eight-day, or "octave," format. From the Book of Genesis to the Gospels and Epistles, the number "eight" is used to signify salvation, covenant, purification, and dedication. Perhaps, more importantly, it is used to indicate the end of one era and the beginning of another in which God is revealed, manifested, and present to His children in a new way.

Q. *What kind of feast day does the Father request?*

A. *The Holy Octave of Consecration to God Our Father,* in its most powerful form, is intended as a formal eight-day feast for God our Father culminating on the first Sunday of the "eighth" month, God our Father's month—August. The solemn eighth day of *The Holy Octave of Consecration to God Our Father* would be celebrated under the title of "The Feast of the Father of All Mankind." On this day, the children of God would come together to know, love, and honor their one true Father.

Q. *Is this related to Mother Eugenia's (1932) revelations?*

A. Several years ago, I read the messages of Mother Eugenia and was stunned. I found them absorbing and but also unsettling. I found them unsettling because I had never really thought of God our Father as a real person before—not one who really wanted to have a relationship with His children. And unsettling because I wasn't sure how to relate to more than one person in the Holy Trinity. It almost felt like I was being disloyal to Jesus, or worshiping more than one God. After I realized the relational process of the Holy Trinity and that we pass through the gate (Jesus) to get into the sheepfold (Heart of our Father), I understood better. We are all intended for the Heart of our Father. God our Father's message to Mother Eugenia helped me begin to think about these things and to discover my Father. Nearly a year later, I heard the voice of our Father tell me to look up—and that's when I saw the eight lights. That's when the work on *The Holy Octave of Consecration to God Our Father* began.

Through both Mother Eugenia's messages and through the dialogue, our Father has asked for a feast—a feast entitled *The Feast of the Father of All Mankind*. He also asked that the feast be on the first Sunday of August, the eighth month.

For some reason, Mother Eugenia's messages were approved by the Church, but were sealed away without explanation. I believe *The Holy Octave of Consecration to God Our Father* is the fruition and culmination of that earlier effort.

Q. *Why is this feast day necessary? Why August?*

A. I believe that our Father desires a special feast that specifically honors Him. The Church has feast days for Jesus, the Holy Spirit, Mary, and the Saints—but none for our Father. Through the dialogue, I understand that this Feast Day is necessary at this time, that the Church is somehow incomplete until this is done. I also understand that this Feast is directly related to our Lady's Triumph and the Era of Peace.

This cannot be a Feast for the sake of adding another feast to the Church calendar. Instead, it is what the Feast would accomplish:

mankind understanding that God is our Father, that we choose to know, love, and honor Him, and that we say "Yes" to His Will. This is accomplished by consecrating ourselves to Him and more clearly understanding the Holy Trinity.

I understand that our Lady will Triumph when the prodigal children return to their Father. Only then will an Era of Peace be granted because God will live among us in a new and special way. Our lives, our culture, will be built around God—God will not be separated and set apart from our daily lives.

Until we know, love, and honor our Father, how can the prodigal children return home? How can the children be reconciled with each other and with God? How can there be peace among men— the peace of God?

Our Father has asked for this Feast in August, specifically the first Sunday of August. This consecration feast, I believe, will help usher in a new era.

Q. *Tell about the Eternal Father and His Fatherhood, as our Father?*

A. When we read Holy Scripture, we see that our Father has always been with His prodigal children, from the day they exiled themselves from Him in Paradise to the present. He has never left us as orphans. His words and actions in Holy Scripture demonstrate that He is a loving, compassionate, protective father, not only in the Old Testament, but also as revealed by His Son Jesus in the New Testament. God's Fatherhood may seem distant and non-related to us, something in ancient books. "What does this have to do with us," we might ask. But it has everything to do with us—personally.

Jesus offered His life for each one of us, so that we might know the Truth—that God is our true Father and we are His true children. These are not just words, it is reality. And God our Father desires a real relationship with each one of His children. He is the most tender of Fathers. Never absent, He is always with us—in every time, place, and circumstance.

He knows us intimately—He made us and has been present with us always He loves us completely, and wants us to choose to know, love, and honor Him so that we might live with Him eternally.

He cares for us like a tender mother with her babe and protects us like the fiercest warrior. He wants to be involved in every aspect of our lives.

God is "the" Father and His is "the" family—how great and wonderful and awesome this is—we are known, loved, cared for, and protected by the Creator of the entire universe, of all that is: He is our Father.

Q. *Why do you call him, "The Father of All Mankind."*

A. I refer to Him as the Father of All Mankind because that is what He refers to Himself as in the dialogue. This title is very important and illuminating because it establishes that (1) God is our Father and (2) He is the Father of all men—no exceptions. If we ponder this, we will realize that we are all brothers and sisters. We belong to one family and have one Father and one Mother. We are all made in the image and likeness of God, and God lives in all of us.

Certainly, if we truly understand the implications of this, we would never fight, never hate one another. We would freely choose to live in the peace and love of God.

When the world comes to embrace our Father and this title, peace will come to the world.

Q. *The Father speaks to you about teaching His*   *children "after the storm." What does this means? What storm?*

A. Based on our Father's comments in the dialogue, I understand that an imminent upheaval is coming—in our Father's words,

"Soon." I think this is supported by events that have been occurring during this century. As we evolve more and more into a Godless global culture, we generate consequences. I believe that the consequences for our ill-advised choices constitute the "storm," our Father refers to. We are bringing chaos and havoc down upon ourselves. As with storms in nature, there will be darkness and damage—but after this will be clearing and the fresh air of renewal and transformation.

After the storm our Father refers to is over, mankind will relate to Him differently. A transformation will have occurred, and life will be lived in a new way—life lived intimately with God our Father.

I understand that all the revelation and work that are taking place to help mankind see the true face of our Father are desperately needed.

Early in the dialogues, I symbolically saw a green valley with sheep—and Jesus, Mary, and the Apostles were up on the hillside watching over and caring for these sheep. There were passes at both ends of this valley. The sheep entered at one end through a narrow pass and exited at the other end—a very rocky, craggy pass. And as the sheep approached to pass through this opening, there was an intense, dark storm. A Cross of Light illuminated the sky above the opening. On the other side was a large, bleak, dry desert. And our Lady, Jesus, and the Apostles led the sheep. But there were sandstorms and many of the sheep wandered off. Finally, they came to a lush area near a great body of water. Here life was begun over again—simply and purely with God.

Q. *Has He spoken to you about chastisement? Have you had visions of the world in chastisement or after?*

A. Yes, I have had experiences during prayer where I have seen chastisement—again, I believe through man's own choices. During one experience, I was outside and across a great wide field of grain. I saw a city far off in the distance. Suddenly, the city exploded into smoke and flames; it was hot, red, and glowing. Another time, our Lady showed me the earth and it was desolate and there were men's bones scattered about. It seemed sterile and lifeless.

Not only did I see the vision of the valley, the storm, and the desert, as I mentioned previously, but I also saw a lush area near water which I believe represented a new way of life after the storm. I have also seen a radiant city where I was with our Father. However, the city was still empty. And our Father seemed to be waiting.

Q. *What is His plan for mankind, as you understand?*

A. God our Father's only Plan for mankind is that His children return to Him—it is as simple as that. The more we pull away, run away, from our Father and His Will, the farther we will have to go to return to Him, the more our hearts will be hardened, the more we will need to undergo to be purified and refined.

Our Father wants to live with us and in us forever—this is His Plan for mankind.

Q. *Will many people die if there is a chastisement? Has He said?*

A. Again, our Father doesn't use graphic visions of death and destruction to terrify me. I see things symbolically and I understand what "could" be: desolate earth and bones, burning cities–or new life in God.

If only we understood what could happen if we keep making the wrong choices—choices not in God's Will, but outside it. Desolation and death are the consequences of being outside God's Will.

Q. *The Father speaks about all "being transformed into Him." What is this transformation?*

A. I understand that some sort of transformation will take place—man and the world will undergo a change. I don't quite know how to explain this except to say that God will be more fully in those who invite Him, who are open to Him. This process will have an effect—those who are not prepared will experience great suffering, perhaps even death. But all will be reborn in God.

Q. *Will all souls be transformed into Him?*

A. This is God's sincere desire. This is God's Will for His children. We can choose to be in or outside God's Will. It is our choice.

Q. *Has the Father spoken to you about suffering? About sin?*

A. Suffering is a sacred thing. It brings us closer to God. When we suffer, we are like Jesus. When we suffer, we can choose to reach out to God, to ask Him to help us. This shows our dependence on God, our childlikeness. And we can choose to offer our suffering to God to be used for the good of our souls and the souls of others. No suffering should ever be wasted. It is a gift from God.

The term "sin" has fallen from favor in our times. However, all "sin" means is that we have chosen to do, say, or think something that is outside God's Will. We have separated ourselves from God by our free will. God's Will is where God is—it is Paradise, Heaven, His Kingdom—His Heart.

Q. *What is the most fascinating thing He has told you?*

A. That He loves Me and that I am His child—I belong to Him. This applies not only to me, but to all of us.

Q. *The Father has often spoken to you about David, Isaiah, Judith, Daniel, Abraham and other Old Testament figures. Have you seen these people in visions? Why are they so important now?*

A. I believe that our Father has used several figures and stories from the Old Testament to show me that they exist outside time and space to teach us in the present. They were not only relevant then, but for all times and places. There is a sense in the dialogues that something very profound is going to happen—soon. David, especially, has been an integral part of the dialogues. I have often seen David beckoning me,		running ahead of me to the top of a hill where there was a newly built Church. But I haven't been allowed to go in. David shows it to me and smiles with great excitement and joy. Abraham was shown to me to teach me about fatherhood and sacrifice. Judith, Mary Magdalene, and Daniel demonstrated faith, fidelity, courage, and trust. Isaiah, Ezechial, Daniel, Jeremiah, Hosea, Joel, and Micah revealed the prophetic element.

Q. *Has the Father spoken about Mary's apparitions?*

A. Yes, our Father has said that our Lady has come to mother us and prepare us to return to Him. He has specifically referred to Fatima and the Miracle of the Sun. Our Lady's mission will be completed when the one who attempts to separate us from God is defeated and we are restored to our Father.

Q. *Is now the time for the fulfillment of the Lord's prayer, "Thy Kingdom Come on Earth?"*

A. This has always been our Father's desire, His Will. According to the prayer Jesus taught us, "Thy Will be done. Thy Kingdom come on earth as it is in heaven." Doing God's Will is necessary for the full coming of His Kingdom on earth. The process is ongoing and it comes in degrees, in stages. Where God is, there is His Kingdom. So the Kingdom is inside us, around us, and apart from us in a place we will go to after we die. As St. Paul tells us, we can only see through the glass darkly now. This will change, however, when heaven touches earth. Through us, the kingdom comes when we know, love, and honor our Father, when we give Him our Fiat. It has been coming like small specks of Light, connection points, but will come more fully when mankind embraces our Father. *The Holy Octave of Consecration to God Our*

Father will, I believe, help facilitate this. And our Father is asking for this now.

Q. *Are your messages in any way connected to Luisa Piccarreta's message about Divine Will and the Kingdom of the Divine Will on Earth?*

A. I am familiar with Piccarreta's writings in a general way, having read introductory material. I have not read her advanced works, however. My sense is that what she writes about may refer to what takes places after what is transpiring now. But again, I cannot respond to this question properly because I am not fully familiar with the material, nor has our Father spoke of it to me.

Q. *How important is this feast day for the Father? What will it mean to the world? To the Church?*

A. I think much has been leading up to this Consecration Feast Day. In a sense, the Church will be more "complete," having revealed and celebrated the Three Persons of the Holy Trinity more fully—especially the Source of All, God our Father.

It will not be a "new" Church in the sense that it does away with the old. Rather, it is a more complete revelation and fulfillment of the Church—the prodigal children returning to their Father. Our Father's children will truly know, love, and honor Him—as well as the entire Holy Trinity. He will be with us, living with and in us in a new way.

I understand that the Consecration Feast would bring the Presence of God and His Peace to the world in a way previously unknown to mankind.

Q. *Is the feast day related to Mary's Triumph?*

A. Yes, I believe it is. In the Book of Genesis, God tells us the woman (Mary) will crush his (Satan's) head. This passage is positioned between the disobedience of Adam and Eve (having been seduced by Satan) and the revelation of the consequences for this act (exile from our Father).

My understanding is that Mary will triumph over Satan when the children of God are exiled no more, when they finally return back home to their Father. Jesus was sent to ransom us (pay for our sin) so we "could" return; He was also sent to show us the way back home. Jesus revealed the Truth that God is our Father and we are His children, so that we could "choose" to have Eternal Life with our Father. He also sustains us and is present with us on that journey. Like Mary and Jesus, we, too, must freely offer our "Yes" to God's Will.

The Consecration Feast Day provides us with the opportunity to do all these things. When mankind *returns* to its heavenly Father, Mary will have *triumphed* over the seducer who tempted the children into exile.

Q. *Has He spoken about the Church and Mary's Final Dogma?*

A. Yes, our Father says the dogma is right and true. However, I have been asked to separate myself from the work of promoting the dogma. I was told by our Father that I would understand this later.

Q. *Has the Father spoken about the Second Coming of Christ? Is this near?*

A. Our Father has spoken only of His coming to us and the coming of His Kingdom.

Q. *When does He want this feast day to be celebrated?*

A. Our Father has asked that His feast day be celebrated on the first Sunday of August.

Q. *Tell us about the history and meaning of the medal? What does it signify with the harp on the back of the medal?*

A. In the dialogue our Father told me that He wanted a medal struck which should be given to each individual who consecrates himself to Him. He showed me what He desired for a medal, saying that the medal was His gift to us, that it showed His Love for His children. He described it as a road map back home to Him. He asked that the medals be blessed, saying that many miracles would come about through the Consecration and Medal. Our Father explained that the medal should be worn as an outward sign to all His children and that embracing this symbol would show His children's love for Him.

Therefore, a special medal was designed to illustrate the process of this consecration. On the front of the medal is the actual consecration process. God our Father is seen in heaven reaching down to us on earth; man is seen on earth reaching up to God our Father in heaven. The force of God's Love for us is shown in the rays that proceed down from His hand; the force of our love for Him is pictured in our "fiat" radiating up to Him. These rays intersect through the Cross of Jesus. This Cross is the bridge or link between God our Father and His children. At one end, it is grounded in the earth through Mary, our Mother. It then proceeds up through the sanctifying power of the Holy Spirit into Heaven at the other end. Eight lights, signifying the Scripturally-supported Octave, are shown on the horizontal beam of the Cross. These eight lights serve to guide us on our journey back home to God our Father.

The back of the medal displays the eight-stringed harp of David, as mentioned in Psalm 6. St. Augustine understood this mystically, as symbolizing the octave—seven days of this mortal life followed by the last resurrection and the world to come. And that during our mortal life, like David, we must also feel sorrow for our sins and repent of them while here on earth. On this eight-stringed harp we have placed the eight themes or steps of the Holy Octave of Consecration to God our Father—praise, thanksgiving, offering, repentance, inheritance, fiat, fidelity, and consecration. Inside the bow of the harp are printed the words: "The rhythm and harmony of God's Will." This reminds us that when we pluck the eight strings or themes of this consecration to God Our Father, a beautiful music ascends to heaven—we are choosing to live in the rhythm and harmony of His Will.

Q. *The Father said He will come on August 1999. What does this mean?*

A. Our Father said He would come if mankind celebrated His Feast Day in 1999, which has been designated by the Church as the Year of our Creator and Father. My understanding is that our Father is telling us that if mankind knows, loves, and honors Him—if we love Him and give ourselves to Him—He will indeed come to be with and in us in a special way.

Q. *Tell us about the God the Father Scapular that He asked for. Why is it white?*

A. On day during dialogue, I saw laundered white, linen sheets hanging out to dry in the sun. My two grandmothers (who are deceased) and Our Lady came out from behind the sheets. They had been tending them. Then our Father placed the white linen scapular in my opened hand and I was told that it signified our souls and that in offering ourselves to God, our souls must be clean and white. I was told that the scapular would serve as a visual aid, so that people would understand that in offering themselves to God, they must be cleansed and purified. The scapular looks the way our souls should look before God.

Q. *"Eight" is the Peace of God, the Father said. What does this mean?*

A. I understand the meaning of this on three levels: (1) "eight" signifies the end of one era and the beginning of a new one, e.g., the Sunday of a new week. (And for us in this time, the new era, I believe, will be an era of peace.), (2) the "eight" graphically illustrates two circles intersecting and flowing into each other— the higher into the lower and then the lower into the higher— God in us and us in God, the connection of heaven and earth, His Kingdom coming to earth as it is in heaven, (3) the "eight" represents the Holy Octave which our Father referred to as an [eight-runged] ladder to Him. Through *The Holy Octave of Consecration,* we return to God and we are in His Heart, His

Kingdom, His Will, His Peace.

Q. *Tell us about the Father and Fatima. Has He spoken of Himself being involved with the message of Fatima?*

A. Yes, our Father explained that Mary's Heart will Triumph when His children return to Him; that when this occurs, there will be an Era of Peace; and that the consequences of our choice was graphically depicted in the Miracle of the Sun at Fatima.

Q. *Tell us about the "Miracle of the Sun" at Fatima with the Father. What about Russia?*

A. In the dialogue, our Father explained that He was represented in the Sun at Fatima's Miracle of the Sun. He showed me that when the Sun danced in the sky and its many colors seemed to penetrate everything it touched, that He was trying to show us that He is with and in us— in all His Creation. He also showed me that when the Sun fell toward earth, this was an attempt to show us that He was coming to us.

The reaction of many was sheer terror. The people weren't ready. And He also wanted me to know that we have choices and that there are consequences for our choices. I was made to understand that the power of the Sun was used specifically to demonstrate that if we continued to pursue and apply knowledge (Science, Medicine, Technology, etc.) "outside" His Will, that we would reap the consequences (possibly nuclear consequences which "ape" the power of the sun). However, if we chose God and His Will, our Father would come and warm us (as He did to the cold and rain-soaked people at Fatima) and fill us up with His Love and Peace.

The choice is ours. That's what my understanding is of the Miracle of the Sun at Fatima.

Q. *The Father said to you, "All that is present will cease and become new." What does this mean? When will it happen?*

A. Our Father is referring to transformation here. Only our Father knows the time when this will be accomplished. Again, my understanding is that all will be made new "in" God. God is present in His Creation now, but He will be present more fully and in a new and different way. As the world pulls farther and farther away from God, the time for consequences and eventual transformation comes ever closer. Our Father has often said, "Soon."

Q. *Who are the remnant that the Father speaks of to you?*

A. When our Father uses the term "remnant" I believe He is referring to those who are in union with Him, in the rhythm and harmony of His Will. Those who have been loyal. Those who know love, and honor God—the entire Holy Trinity, all Three Persons. Those who have overcome all obstacles to the Father.

Remnant indicates a part that remains after the remainder of the whole is removed. Many of God's children have been absorbed into our worldly culture, leaving a "remnant" that has stayed loyal to God—those who have and will survive these times of purification. Remnant can also pertain to those who are left after a chastisement. However, this term should never be used in an *elitist* sense. We must always remember that it is God's Will that not one of His little ones be lost.

Q. *Should people store food and prepare?*

A. I think it is good to want to live a more simple, basic life— closer to God and His Creation. But I have not been given any indication in the dialogue that we should head for the hills and store food and water. I'm not certain if this is necessary or appropriate for the consequences we may be enduring. I think the most important thing is to know, love, and honor God our Father—and trust in Him always.

Q. *What does the Father mean when He speaks of the Rhythm and Harmony of His Will?*

A. Our Father's Will is like beautiful music. When we are in our Father's Will, we are in "sync" with Him; we are immersed in the rhythm and order of it; we are in complimentary harmony. When we are outside our Father's Will, we are not in sync with Him; we are outside the rhythm and order of it; and our lives are discordant.

When instruments and voices are out of tune, out of rhythm, and out of harmony, the music is unpleasant because it is discordant. This is what we are like when we are outside God's Will.

Q. *How can we get closer to the Father's Will?*

A. Our relationship with our Father begins by spending time with Him. This can be done through the Sacraments or by praying the Chaplet and other prayers. It can also be done without praying or talking, by quieting ourselves and becoming immersed in His Presence. We can share our joys and sorrows with Him. We can also ask Him for His help. Or we can request that He guide us in our daily lives. And always, we can come to Him when we have offended Him and ask for His mercy and forgiveness.

Our Father desires to have an intimate relationship with us all. As we begin to know, love, and honor Him, we become more and more immersed in His Holy Will. Gradually, we begin to more closely resemble our Father in thought, word, and deed.

When we are uncertain about God's Will in any given situation, we can ask ourselves what our Father would want us to do. We can refer back to His commandments and Jesus' teaching. Every time we say, "I love you, Father, and I give myself to you," we are freely offering ourselves to Him and asking Him to take us to Himself. And where our Father is, that is Paradise, Heaven, His Kingdom—His Holy Will.

Q. *Can we come to hear His voice, too? He has said hearing His voice "is possible for all of you," hasn't He?*

A. Yes, I believe all of us are born with the right equipment — our soul. As temples of the Holy Spirit, I believe all children of God are capable of hearing the voice of their true Father.

We hear the voice of God in Holy Scripture, in each other, and deep within our hearts. The children of God have been in exile since our first parents left Paradise, so our Father may seem very far away. But He has never abandoned us. He is always with us.

If we slow down our pace, if we take time to spend with our Father, if we quiet ourselves and listen—we will hear His voice inside us.

This is not to say discernment isn't needed. But a complicated set of instructions isn't needed for the children of God to speak to their Father and to listen to His voice. This is a gift we are all born with—it is part of our inheritance as the children of God.

Q. *What do you know about the "purifying fire" that He told you about? He told you it "will sweep across the planet." Is this a real fire? A nuclear fire? A spiritual fire?*

A. Only God knows in what form this purifying fire will come. I know only its purpose—it will purify us. This may be strictly spiritual, or it may be physical. Perhaps it will be both. Whatever its form, it will serve to purify us. This is not necessarily bad or frightening—mankind and the entire planet are in great need of cleansing and purification.

Q. *What does this mean when He says, "The end of an era is hurtling toward you, My children."*

A. Based on the dialogues, I believe that we are moving swiftly toward the end of one era and the beginning of the next. In this particular phrase, I believe our Father meant that the end of this era is fast approaching because of our own choices and decisions.

We are causing a set of circumstances to occur in this world that will most definitely have destructive consequences—physically and spiritually. We have only to look at the world today and see that this is true.

Q. *You had visions of a powerful man rising. The Father said, "This man means to break the back of My children." Who is this man? Is he the antichrist?*

A. Several times in the dialogue and readings there have been references to a powerful man rising. In prayer, I have seen a man at what appeared to be a rally. There seemed to be economic and political chaos. This man assured the people that everything would be all right. That the world could be united. That we could be better than we had ever been. But this was an empty promise because he was offering a "Godless" peace—this was not the peace of God. Unfortunately, no one at the rally seemed to notice or care about this omission.

I have also been given readings from Daniel regarding the antichrist. These readings specifically refer to a person who would disregard God's Laws, making his own. Our Father seems to be emphasizing the importance of "His Laws" in this time.

Q. *What is the meaning behind the messages that speak of a "new heaven and a new earth?" The new Jerusalem? Is this the same as the writings in the Book of Revelations? The same as given to Father Gobbi?*

A. Mankind has been moving toward the New Jerusalem—a new heaven and a new earth, the City of God—since the beginning of mankind's salvation history when we lost Paradise. God has promised us this in Scripture, especially in the Book of Revelation.

I understand the New Jerusalem to be that point in time when mankind will be "fully" reunited with its Father—when God will be present with and in His children in a new way. Again, some sort of transformative purifying process will need to take place for this to happen.

I assume that the "new Jerusalem" referred to in the dialogue and Father Gobbi's messages are the same. However, I cannot authoritatively comment on this because I have not closely studied Father Gobbi's messages, nor has our Father spoken to me about them.

Q. *The Father speaks of a new ark? Can you explain?*

A. To understand how our Father is using the term "ark" now, it would help to view it from a historical perspective: (1), Noah's ark housing and physically saving "eight" people in a worldwide purification; (2) the Ark of the Covenant housing the Presence of God; (3) Mary becoming the "new ark," housing the Presence of God (Jesus); and (4) the children of God becoming the ark, when through the Holy Spirit, the Presence of God dwells in them, as in a tabernacle. In all these cases, the evolution of the "ark" has involved movement into a new era.

What is the "ark" in these times? Our Father says that when we are contained and consumed in His Love, nothing can harm us. He refers to this as the ark of His Love. He also says that when we have found our way back home—back to His Heart, His Love— that we are safe. He is in our heart and we are in His. In the dialogue our Father explains that the consecration must go on this ark. My understanding of this is that when the Presence of God dwells in us, we also dwell in the Presence of God. When we have found our way to the Heart of our Father, we are finally home. We are safe and protected. And to find our home to His Heart, he has given us *The Holy Octave of Consecration*.

Q. *How do we learn to "see with the eyes of our soul?"*

A. God has given us the senses of sight, sound, taste, touch, and smell, so that we can perceive our physical world. However, through my experience with our Father, I have come to understand that we are entering a period of time when God is going to be present with and in us in a fuller way. St. Paul said we now see through a glass darkly. But I believe, as the coming of God's Kingdom approaches, as heaven more fully intersects with earth, we will be better able to apprehend God's Presence within our "souls." We will be more sensitive and responsive to God's Presence.

I cannot explain it better than to say it is like a spiritual evolutionary process. We've always had the ability, I think. We are born with the ability. However, at this point in mankind's salvation history, we will begin to explore, discover, and improve our ability to apprehend God through our souls while we are yet in our physical bodies.

Does this mean that we will eventually see God with our physical eyes? I only know that for now He is asking us to know, love, and honor Him better by seeing Him with the eyes of our soul. It is as if heaven and earth are intersecting within us.

When I see our Father with the eyes of my soul, something inside me resonates, like a chord is being struck within me that vibrates on a spiritual frequency allowing me to apprehend our Father in a way my human eyes cannot.

How do we see our Father with the eyes of our soul? This faculty is developed by spending quiet time with our Father: praying, speaking to our Father about our daily joys and sorrows, asking Him to help and guide us. And then by sitting in silence, basking in the warmth of His Presence, listening to His gentle voice inside us. As we develop our relationship with our Father, as we come to know, love, and honor Him more, we will begin to apprehend His Presence with and in us more fully. We will come to know Him as a "real" Person. We will have found our Father.

Q. *What does the Father mean when He says, "Teach My children that they must rely entirely on Me?"*

A. Most of us think we are self-sufficient or that we need the help of other human beings to function and survive. But not many people will admit that they need God. Today, mankind thinks it has an answer and solution for everything. How foolish this must seem to our Father. What I have learned through the dialogue is that if we are going to survive, individually and collectively, we must rediscover and embrace our intimate relationship with God—He is our Father and we are His children. And as children we must look to our Father for all things, great and small, in our lives. Certainly, this doesn't mean we sit passively, expecting our Father to give us everything we "want." Rather, it means that we can, in trust, depend on our Father to provide us with our daily bread—for those things we need to survive physically and thrive spiritually. When we cooperate with our Father's Will, He helps us help ourselves and each other.

What our Father is trying to teach us is to relate to Him as trusting children who look to their Father for sustenance, help, guidance—but most of all, love. This means letting go and letting God. In its most perfect form, this is "living in the Will of our Father."

Q. *Tell us what the Father has said to you about the gift of "choices" and about "consequences."*

A. God has given each one of us the opportunity to choose. This is a gift of freedom. We have the perfect freedom to choose or not to choose God and His Holy Will. God has given each one of us the gift of free-will choice. This is how much He values us. He did not create us as puppets or slaves. Instead, He made us so that we had the perfect freedom to choose. There is no coercion or oppression in our relationship with our Father. There is only Love.

There are consequences for our choices—a built-in cause/effect factor. When we choose God and His Holy Will, the consequence is eternal life in God. When we make choices that are opposed to God and His Holy Will, the consequence is separation from God because we place ourselves outside His Will.

This concept of consequences is important because it helps us understand that God does not separate Himself from us; we separate ourselves from Him. It also helps us see that our bad choices set up a causal chain reaction that produces effects that hurt, damage, and destroy us and those around us, sometimes for generations. Ultimately, it is not God that will destroy us if we continue to make bad choices. It will be ourselves.

Q. *What did the Father mean when He told you to "build the Church and I will come?"*

A. I believe our Father meant this on three levels: (1) the Church in general, (2) actual physical churches, and (3) our hearts—the temples of His indwelling Presence. I believe when we, as a "Church," know, love, and honor our Father, He will come to us in a new and special way. I also think that our Father is asking us to glorify Him by building churches or chapels in His honor. And always, our Father is requesting that we build the church, tabernacle, or temple, that is our heart, so that His Presence may dwell in us.

Q. *Should people spread the new devotion more?*

A. Yes, our Father wants to draw all His children to Himself in this time. It is by means of this devotion that we will come to know, love, and honor Him more fully. Again, I believe that the return of the children of God to their Father is directly related to our Lady's Triumph and the Era of Peace. Therefore, the spread of this devotion is timely.

Q. *Is the Father still speaking to you?*

A. Yes, during dialogues. It is my understanding that our Father wants to have an intimate relationship with all of us.

Q. *How has your family responded to all of this?*

A. Some family members have been very supportive of the work.

Q. *Has the Church investigated your experiences?*

A. No, the Church has not investigated my experiences.

Q. *Do you have a spiritual director? Have any theologians studies these revelations?*

A. Yes, a Catholic priest with a background in spiritual direction and Canon Law is serving as my spiritual director and another priest, an experienced and well-respected theologian, is acting as an advisor.

Q. *Do you publicly speak of these messages and experiences?*

A. I speak privately about our Father to my Family and publicly through my writing. But as a wife, mother, and grandmother, I do not feel called to leave my family to speak publicly. I believe the written work serves that purpose.

Q. *How has your life in the Father changed you?*

A. My life has changed dramatically. Before I was very much engaged with the culture. Now, I focus on our Father and my family. Our Father is the central core of my life. Everything flows from that relationship. Not only do I better recognize the Presence of our Father with us, but also in us. This has given me a profound appreciation and love for all other human beings.

Q. *Tell us about your love for the Father of All Mankind.*

A. I have come to know only one true thing—and that is my love for our Father and the Father's love for me and for all His children. When you love our Father, He is in your thoughts always—even when you are actively engaged with something else. You see Him in His creation, in other people. You come to depend on Him for comfort and guidance. You are constantly in awe of His Creation and, most of all, the realization that He is your true Father and you are His true child. You want to please Him by doing His Will in all you think, say, and do. And when you do something that offends Him or another person, you feel genuine sorrow.

I also realize that our Father is a real Person, and this is who you fall in love with—not an abstract, intellectual concept. This intimate relationship becomes the most important thing in your life. He is all good, all merciful, all loving. He is gentle and yet powerful. He is kind; He has a sense of humor; He loves us beyond all human reason. He loves us unconditionally. How could I not love our Father? He is Love.

Q. *How should souls approach the Father?*

A. I would suggest that we approach our Father with awe, humility, an open heart, trust, and confidence. We can do this through the Sacraments and through our quiet time with Him. We should always seek Him out and invite Him into our lives, because He is always there for us. We should especially approach Him in a quiet environment, with an attitude of giving, not taking. We should praise and adore Him. And rely on Him for all we need.

Most importantly, we mustn't be "afraid" of Him. We should respect Him above all things and we should feel fear of ever offending Him or being separated from Him. But never should we be afraid of Him. This type of fear separates us from Him and keeps us from approaching Him. He is our all merciful and loving Father and we are His prodigal children. He loves us unconditionally—despite of and because of our weaknesses.

In approaching our Father, in establishing a personal, intimate relationship with Him, we learn how to better resemble the Father who made us in His own image.

Q. *How should the world approach the Father?*

A. The world can approach our Father in the same way. He, first and foremost, wants us to embrace Him as our true Father and to recognize that we are His true children. Second, He has given us *The Holy Octave of Consecration* so that all His children can individually and collectively know, love, and honor Him. This Consecration Feast Day, then, serves both to regather all His children and to restore them to their one true Father.

Through this, I believe that our Father will be with us in a special way. His Era of Peace will be granted to the world, and His Kingdom will come on earth as it is in heaven more fully. When we know our Father, we will know His Peace.

CHAPTER FOURTEEN

LUISA PICCARRETA

O
f all the visionaries who have reported experiences with God
and the coming of the new era, perhaps the one who gives
the most profound insight into these mysteries is a woman
from 19th century Corato, Italy, named Luisa Piccarreta. In her
revelations, Luisa did not report an intimate relationship with the First-
Person of the Holy Trinity. However, she did leave a volume of
revelations that meticulously unfold many secrets about the new era, an
era that according to her revelations will embrace to a great degree the
true meaning of the words found in the *Our Father*, especially the
petition for the coming of the Kingdom on earth as it is in heaven.

Luisa Piccarreta was born on the Sunday after Easter, April 23,
1854, in Corato, Italy, a village in the south of Italy not far from the
Adriatic Sea and about 20 miles northwest of the seaport of Bari, where
St. Nicholas is buried. She was baptized the same day she was born and
would spend her whole life in Corato. Besides Luisa, her father and
mother, Vito and Rosa, had four other daughters.

The household was said to be a holy home where no foul
language or deceit was allowed, and the Piccarreta's refused to permit
their children to be entrusted to others. Luisa's childhood is said to have
been marked with signs of her predestination, as she tended herself with
matters of God and reported hearing the voice of Jesus at the age of nine.
By this time, she had already come to spend hours at a time in church,
kneeling immobile and absorbed in contemplation.

Luisa also said she experienced intense nightmares that added to
her timid and fearful disposition. The devil would taunt her in her
dreams, causing her to seek refuge in her prayers, especially the *"Our*

Father" which she prayed to all male saints. She also said she would have dreams of the Virgin Mary who would vanquish Satan and relieve her mortal distress.

Jesus Speaks to Luisa

On the occasion of her first locution from Jesus, she had just made her first Holy Communion and Confirmation in what was to become her life: the willful attempting through prayer and solemn acts for a closer and more intimate relationship with God. At age eleven, Luisa became a Daughter of Mary and a year later she reported hearing the voice of Jesus interiorly on a regular basis, especially when she received Holy Communion. Luisa said that Christ taught her about the ways of God, especially the Cross. The Lord, she said, would correct her, even scold her when necessary. She said she learned from Him about His hidden life, the virtues, meekness, and especially the need to surrender to obedience above all matters and desires. The Lord also taught her meditations.

Biographers write that Luisa Piccarreta's life was, for the most part, one of complete mysticism from the earliest age until her death. She received only a first-grade education and her mystical writings betray this fact with many grammatical errors, although the terminology in them is appropriate.

As Luisa got older, she began detachment from herself and from everything of this world. Then, at age thirteen, while working in her home, and meditating on the passion of Christ, Luisa experienced a powerful vision.

Standing on the balcony of her house, where she went to get fresh air after becoming faint meditating on the Passion of Christ, Luisa gazed downward to behold a vision of an immense crowd of people in the middle of the street surrounding Jesus, who had the Cross upon His shoulder and was dragging it one way and then the other. She saw Christ struggling to breathe as blood dripped from His face. Then Jesus raised His eyes and looked at Luisa on the balcony and said, "Soul, help me!" An immense sorrow filled her, she would later explain, as the vision made a life-long impression on her, causing her to long for her Savior's suffering. Around this same time, her own physical sufferings did begin, as did her hidden spiritual sufferings.

These sufferings increased in intensity as time went by, often causing her illness to be investigated by medical authorities and priests who were openly hostile in their capacity to understand the little victim.

From age 13 to 16, Luisa came under a series of demonic attacks that helped her to better prepare for her life - long mission as a chosen instrument for God's revelations. The devil assaulted her in many ways, especially by temptation and suggestion, and even physical assaults.

Then one day, when she was sixteen, she experienced a particularly brutal demonic attack that left her stunned, but in a state which the Lord used to invite her to become "a victim soul." The following year, Luisa became physically ill, vomiting her food and having to be confined to her bed. After a period of confusion, it was realized that her illness was mystical and this was then the beginning of what would lead to a permanent bed-ridded existence. For the next 64 years, she was "nailed to her bed," but never showed a single bedsore on her body. She also at this time ceased to eat, and never ate food or drank water again. For 64 years, she survived only on Holy Communion.

The Gift of the Divine Will

In bed, Luisa's body assumed a sitting position, the position that caused, upon her death, the need for a special casket. After the age of 22, Luisa never again left her bed. That same year, on October 16, 1888, at the age of 23, Luisa was united to Christ in a mystical marriage. Eleven months later, Luisa reported that she was taken to heaven where in the presence of God the Father, the Son, and the Holy Spirit, and the entire Celestial Court, her union with Christ was ratified. That same day, she reportedly received the "gift of the Divine Will," a mystical gift that permitted her soul to receive great graces, singular graces, that opened her to the sublime secrets of mystery of the Divine Will of God. A short time later, she was married to Jesus again in a "marriage of the cross." Luisa received the stigmata, which remained invisible to the world. The remainder of her life was a mixture of joys, sufferings, writing, sewing, obeying, praying and helping others with the wisdom of her experiences.

Luisa died on March 4, 1947. There was uncertainty about her death for four days as her body did not develop "rigor mortis." Forty seven years later, in 1994, the Vatican directed the Archbishop of Luisa's diocese to begin the process for her beautification. This cause was opened on November 20, 1994, the Feast of Christ the King.

But it is what began in February of 1899 that most accentuates her life. For it was in that year that she began to write, under the obedience of her confessor, the secrets of the mystery of the Divine Will.

The Coming of the Father's Kingdom

Luisa's revelations are primarily centered on the new era, the era foretold at Fatima. It is to her an era of sanctification, and she writes, it will be the fulfillment of Our Lord's prayer that "the Father's Kingdom Come and His Will be done on earth as it is in Heaven."

Once again, this new era is not to be misrepresented as a magical era of human existence. People will still have free will, and as other visionaries have noted, this entire period will be transitory, as the Church marches forward to fulfill its mission.

But Luisa's Piccarreta's writing reveal, through her visitations from Jesus and Mary, that a time of great grace is coming upon the world, a time of peace. But first, she says like all the other prophets of our day, a great purification will occur.

According to Piccarretta, Christ told her that in the order of His providence, God has renewed the world every 2000 year period. In the first period, He renewed it with the flood. In the second 2,000 year period, He renewed it with His coming and manifesting of His Humanity.

Now, at the end of the third period, there will be a third renovation that will witness a purification to be followed by a new era of light upon the truth. Like a rising sun, a great flood of grace from heaven is to descend upon the world, according to Piccarretta, and the minds and hearts of men will be transformed in such a way as to reestablish the Kingdom of God's Will on earth.

This new era, the era of the Kingdom coming on earth, will be the fulfillment of God's ordained will, says Piccarreta, and will be a great gift to mankind, something never before experienced since the fall of man. Most of all, it will be a reign of peace, an era of peace, wrote Piccarreta, where no conflicts will exist and the Church will reign.

The Church is presently studying the messages of Luisa Piccarreta and the process of her beatification is also underway.

EPILOGUE

"I hear within myself something like a sound of running water which says: Come to the Father."

— St. Ignatius of Antioch as he prepared for his martyrdom

F r. Jean Galot greatly contributes to our understanding of the Holy Trinity in his work *Abba Father*. In this book, he notes that in the action of the Three Persons, the Father sends the Son, The Father and the Son send the Holy Spirit, but *"it is never said that the Father is sent."* He is always the one Who sends, and that would suffice, writes Galot, *"to give His action in our world a characteristic that belongs to His person alone."*

With the advent of a new era underway, we see in the words of the prophets of our times how the Eternal Father is again directing the actions of His Son and the Holy Spirit in a special way, a way certainly deserving, according to the prophecies, to be understood as a Second Pentecost. The renewal of the Church and the world is revealing once again how our Father possesses and expresses the fullness of His Divine Fatherhood. In and through the Father, a great plan is unfolding that will fulfill the promises of *"a great era of God"*—promises foretold in both the Old and New Testaments.

But unlike any previous time, a powerful and wonderful feature of the Father's plan will be the hallmark of the new era: the reunification of the First Person of the Most Holy Trinity—Our Father—with His children. This will occur in a unique and unprecedented way. Indeed, the prophets tell us that in the restoration process that will unfold, God the Father will, in a special, "spiritual way," send Himself to regather, assemble, and embrace His children. The Father desires to show that He, Himself, is coming at this time to love, comfort, and sustain them, especially during the initial phase of these new times—the winnowing and threshing stages that have begun and will soon intensify.

The depth of the mystery now underway—the mystery of the coming of the temporal Kingdom of the Father on earth—is one that is impossible to completely explore and even more impossible to completely understand. The visionaries, the voices of God found in this account, have contributed a great deal to our understanding. However, no compendium of testimony, regardless of how vast or authentic, gives us the full picture. It is a mystery that God retains for Himself—once again to be revealed in stages and degrees.

But what do we know? What has the Father revealed of His Face and His coming Kingdom through the words of His chosen ones. A portent has been given through His prophets in this account, and a summary is in order.

The End of an Era

The coming of the Kingdom of God on earth will mark both a beginning and an end. It will be the end of an age, an age of transition, that at its beginning witnessed the redemption of mankind through Christ's sacrifice on the cross. This epoch of time then went on to fulfill the necessary elements of reparation and justice as decreed in God's Divine Order.

Indeed, over the last two thousand years, Christ, True God and True Man, was born of a chosen people and proclaimed and proven to be the True Messiah, the Redeemer of the universe. In Christ, religion became no longer a "blind search for God" (Acts 17:27), but the response in faith to a God Who had revealed Himself. Christ instituted the Sacraments which would begin to restore to man the grace lost through sin. These graces were also necessary to restore the unity of creation in the order of the Divine Will. This revelation in Christ also bore witness to the truth of the Holy Spirit and the Eternal Father. Together, the Most Holy Trinity's plan for creation was advanced with the hope of uniting all things in Christ—things in heaven and on earth.

The last two thousand years also bore witness to the fact that the Christian faith is the true path in man's desire to overcome evil, to crush the Deceiver, and to find "full self-realization" in God, as revealed by Christ. The Christian religion was revealed to be a religion of glory and over time the Gospel, as Christ asked, was spread by His followers to the far corners of the earth. Generation after generation maintained and proved these truths through their holy lives, heroic deaths, and in their miraculous deeds. By such witness, they also demonstrated that Christ truly is the Lord of history, the Alpha and the Omega, *"the beginning and the end."* In Him, it has been proven that the Father has spoken the definitive word about mankind and its history. And against His Church, His Mystical Body, not even the gates of Hell have been able to prevail, as was prophesied in Scripture.

Withstanding the Gates of Hell

Moreover, now, at the end of this age, the world has witnessed "Hell" desperately attempting to prevail over Christianity and the truth of it's teachings. But all of this oppression has been to no avail. The Church has withstood every assault from outside and within, and in the Chair of Peter, the Truth of Christ still prevails. Soon, the complete failure of an unprecedented age of evil will be witnessed as the errors of Humanism evaporate before the eyes of the world through the painful dissolution of a civilization built on illusion.

This pending climax to our age has been moving at an increasing pace for almost two hundred years, as the world has gradually and visibly come to embrace evil for good and institutionalized the legitimacy of sin. Yet, God's prophets of the age have persistently illuminated the truth of the events at hand. They have revealed the signs of the times as marked in Scripture, and have accurately foretold that God is directing the world through such dark times in order to arrive in the new era of light and peace. And although the opposite may seem to be true, faith and trust in God will prevail in the end. Indeed, through the resolute intercession of the Queen of Peace, heaven's prophetic words of hope for the "coming of the Kingdom on earth" are about to be completely realized. The door will now close on an age of unprecedented death and misery, and will open on an era of peace to be reportedly unlike anything on earth since the Garden of Eden.

A Painful Transition?

For individuals, the passage from one era into the next will be most of all, a matter of perspective and choice, the prophets tell us. Belief in all that is of this world, the materialism, sensualism, and intellectualism, may be painful to surrender and will result in confusion and despair if one is not grounded in Christ, they say. Surrendering oneself to the truth of the eternal soul now, before it is too late, has been the Virgin Mary's call. It is the age-old call to conversion every sinner must face, but has been elevated to an almost audible level in the drama of our passing age.

Indeed, not since the heralding of John the Baptist has the urgency of the call to conversion been given to a generation, so steeped in incredulity, that it has chosen to deny the generous outpouring of signs and wonders that have marked God's urgent words. Tragically, time is running out, we are told, and soon many will be lost in the storm that will purify God's children.

In harmony, the prophets continue to tell the world that the safest and easiest way to understand the times at hand is to surrender to the glorious reality that nothing of the present world is worthy of the hope promised for the future. It is not an end, but a beginning people must seek. A culture steeped in death needs to surrender to a new culture of life—one that is founded in God's Truth. Therefore, the new era invites mankind to embrace God in confidence, free from all of the temptations of false happiness and peace, and to say from its heart *"Abba! Father!*

The New Era

As they have done in revealing the truth about the close of this era, the prophets have also revealed to us much about the new era—the Era of Peace—the coming of God's Kingdom on earth. In the light of Christ, the Lord and Master of history, the new times will give rise to a path of unity—unity of faith, people, and nations. The future will belong to Christ Who will embrace all within His redemptive power. Jesus Christ is the same yesterday, today, and forever, and unlike ever before, this truth will be clearly understood and acknowledged. In a special way, the Church will give to the world this witness of truth. The new era will be one that will see a great evangelization of the world in fulfillment of the Scriptural prophecies.

In this new era, visionaries tell us that God will bring to fruition mankind's salvation history, the ultimate completion of our long journey. Over time, the complete "Triumph" will be realized in the world and God's peace will come to reign. What will this complete Triumph be? The return of all of God's children to their Heavenly Father.

Through Our Lady's revelations, it has been revealed that this return will be a gradual process, but is to begin with a blast of transformation. Soon, visionaries say, a critical phase will introduce a great light into the world. This phase will seem, to many, like a violent storm, painful and destructive. It will force a change in the world, as if moving a flock of sheep from the safety of a mountain meadow into a barren hostile desert. But through such action, God's family, His new family, will be formed. A new culture will arise, as survival in the old culture will be seen as impossible and people will realize that "consequences" in the Divine Order have served as divine justice. Thus, this will hasten the return of God's children to Him, for they will be in need of safety and protection.

Visionaries say that all of this will be a restoration process—a restoration of God's Kingdom on earth—as it was in the beginning. This is because God never intended that His children build a world of false gods and passing pleasures. Rather, He created His children to resemble Him in all things. Now, they too will desire this—not the allure of the world and its hollow promises.

An Age of Great Faith and Trust in God

As this new era begins to unfold and take shape, God's children will begin to seek His voice in all things. They will see that what has been lost has actually been a liberation. They will develop great trust and faith and they will learn to listen to Him with their hearts. Consequently, over time, they will come to see God more clearly, unlike any generation before. Many souls will be truly fashioned, the prophets say, in Christ's likeness. This will be their desire and they will occupy themselves with love, love of their God and their fellow men. Indeed, they will keep God company all day and all night, and will honor Him everywhere.

Not surprisingly, great faith will arise in the new times, as such vigilance in God will reap rewards. There will be no place for politics and intrigue, as God's Will is to be served in truth and in the light of such truth. Likewise, the Church will breath new life into its teachings. Thus, the family of man will be forged into an image of the Holy Family, making it a Divine Family of God's children with their heavenly Father.

It must be noted that all of this will come about not only by God's children responding through their own free will, but also because of God's grace, an ordained peace, which will be like a new covenant between God and man. This peace will permit mankind and the Church to make great strides throughout the world as whole nations come into the Church. But most of all, it will be the teachings of the Church that will be embraced. Especially, the concept of God and His Kingdom being a family—one which, like earthly families, has a loving mother and a devoted father.

Honoring our Heavenly Father and Mother

This profound realization will then enkindle in God's children a greater desire to honor their heavenly Mother and Father. Mary will be universally accepted as the Mother of all mankind, as its Co-Redemptrix, Mediatrix, and Advocate. She will be appreciated as its Queen, especially for bringing the long prophesied defeat, the crushing of the head of the adversary. She will be loved and cherished for submitting to God's Will in her victorious efforts, and in honor of the name of Mary, she will once again be recognized as the Lady of all Nations.

God the Father, the Father of all Mankind, will also receive the honor and glory He deserves. His Kingdom will truly have come because it will be a Kingdom that will dispense peace and justice, a Kingdom of the heart, which will finally be realized on earth. As in the parable of the prodigal son, God's children will be received by their Father with celebratory joy, and God will finally dwell in the hearts of His children.

God's children will seek to honor the Father of all Mankind with a Feast. The one true God and Father will be offered enduring love and honor and, as Christ said, will be worshiped in spirit and truth. The prophets tell us that this is what the human heart was made for. And so God's people will sing praises to His name and will rejoice in their enthusiasm, for all they do, they will do for God. Indeed, nations will revel in the beauty and splendor of the Father, His Kingdom, and His peace, and they will realize they are truly blessed. The Face of the Father will be honored in homes, workplaces, and churches throughout the world.

Moreover, through intimate prayer, many souls will dialogue with their Father in a new and profound manner, apprehending Him in a special way in their souls. All life, then, will be a joyful sacrifice, as many people's hearts and souls will connect with God, like heaven will connect with earth. Indeed, the Spirit will engineer, through faith, great possibilities.

The Reign of the Divine Will

Conscious choices to live in God's Will, His Divine Will, will eventually be the hallmark of the new era — the era of the Divine "fiat." In humility and repentance, many people will turn to their God for everything, not just protection and sustenance. Trust and love, through trial and triumph, will breathe in the souls of God's faithful. And the children of the new era will be seen more as truly reflecting the image of their Creator and especially His Divine Will. They will also, in turn, see God with the eyes of their souls.

All of this is the Kingdom to come, a Kingdom, that as Christ said, will truly reign within souls. Indeed, the new era will find great churches and shrines dedicated to God the Father, God the Son, and God the Holy Spirit. Peace will reign and the Eucharistic presence of God will be found everywhere.

The Trumpet Calls

According to the prophets of today, these times are closer than we think as God seeks to now come and begin this glorious era. He seeks to wait no longer for the return of His children. Perhaps the following message from the Eternal Father to Barbara Centilli provides the most fitting conclusion to this account:

These times cannot be turned back. Why? Because, My little one, to do so would forestall the glory that is to come. My Divine Glory brought down amidst My children. How can

this be if none are waiting, if none are prepared, if none are willing to welcome and greet their Father? It cannot be. All must be made ready. All must know, love, and honor Me. And then I will come in Truth. For this is the final hour. The final hour of an era best left behind by My children on their journey home.

Sensational as it may seem, daughter of My Heart, I grow impatient and will use whatever means are necessary to gather My children to Me. Am I a thoughtless Father? Do I forget and neglect My children? No, never. And as any human parent, I am intense in My desire that My children be well, protected, and provided for. But for this to occur, they must be in My Heart; they must come home. Draw them nearer with the sweet song of your prayers, with a promise of restoration and transformation for all those who respond with a "Yes" freely given to their Father.

Speak of this to those who will listen, Barbara Rose. Tell them they are so deeply loved—each one. That My Heart is torn asunder with grief at the thought of losing even one. Know this and ponder the choice before you in this time: Do you choose to know, love, and honor your Father and God? In knowing, loving, and honoring Me, you reside in My Holy Will. You reside in Me.

When My children know, love, and honor Me, then will they be transformed and realize the Kingdom within them-—My Divine Presence. My Will is communicated to My children through My Spirit. In this way, My Presence dwells in them. Do you comprehend what this means? Think for awhile, little one. Do My children even begin to grasp what it means to have their God dwell in them as precious temples—dedicated to their one True God and Father.

They say they do not know Me. They say I do not exist. Yet I am closer than two human bodies touching one to the other. I dwell within you—in the heart of your soul. What does this mean, My smallest daughter? I will dwell among My children on earth more fully when they allow Me to dwell within the temple that is their soul. Then My Kingdom will truly have come on earth as it is in heaven.

I have come in degrees. Drawing toward you throughout mankind's salvation history. But now you must stop, become attentive and resolute, and approach Me so that we can meet—one to one, Father and child, and re-unite, in the way that was intended. Do you still not see? This was your rightful inheritance—from the beginning. The shell that has been man, made in My image, will now become man, son of the Living God. You are My children. Comprehend the meaning, daughter of My Heart. This is not a gift to be thrown carelessly away. This honor exceeds man's understanding.

Know Me so that you may love Me intimately and honor Me, not out of duty, but choice—choice for the One Who gave you life and Who will someday take it away [in physical death]. Establish the Consecration and Feast Day devotion to My Fatherly Heart and I will truly come in a way unprecedented in time and place. Know who you are, My children. The trumpet calls all Mine home in this time. Come—and be at peace—the peace freely given by Me, your God and Father— in these times. Draw each breath you take from My Holy Spirit. Live in Me as I desire to live in you. This is the glory of the Lord. My Peace, child—now and forever. Purify and dedicate the Temple of the Lord God on earth.

Reading Is 60:14-15 — "And the children of them that afflict thee, shall come bowing down to thee, and all that slandered thee shall worship the steps of thy feet, and **shall call thee the City of the Lord, the Zion of the Holy One of Israel**. Because thou wast forsaken, and healed, and there was none that passed through thee, I will make thee to be an everlasting **glory**, a joy unto generation to generation."

NOTES

CHAPTER ONE: I AM A FATHER TO ISRAEL
1. Pope John Paul II, *God Father and Creator* (Volume One), Boston, Massachusetts: Pauline Books & Media, 1996, p. 162.
2. Jean Galot, SJ, *Abba Father, We Long to See Your Face*, New York; Alba House, 1992, p. 40.
3. Ibid., p. 41.
4. Ibid., p. 50.
5. Ibid., p. 49.
6. Ibid., p. 81.
7. Ibid., p. 82.

The theology in this chapter comes from various texts, primarily Pope John Paul's book *God, Father and Creator* and Fr. Jean Galot's book *Abba Father*. Both are highly recommended.

CHAPTER TWO: MY FATHER AND YOUR FATHER
1. Galot, *Abba Father, We Long to See Your Face*, p. 50.
2. Michael O'Carroll, *Trinitas*, Collegeville, Minnesota: The Liturgical Press, 1987, p. 107.
3. Galot, Op. Cit., p. 54.
4. ———. *Catechism of the Catholic Church*. New Hope, Kentucky, St. Martin de Porres Comminity, 1994, p. 71.
5. Ibid., p. 71.

The theology in this chapter comes from various texts, primarily Pope John Paul's book *God, Father and Creator* and Fr. Jean Galot's book *Abba Father*.

CHAPTER THREE: OUR FATHER
All Biblical quotes are from The Holy Bible, Douay Rheims Version and the New American Bible.
The theology in this chapter comes from various texts, primarily Pope John Paul's book *God, Father and Creator* and Fr. Jean Galot's book *Abba Father*.

CHAPTER FOUR: GOD SHALL REIGN OVER THE NATIONS
Biblical quotes are from the Holy Bible, Douay Rheims Version and the New American Bible. The material referenced from the *Catechism of the Catholic Church* came from Part Four, Section Two, The Lord's Prayer - *"Our Father"* and from Part One, Section Two, The Profession of the Christian Faith - The Creeds. Desmond Birch's book, *Trial, Tribulation and Triumph* was of considerable help in examining the writings of the Fathers and Doctors of the Church.

CHAPTER FIVE: THE KINGDOM COME
All of the reference material concerning St. Thomas Aquinas' writings on the *Our*

Father are from Fr. William McCarthy's book *The Our Father, Four Commentaries on the Lord's Prayer* (St. Andrews Productions, 1999.)

CHAPTER SIX: ON EARTH AS IT IS IN HEAVEN
        The information in this chapter comes from a compendium of sources on Church Tradition, private revelations, the Saints and prophecy (see bibliography). Some of the information on the Apostolic Fathers and the Doctors of the Church is from Fr. Joseph Iannuzzi's book, *The Triumph of God's Kingdom in the Millennium and End Times, A Proper belief from the Truth in Scripture and Church Teachings.* (St John the Evangelist Press, 1999.)

CHAPTER SEVEN: AN ERA OF PEACE
        The information on apparitions in this chapter is from many sources (see bibliography). The messages of Father Stefano Gobbi are from the book *To the Priests, Our Lady's Beloved Sons* and are used with the permission of the Marian Movement of Priests.

CHAPTER EIGHT: MOTHER EUGENIA RAVASIO
        The information in this chapter is from the book *God Our Father*, no publisher. This book has appeared in many forms and under different titles and can be obtained from Casa Pater, Padre Andrea D'Ascanio, Edizioni (Pater), Box Mail 135, 67100 L'Aquila, Italy.

CHAPTER NINE: THERESA WERNER
        The information in this chapter on Theresa Werner is from the book, *Queen of Mary, Lubbock Texas - The Message... The Story* published by the Queen of Mercy Center and is used with the permission of one the authors, Celeste Lovett.

CHAPTER TEN: GEORGETTE FANIEL
        The information in this chapter is from the book *Mary, Queen of Peace Stay With Us*, by Fathers Armand and Guy Girard. The author's own interview with Georgette Faniel, as well as information provided by Fr. Guy Girard, were also used.

CHAPTER ELEVEN: CHRISTINA GALLAGHER
        The chapter on Christina Gallagher was excerpted entirely from the author's book, *The Sorrow, The Sacrifice and the Triumph, The Apparitions, Visions and Prophecies of Christina Gallagher,* (published by Simon and Schuster, NY,NY, 1995)

CHAPTER TWELVE: MATTHEW KELLY
        The information on Matthew Kelly was taken from Kelly's three books, *Words from God, Our Father* and *Call to Joy.* The author also conducted the interview with Mr. Kelly.

CHAPTER THIRTEEN: BARBARA ROSE CENTILLI
        The information on Barbara Centilli is from the book *Seeing with the Eyes of the Souls, Volumes One and Two.* The interview with Mrs. Centilli was conducted by the author.

CHAPTER FOURTEEN: LUISA PICCARRETA
        The information on Luisa Piccarreta is from *The Kingdom of Divine Will* series and was used with the permission of the Center for the Divine Will in Jacksonville, Florida.

EPILOGUE
        The message from the Eternal Father to Barbara Centilli is from the book *Seeing With the Eyes of the Soul, Volume II.* (St. Andrews Productions, 1999.)

SELECTED BIBLIOGRAPHY

Abbe, Richard M. *What Happened at Pontmain*, Washington, New Jersey: Ave Maria Institute.

Aquinas, St. Thomas. *Summa Theologica* (Vol I). Westminster Maryland: Christian Classics, 1948.

—. "*As the Third Millennium Draws Near*: in Inside the Vatican. New Hope, Kentucky: St. Martin de Pores Lay Dominican Community Print Shop, January, 1995.

Birch, Desmond A. *Trial Tribulation & Triumph Before, During, and After Antichrist*. Santa Barbara, California: Queenship Publishing Company, 1996.

Bloy, Leon. *Le Desespere*. (Publisher Unknown)

Bunson, Matthew. *Our Sunday Visitor's Encyclopedia of Catholic History*. Huntington, Indiana: Our Sunday Visitor, Inc., 1995.

—. *Catechism of the Catholic Church.*, New Hope, Kentucky: St. Martin de Porres Community, 1994.

Connor, Edward. *Prophecy for Today*. Rockford, Illinois: TAN Books and Publishers, Inc., 1974.

Culleton, Rev. R. Gerald. *The Prophets and Our Times*. Rockford, Illinois: TAN Books and Publishers, Inc.., 1974.

Culligan, Emmett. *The Last World War and the End of Time*. (no publisher or date listed).

Dirvin, Father Joseph I., C.M. *Saint Catherine Laboure of the Miraculous Medal*. Rockford, Illinois: TAN Books and Publishers, Inc. 1984.

Evely, Louis. *We Dare to Day Our Father*. New York, New York: Herder and Herder , 1965.

Freze, Michael, S.F.O. *Voices Visions and Apparitions*. Huntington, Indiana: Our Sunday Visitor, Inc., 1993.

Galot, Jean SJ. *Abba Father, We Long to See Your Face*. New York: Alba House, 1992.

Girard, Father Guy and Father Armand Girard and Father Janko Bubalo, *Mary Queen of Peace Stay with Us*. Montreal Canada: Editions Pauline, 1988.

Gobbi, Don Stefano. *Our Lady Speaks to Her Beloved Priests*. St. Francis, Maine: The National Headquarters of the Marian Movement of Priests in the United States of America, 1988.

—. *God Our Father Consecration and Feast Day for The Father of All Mankind*. Pittsburgh, Pennsylvania: Father of All Mankind Apostolate.

Hahn, Scott, Ph.D. *A Father Who Keeps His Promises*. Ann Arbor, Michigan: Servant Publications, 1998.

Iannuzzi, Joseph, OSJ *The Triumph of God's Kingdom in the Millennium and End Times, A Proper belief from the Truth in Scripture and Church Teachings*. St. John the Evangelist Press, 1999.

John Paul II, Pope. *Crossing the Threshold of Hope*. New York: Alfred A. Knopf, 1994.

John Paul II, Pope. *God, Father and Creator* Volume One. Boston Massachusetts, Pauline Books and Media, 1996.

Kelly, Matthew. *A Call to Joy*. San Francisco, California: Harper Collins Publishers, Inc., 1997.

Kelly, Matthew. *Our Father*, Baresman Bay, N.S.W. Australia: 1993.

Lovett, Terry and Celeste, Queen of Mercy, *Lubbock, Texas, The Message … The Story*. Earth, Texas, Queen of Mercy Center, 1991

Metzger, Bruse Professor and Dr. David Goldstein and John Ferguson MA, BD (editors). *Great Events of Bible*, Times New York: Crescent Books, 1995.

McCarthy, Rev. William, MSSA. *The Our Father, Four Commentaries*. McKees Rocks, Pennsylvania: St. Andrew's Productions, 1999.

Ocariz, Fernando. *God as Father*. Princeton, New Jersey: Scepter Publications, 1994.

O'Carroll, Michael Cssp. *Corpus Christi*. Collegeville, Minnesota: The Liturgical Press, 1988.

O'Carroll, Michael Cssp. *Theotokos*. Collegeville, Minnesota: The Liturgical Press, 1982.

O'Carroll, Michael Cssp. *Trinitas*, Collegeville, Minnesota: The Liturgical Press, 1987.

O'Carroll, Michael Cssp. *Veni Creator Spiritus*. Collegeville, Minnesota: The Liturgical Press, 1990.

Poarachin, Victor M. *Our Father A Prayer for the Grieving*. Liguori, Missouri: Liguori Publications, 1993.

Petrisko, Thomas W. *Call of the Ages*. Santa Barbara, California: Queenship Publishing Company, 1996.

Petrisko, Thomas W. *The Fatima Prophecies; at the Doorstep of the World*. McKees Rocks, Pennsylvania: Saint Andrew's Productions, 1998.

Petrisko, Thomas W. *The Sorrow, the Sacrifice and the Triumph: The Apparitions, Visions and Prophecies of Christina Gallagher*. New York: Simon and Schuster, Inc., 1995.

Petrisko, Thomas W. *Glory to the Father, A Look at the Mystical Life of Georgette Faniel*. McKees Rocks, Pennsylvania: Saint Andrew's Productions, 1999.

Piccarreta, Luisa. *The Kingdom of the Divine Will (Vols. 1-20)*. Jacksonville, Florida: The Luisa Piccarreta Center for the Divine Will, 1995.

—. *Queen of Mercy, Lubbock, Texas, The Message… The Story*. Earth, Texas: Queen of Mercy Center, 1991.

Ratzinger, Joseph Cardinal with Vittorio Messori. *The Ratzinger Report*, San Francisco, California: Ignatius Press, 1985.

Saint Catherine of Sienna. *The Dialogue of Saint Catherine of Sienna*. Translated by Algar Thorld. Rockford, Illinois: TAN Books and Publishers, Inc., 1974.

—. *Seeing with the Eyes of the Soul, Volume I*. McKees Rocks, Pennsylvania: St. Andrew's Productions, 1998.

—. *Seeing with the Eyes of the Soul, Volume II*. McKees Rocks, Pennsylvania: St. Andrew's Productions, 1999.

Stravinskas, Reverend Peter M.J., Ph.D., S.T.L. *Our Sunday Visitor's Catholic Encyclopedia*. Huntington, Indiana: Our Sunday Visitor, 1991.

—. *The Father Speaks to His Children*. Italy: "Pater" Publications.

—. *The Holy Bible* — Douay Rheims Version. Rockford, Illinois: TAN Books and Publishers, Inc.

—. *The New American Bible*. Wirtchita, Kansas: Catholic Bible Publishers, 1984-85 Edition.

Casa Pater
Padre Andrea D'Ascanio
Edizioni (Pater)
Box Mail 135
67100 L'Aquila Italy

Help Spread the '*Queen of Peace*' Newspaper!

Secret of Fatima Edition
This 2001 edition takes a closer look at the Secret of Fatima, and in particular, the 'Third Secret' which was revealed by the Church on June 26, 2000. Included is the commentary written by Cardinal Ratzinger, which accompanied the secret's release.

Afterlife Edition
This edition examines the actual places of Heaven, Hell and Purgatory through the eyes of the Saints, Mystics, Visionaries, and Blessed Mother herself. Will you be ready come judgment day?

Illumination Edition
This edition focuses on a coming 'day of enlightenment' in which every person on earth will see their souls in the same light that God sees them. Commonly referred to as the 'Warning' or 'Mini-Judgment', many saints and visionaries, particularly the Blessed Mother have spoken about this great event, now said to be imminent.

Eternal Father Edition
This edition makes visible the love and tenderness of God the Father and introduces a special consecration to Him. Many of His messages for the world today tell of the great love He has for all of His 'Prodigal Children.'

Holy Spirit Edition
This edition reveals how the Holy Spirit continues to work through time and history, raising up great saints in the Church. Emphasized in the hidden, yet important role of St. Joseph.

Eucharistic Edition
This edition contains evidence for the Real Presence of Christ in the Eucharist. Many miracles and messages are recorded to reaffirm this truth.

Special Edition III
This edition focuses on the great prophecies the Blessed Mother has given to the world since her apparitions in 1917 at Fatima. Prophetic events related to the 'Triumph of Her Immaculate Heart' are addressed in detail.

Special Edition II
This edition examines the apparitions of the Blessed Mother at Fatima and in relation to today's apparitions occurring worldwide.

Special Edition I
The first in a trilogy of the apparitions and messages of the Blessed Mother, this edition tells why Mary has come to earth and is appearing to all parts of the world today.

GOD OUR FATHER

Consecration and Feast Day for the Father of All Mankind

This beautiful, eight-day consecration prayer booklet to God Father is based entirely on Scripture passages from the Old and New Testament.

Includes a 'Date of Consecration' Prayer card 48 pp. **$3.75**

SEEING WITH THE EYES OF THE SOUL: VOL. I-IV

Revelations from God the Father to Barbara Centilli

These prayer journals take an extraordinary look at a conversation between God the Father and Barbara Centilli that began to unfold in the mid 1990's.

Seeing with the Eyes of the Soul:
Vol. I $3.00
Seeing with the Eyes of the Soul:
Vol. II $3.00
Seeing with the Eyes of the Soul:
Vol. III $3.00
Seeing with the Eyes of the Soul:
Vol. IV $3.00

'Eternal Father' Painting

Eternal Father Poster 11 x 17"
$5.00 EACH!

God the Father Consecration Medals

Small Medal - $2.00
Large Medal - $3.00

'God the Father' Picture

Consecration Card: $ .75
4 x 6 with Litany: $ 1.00
10 x 15" Picture: $5.00

God the Father Consecration Chaplets

Plastic Chaplet – $4.00 ea.
Crystal Chaplet – $18.00 NOW – SALE $6.00 ea.

Scapular Offering Cloth
Representing our soul, this cloth is made of pure white Linen. **$3.00 ea.**

Best Sellers by Dr. Thomas W. Petrisko!

Inside Heaven and Hell

What History, Theology and Mystics Tell Us About the Afterlife
Take a spiritual journey with the saints, mystics, visionaries, and the Blessed Mother - inside Heaven and Hell! Discover what really happens at your judgment. With profound new insight into what awaits each one of us, this book is a ***must read for all those who are serious about earning their 'salvation.'***   **$ 14.95**

Inside Purgatory

What History, Theology, and the Mystics tell us about Purgatory
The follow up book to the best-seller '*Inside Heaven and Hell*' this books continues on in the same 'reader-friendly' format. Guiding the reader through the teachings of the Church and Scripture, this book is also enhanced by what mystics, visionaries, saints and scholars tell us about this mysterious place.   **$10.95**

The Fatima Prophecies

At the Doorstep of the World
This powerhouse book tells of the many contemporary prophecies and apparitions and how they point to the fulfillment of Fatima's two remaining prophecies, the 'annihilation of nations' and 'era of peace'. Is the world about to enter the era of peace or will there be a terrible chastisement? Contains over 60 pictures.   **$16.95**

The Miracle of the Illumination of All Consciences

Known as the 'Warning' or 'Mini-Judgment' a coming "day of enlightenment" has been foretold. It is purported to be a day in which God will supernaturally illuminate the conscience of every man, woman, and child on earth. Each person, then, would momentarily see the state of their soul through God's eyes and realize the truth of His existence.   **$12.95**

Toll-Free (888) 654-6279 or (412) 787-9735 www.SaintAndrew.com

St. Andrew's Productions Order Form

Order Toll-Free! 1-888-654-6279 or 1-412-787-9735
Visa, MasterCard Accepted!

_____ Call of the Ages (Petrisko)	$12.95
_____ Catholic Answers for Catholic Parents	$ 8.95
_____ Catholic Parents Internet Guide	$ 3.00
_____ Face of the Father, The (Petrisko)	$ 9.95
_____ False Prophets of Today (Petrisko)	$ 7.95
_____ Fatima Prophecies, The (Petrisko)	$16.95
_____ Fatima's Third Secret Explained (Petrisko)	$12.95
_____ Finding Our Father (Centilli)	$ 4.95
_____ Glory to the Father (Petrisko)	$ 8.95
_____ God 2000 (Fr. Richard Foley, SJ)	$11.95
_____ Holy Spirit in the Writings of PJP II	$19.95
_____ In God's Hands (Petrisko)	$12.95
_____ Inside Heaven and Hell (Petrisko)	$14.95
_____ Inside Purgatory (Petrisko)	$10.95
_____ Kingdom of Our Father, The (Petrisko)	$14.95
_____ Last Crusade, The (Petrisko)	$ 7.95
_____ Mary in the Church Today (McCarthy)	$14.95
_____ Miracle of the Illumination, The	$12.95
_____ Prophecy of Daniel, The (Petrisko)	$ 7.95
_____ Prodigal Children, The (Centilli)	$ 4.95
_____ Seeing with the Eyes of the Soul: Vol. 1	$ 3.00
_____ Seeing with the Eyes of the Soul: Vol. 2	$ 3.00
_____ Seeing with the Eyes of the Soul: Vol. 3	$ 3.00
_____ Seeing with the Eyes of the Soul: Vol. 4	$ 3.00
_____ Sorrow, Sacrifice and the Triumph	$13.00
_____ St. Joseph and the Triumph (Petrisko)	$10.95

Cassette
_____ Mary, and the
World Trade Center *(2) 40 min* $10.00

Name:_____

Address:_____

City:_____St____Zip_____

Phone:_____Fax_____

Visa/MasterCard_____

Total Enclosed:_____

PLEASE ADD SHIPPING/TAX
$0-24.99...$4.00, $25-49.99...$6.00, $50-99.99...$8.00, $100 + Add 8%
PA Residents Add 7% Tax
OR MAIL ORDER TO:
St. Andrew's Productions, 6111 Steubenville Pike, McKees Rocks, PA 15136
www.SaintAndrew.com

Printed in the United States
1262400003B/1-20

9 781891 903182